Harm in American Penology

*SUNY Series in New Directions in
Crime and Justice Studies*

Austin T. Turk, Editor

Harm in American Penology

Offenders, Victims and Their Communities

Todd R. Clear

STATE UNIVERSITY OF NEW YORK PRESS

Published by
State University of New York Press, Albany

© 1994 State University of New York

Printed in the United States of America

Marketing by Bernadette LaManna
Production by Laura Starrett

For information, address State University of New York Press,
State University Plaza, Albany, New York 12246

Library of Congress Cataloging-in-Publication Data

Clear, Todd R.
    Harm in American penology : offenders, victims, and their
communities / Todd R. Clear.
        p.   cm.—(SUNY series, New directions in crime and justice
studies)
    Includes bibliographical references and index.
    ISBN 0-7914-2173-2 : $74.50. — ISBN 0-7914-2174-0 (pbk.) : $24.95
1. Corrections—United States.   2. Punishment—United States.
3. Imprisonment—United States.   I. Title.   II. Series.
HV9469.C6   1994
364.6'0973—dc20   94-281
                                                                    CIP

10   9   8   7   6   5   4   3   2   1

Contents

List of Figures and Tables

Figures

Tables

This book is dedicated to Vince O'Leary
and to Donna Richardson

Acknowledgments

For his book I owe many debts. The first draft was written in England while I was on sabbatical: the London School of Economics provided library support, and my friends there, Derek Cornish, George Mair, and Judith Rumgay gave me moral support and good ideas. Several students at the Rutgers School of Criminal Justice worked long hours helping with the library research: J. B. O'Kane, Paul Konicek, Venitha Puliankalath, Tracey Rutnik and Hui-Lung Su. Phyllis Schultz, librarian for the Rutgers-NCCD Criminal Justice collection, was an invaluable resource—she kept my desk crowded with documents, most of which found their way into the book. Friends and colleagues who read drafts and gave insightful feedback included Patricia Hardyman, Robin Mace, Margaret Smith, and Bruce Stout. (Of course, they cannot be blamed when I did not follow some of their suggestions.) Special thanks are owed to Andrew von Hirsch and Doug Husak, who commented on my argument in chapter one. The reviews of Frank Cullen, Joan Petersilia, and John Smykla also helped sustain my optimism for the topic. Finally, I want to thank Laura Starrett, Alicia Mahaney Minsky, and Chris Worden for their able editorial work, which improved the manuscript immensely.

My father gave me the spirit for these arguments.

Preface

This book grew out of the reading and writing I did during my 1990–91 sabbatical. The sabbatical, in turn, grew out of my despair at the changes taking place in the criminal justice system, especially changes in the use of corrections. After over 15 years of immersion in correctional change; after working with literally hundreds of correctional projects of various forms and directions; after gaining something of an insider's reputation in the field of corrections and winning awards for my work, I was spent. I had lost my heart and my head for the work, and like so many probation officers, correctional counselors, prison workers, and treatment providers I had known over the years, I desperately needed a break. In a sense, then, this book grew out of my frustration at the field, my disillusionment about reforms, and my personal exhaustion with the day to day effort of trying to make sense of it all.

When I first started telling people about what I was writing, I found the reactions were quite curious. People often had much to say about my topic, and usually their remarks contained a powerful grounding of self-confidence in their opinions that far surpassed my own confidence in the topic. This worried me, as I began to think I was about to write a book on a topic everyone else understood far better than I did.

The most common reaction was a kind of a snort at the title of the book—and at my phrasing of its subject: "penal harm." The words, said aloud, conjured visions of male sexual aggression in people's minds, it seemed, or else they conjured no vision except that of a paltry essay on bad things that sometimes happen to people while they are confined.

So I went looking for another phrase. There were several candidates: penological harm, criminological harm, correctional harm, among others. Most were unacceptable, because they carried imagery of science as the cause of the harm—and not only that, they provoked an idea that this was to be a scientific study of the phenomenon. The image was poor, because in the book I argue that penal harms are not based in science, nor are they contrary to science. And the idea was wrong, since I would never claim this essay to be a scientific study.

The more I looked about for a suitable title, the more I came back to the short, simple phrase 'penal harm.' The phrase, I thought, had several advantages. First, its sound was stark and direct, without namby-pamby allusions to science or expertise. Second, the phrase was something of an invention on my part, and therefor I was more or less free to define its meaning in whatever way suited me. The final decision was made as I sat in a hot bath, thinking about reorganizing the chapters, as authors so often do in their unselfconfident way. It struck me that the very snortling reaction of my male peers who, when they heard the term 'penal harm,' immediately thought of their (and, I suppose others') sexual organs on a rampage was precisely consistent with the kind of imagery I had in mind about the topic. There is a kind of a masculine brutality in the cold, careful, self-exculpatory way we use the justice system to try to conquer offenders in our midst.

The words also connote a grand deception of the system. We claim, on the one hand, to be in pursuit of punishment, of penal justice; we find ourselves, however, continually caught up in the web of desires to hurt one another. We claim, as well, that if only we could deliver enough pain to the offenders among us, our lives would be better. Yet, virtually no one living through a time period of the most extreme increases in penal harm in our history would venture the opinion that we feel the better for it. The notion of penal harms contains some of our most pressing social contradictions.

This book has two purposes, one contained within the other. The primary purpose is to explore, maybe expose, the ideologies of harm that undergird contemporary penological thought. This can be summarized as a very simple intention: many aspects of correctional or penological practice contain implicit and explicit ideas about harm as a method of society, yet this basic reality of the field has been subjected to little critical comment.

The secondary purpose of this book is to use the analysis of penal harm to construct an argument about contemporary corrections policy: That the punitiveness—the harms—of corrections have become more excessive than is useful to our society, and there is a need for deescalation.

It may help the reader to know from the outset that a comprehensive review of correctional literature is not intended here. Such a study would be useful, of course, but not necessary to the purposes of this book, which are to enter a debate on correctional methods, or perhaps to urge that such a debate is needed. Exhaustive study is not required to know that modern corrections has gotten itself into deep difficulties with both methods and ideas, and we do not necessarily get out of those difficulties by reviewing every study ever made of the field. What is intended is a selection of studies central to the themes of the essay, which are that the claws of corrections are sharp and in need of trimming.

Throughout this book, the terms *penology* and *corrections* are used virtually interchangeably. It is worth noting that these terms are not very different. According to the 1990 Oxford Dictionary, penology is "the study of the punishment of crime and prison management," whereas correction is an archaic form meaning "punishment." To the many people who are employed by the various departments of corrections, it will probably come as a surprise to learn that their agency is named after an archaic idea of the function of punishment—though perhaps, in this day and age, it will not seem at all surprising. When speaking of the idea of punitive harm, it seems preferable sometimes to use the term *penology*. When the term *corrections* is used, it is not meant to connote some softer idea of the harm, but instead to simply avoid the overrepetitive use of the word *penology*. For much these same reasons, Garland (1990) uses the term *penality*.

I will sometimes also use the term *penal policy*. Again, I do so advisedly, as the term seems to suggest that what we do in corrections is thought out and purposeful. A few years ago, I reflected on the idea that what we seem to have in this country is more of a punishment lifestyle, an almost compulsive attachment to toughness. In this respect, the use of the rational-empirical term *experiment* is also inappropriate, although the metaphor of trying something new and seeing if it works does apply to what we've been doing since about 1973. This is also as good a place as any to admit that my choice of the year 1973, though arbitrary—marks the point in time when it looks like we started changing the amount of penal harm we applied to our fellow citizens.

But I also felt that the central ideas of the so-called "get tough" movement—the ideas that drove the experiment—were not necessarily wrong ideas. Deserved punishment, career criminal models, risk classification and prediction, victim's needs, community protection: these were all ideas that had played prominently in my own work over the last few years. The problem, I believed, was that the get-tough ideology got these ideas wrong. What I wanted to do was to write a book that would take those ideas as legitimate, and describe why they do not lead, inexorably, to getting tough.

That is what I have tried to do here. Chapter 1 enters the debate about the justifications of punishment—in many respects, this debate was the jumping-off point for penal harm growth since 1973. Chapter 2 describes that growth and asks, "what caused it?" and, "what resulted from it?" We then consider the three main arguments in favor of penal growth: criminological research is discussed in chapter 3, victim's needs in chapter 4, and community protection in chapter 5. In chapter 6, I summarize my main points and offer some cautious suggestions about what we must do to change course.

Penal Harm and Its Justifications

We halted before the door of a cell, and
the journeyman on duty rattled his key into
the lock. Inside, the client lifted her head,
opening dark eyes very wide. Master
Palaemon wore the sable-trimmed cloak and
velvet mask of his rank; I suppose that these,
or the protruding optical device that enabled
him to see, must have frightened her. She did
not speak, and of course none of us spoke
to her.

"Here," Master Palaemon began in his
driest tone, "we have something outside the
routine of judicial punishment and well
illustrative of the modern technique. The
client was put to the question last
night—perhaps some of you heard her.
Twenty miniums of tincture were given before
the excruciation, and ten after. The dose was
only partially effective in preventing shock
and loss of consciousness, so the proceedings
were terminated after flaying the right leg, as
you will see." He gestured to Drotte, who
began unwrapping the bandages.

"Half boot?" Roche asked.

"No, full boot. She has been a
maidservant, and Master Gurloes has found
them strong-skinned. In this instance, he was
proved correct. A simple circular incision was
made below the knee, and its edge taken with
eight clamps. Careful work by Master
Gurloes, Odeo, Mennas and Eigil permitted

*removal of everything between the knee and
the toes without further help from the knife."*

*We gathered around Drotte, the younger
boys pushing in as they pretended to know
the points to look for. The arteries and major
veins were all intact, but there was a slow,
generalized welling of blood. I helped Drotte
apply fresh dressings.*

*Just as we were about to leave, the
woman said, "I don't know. Only, oh, can't
you believe I would tell you if I did? She's
gone with Vodalus of the Wood, I don't know
where." Outside, feigning ignorance, I asked
Master Paleamon who Vodalus of the Wood
was.*

*"How often have I explained to you that
nothing said by a client under questioning is
heard by you?"*

"Many times, Master."

*"But to no effect. Soon it will be
masking day, and Drotte and Roche will be
journeymen, and you captain of the
apprentices. Is this the example you'll set for
the boys?"*

"No, Master."

—Gene Wolfe, *The Shadow
of the Torturer*

The point is so obvious that it is generally ignored: punishment, in
the classic sense, involves a government's organized infliction of
harm upon a citizen. Corrections is a bureaucracy established by
government to carry out these harming acts.

In the United States, we allocate $25 billion a year to the penal
harm bureaucracy, and we currently apply these harms to 1 in 43
adults. Such a large and expensive social program requires justification, and many writers have sought to offer reasons for penal harming. My purpose in this chapter is to explore those reasons and ask if
they provide a sufficient rationale for penal practices that are composed of officially sanctioned harms imposed upon citizens.

There is no simple answer to this question, as the many writers
who have preceded my analysis would agree. My argument is that

when other writers have used value-positive terms such as *punishment* or *sanctions* to investigate this topic, it enables them to sidestep the harming intent and harmful content of the actions they seek to justify. In this chapter, I recall the common justifications of penal harms, and discuss them in light of the harm being advocated. When approached from this angle, the common justifications of these harms seem to rest on much more shaky ground. The importance of recognizing the harmful content of penal practice for its advocacy is illustrated by comparing the intuitive reaction to these three assertions: (1) It is good that we censure one another for certain conduct; (2) It is good that we punish one another for certain conduct; (3) It is good that we harm one another for certain conduct. If there is any uneasiness about the latter statement, it comes from our natural doubts about the wisdom of being instrumentally harmful.

In this chapter, I explore the justifiability of penal harm. I begin with a definition of the term, showing that what sets punishment apart from other governmental actions is that it seeks to harm the well-being of the citizen (offender). Such an action begs for justification, and I summarize the traditional retributive and utilitarian justifications of penal harm. After describing contemporary penal practice, I return to these justifications and consider how well they withstand scrutiny, given the nature of today's penal system. My conclusion is that our original doubts about penal harms are well taken.

I will argue that recognizing these doubts—bringing them into the penal harm debate—shifts slightly our understanding of the justifications of penal action, for it calls to our attention the deeply ingrained ambivalence we have about it. Specifically, I will argue that neither of the traditional retributive or utilitarian arguments survive scrutiny about the way they justify penal harms. If this is so, then the intellectual basis for our system of harms is wanting.

The phrase *penal harm* receives a more detailed definition below, but a brief explanation of my adoption and usage of the term in these opening paragraphs will be helpful. It is not meant to refer only to the indirect consequences of penal sanctions for those upon whom they are imposed. Indirect suffering of punished offenders and their families[1] has received wide attention in the literature: men in prison are exposed to severe deprivations (Sykes 1958), experience attacks upon their coping abilities (Toch 1989), are exposed to a range of medical (Hammet 1989) or other environmental threats (Wright 1989); for example, about one in five are victims of sexual attack (Lockwood 1980). Even though recent studies have suggested that the impact of physical and psychological stresses in prison has been exaggerated

(Bukstel and Kilman 1980; Zamble and Porporino 1988), it is undeniable that most prisons are not healthy places.

But even if prisons were healthy places, the penal sanction would be an act of harm; not merely because of the loss of freedom, but because the very content of punishment is harm. If it does not contain harm—if the offender does not suffer—then we do not think the offender has been punished (Hart 1963).

Nor is the term meant to refer primarily to the harms that accompany attempts to control offenders and to protect society from them. Modern methods of behavior control often have undesirable side-effects, especially drug controls and electronic controls (Ball, Huff, and Lilly 1988; Baumer 1990). Nobody should underestimate the discontents that coincide with being under someone else's control.

Yet even if we were to follow the proposals of some to do away with behavior control as a goal of sentencing decisions (Singer 1979; von Hirsch 1976), penal sanctions would be acts of harm. Indeed, according to those advocates, they would then be pure acts of harm against offenders, and this would be a philosophical advance.

It is in this sense that the term *penal harm* is used here—it refers to the essence of the penal sanction—that it harms. It refers as well to its special status as a planned governmental act, whereby a citizen is harmed, and implies that harm is justifiable precisely because it is an offender who is suffering.

The pains of imprisonment and the collateral consequences of control are important considerations to the concept of penal harm, but are incidental to my usage of the term. Terry Baumer (1989) tells a story that illustrates the point. In an exit interview of one woman in his study of electronic monitoring of pretrial offenders, he learned that the anklet had caused a serious rash on her leg. When he asked her why she didn't tell the authorities about the problem, she answered that "she thought it was supposed to be that way."

It is precisely this aspect of the penal sanction that offers the best understanding of penal harm: it is supposed to hurt. When it does—when prisons are painful, when controls are demeaning—we are no more surprised about it than the torturer's apprentice is by the strategic choice of the "full boot."

AMBIVALENCE ABOUT HARM

There is a great deal of ambivalence about making prisons harmful places. (There is less ambivalence about sending citizens to prisons in order to harm them.) Our Constitution places restrictions on how onerous a prison can be, at least with regard to the indirect pains of being incarcerated. Professionals in the field of corrections are loath to admit that they are bureaucrats whose job it is to implement judicially decreed harms. It is popular to portray the offender as benefitting from the harsh regimes of correctional programs—getting better due to boot camp, or improving from being "scared straight" (Finckenauer 1982).

It is odd that so many people seem to want to downplay the essential harmfulness of the penal method, as though it were some sort of community secret. It is curious also that the simple statement of the nature of punishment and the task of corrections often provokes defensiveness among the officials of government who bear some role in the punitive process—legislators, judgers, managers, and workers. Almost nobody wants to acknowledge they are in a business that harms people, and to state the obvious dismays many who work in the corrections field.

They react as though they have been accused of cruelty. They protest in one way or another: "But these are people who have injured others"; "Somehow, criminals have to be stopped"; "Just think what life would be like if the government did nothing about crime"; and so forth. Or they proclaim: "The punishment must fit the crime"; "An eye for an eye, and a tooth for a tooth." They object to the implication that there might be something wrong with a government-run harm business. In general, two types of objections are voiced. It is said that we must harm offenders because crime must be eradicated, and that we must harm them because to not do so would be morally wrong.

The important point is not whether these protests are right or wrong. They serve to divert attention from the essential nature of punishment—it is organized, intentional harm against a fellow citizen. In recent years, the industry of penal harms has become a carefully calibrated procedural machine. Responding to complaints of arbitrariness and capriciousness in the allocation of penal harms, the makers and managers of the correctional process have produced a host of reforms that establish an overlay of due process and commensurability on the centuries-old Anglo Saxon traditions of law. The aim has been to eliminate irregularities in the production of penal harms and to solidify the justifications of its foundation institutions; in other words, to pursue

the control of pain delivery, rather than the control of pain itself. Regulation of pain becomes so important that the necessity of inflicting pain is more or less taken for granted . . . Sufferings disappear in a fog of regulating mechanisms. Somewhere, far behind, is an activity of dubious repute. But we do not come quite

close to it because we are so intensely preoccupied with building up
regulatory mechanisms. (Christie 1981: 49)

The harm is justified because it is right, and it is necessary because
it helps both citizens and offenders alike. These are the easy—the
commonsense and everyday—justifications we use in our self-defen-
sive reflections about harming law violators. How persuasive are
these arguments?

Historically, social philosophers have spent considerable time
exploring and explaining the justifications for government-sponsored
injury against its citizens. Before turning to these justifications, we
need to consider at more length the nature of the official harm invoked
through the punitive apparatus.

<h3>PUNISHMENT DEFINED AS PENAL HARM</h3>

The traditional view of the definition of punishment can be summarized as follows: punishment is an evil or unpleasantness imposed by
personal agency of properly constituted authority against an offender
because of the offense (Flew 1954). Lest the point be missed, the
philosophers of criminal law have gone on to stress that the harm (or
pain) is central to the punitive act, not merely its by-product (Benn
and Peters, 1959), that punishment "always involves an expressed
intention to inflict pain" (Westermarck 1932: 78); that "punishment is
an Evil inflicted by a Publique authority" (Hobbes 1937: 164).

This definition has generally been used to distinguish the various
types of gratuitous harm caused by individuals from official harm
that is permissible because it is legitimate punishment. It is merely a
definition, and is not meant to excuse the harm of governments—
justifications of government harm are more complex and are considered below. Moreover, as a definition, it does not indicate how much
pain or hardship is needed before an act is a punishment, but only
that the intention of harm, under certain limitations of proper authority and proven citizen misbehavior, can be considered a punishment
and therefore permissible.

One of the ironies of penal harm is that it is invoked as a response
to the harmfulness of crime. It is a distorted inversion of an old
axiom: we are told that "two harms make a good." In the case of
modern punishment, criminal harm begets penal harm. For this
reason, it is not surprising that legal philosophers have gone to some
lengths to distinguish among the various types of harm, so as to
excuse some harms by elevating them to the level of penality.

That criminal harms require official attention is a well-established
idea. John Stuart Mill (1926) provided the classic argument that acts

should not be criminalized unless they produce harm—that harm is a limiting principle to criminalization—since this would guarantee that the behavior is being repudiated simply because it is objectively reprehensible, and not "purely or even primarily because it is thought to be immoral" (Packer 1968: 268). Since one role of government is to protect the rights of its citizens, the negative right to live without injury from others is thought to be the proper province of the law. Indeed, the very existence of interpersonal injury or its threat produces the need for a criminal law in the first place. This relationship is so direct that some legal philosophers have argued that criminal harm "is required of any crime validly on the books of our legal system" (Gross 1979: 114).

To use the existence of a criminal harm as a justification for a penal response is to leave two questions unanswered. First, what constitutes a harm that is rightfully subject to criminalization? Second, why is a *penal* response required, rather than some other response?

In a series of books, Feinberg (1984; 1985; 1986; 1988) has developed an elaborate theory of what constitutes harm, and of the bases on which distinctions may be drawn about criminal and noncriminal harms. A full description of this work is neither possible nor necessary here; rather, it suffices to summarize his main thesis: a harm exists when there is an unjustified setback to legitimate interest to which a person has a claim. For this reason, a citizen may be publicly blamed for action that causes harm. Thus, harm occurs when there are setbacks to a person's legitimate interests sufficiently blameworthy to call for a public condemnation. The language of public blame and condemnation is the penal action.

Therefore, the discomforts resulting from penal sanctions do not meet Feinberg's test as true harm. Crimes occur when offenders cause illegitimate setbacks to legitimate interests of the victim. Therefore, the sanction which follows the crime is not harm, for it is an entirely legitimate setback to illegitimate (criminal) interests.[2] Feinberg lists penal harms as precisely the kind that are excluded from criminalization, because to criminalize them would be patently illogical: the remedy for a criminal harm is a penal sanction; how then, logically, could the use of a penal sanction become the basis for invoking that sanction as a remedy? Not only would it be troublesome to identify the perpetrator, it would be ridiculous to subject the state's agents of penal harm to a sanction of harm, merely for having carried out their duty. At a minimum, there would be an unending trail of criminal culpability.

Yet simply because a penal harm can never be considered a criminal act does not mean it is not harmful (and, perhaps as a consequence, regrettable). Nor does it mean that the invocation of penal harms raises no moral problems.

In a persuasive argument about the moral content of the criminal law, Husak (1987) has criticized those who would treat harm as an objective component of conduct that can be properly criminalized. Drawing on Feinberg's earlier work, Husak demonstrates numerous examples of circumstances in which harm occurs to a citizen as a result of intentional action by a fellow citizen, for which the application of the criminal sanction is at least questionable, if not downright inappropriate (234–36).[3] Because this is the case, Husak suggests that a "moral and political theory is required to justify whether and under what circumstances the criminal law should recognize a harm" (235)

It follows, of course, that the only distinction between the harms of punishment and the harms of criminality is a moral/political one. The law violator's harms are an attack upon the victim (discussed in detail in Chapter 4) and a breach of the imperatives of government, whereas the government's harms are the realization of those imperatives. In fact, what is abhorred about the lawbreaking cannot be solely the harm that results, because harm is precisely the instrument of punishment. This is why the criminal law must appeal not to some objective dislike of the harms committed by select citizens, but to a vision of a moral/political order by which the government's use of power is justified, indeed by which its very function as arbiter of the uses of harm is certified. When it comes to the issue of imposing harm, the idea of government is that it may harm according to its rules when its citizens harm in their breach—indeed, some influential theorists have argued that on this occasion the government is *compelled* to harm its citizen (Mabbot 1939; Van den Haag 1975).

Why, then, does the government get to do what its citizens cannot? One answer, admittedly inadequate but nonetheless worth saying in passing, is that the government makes the rules and reserves for itself that power. This answer is not only obvious, but also tautological. It suggests a revised version of our second question about penal harms: What interests would justify requiring the government to do what it forbids for its citizens? To answer this question, we must explore the traditional moral/political justifications of the use of coercive power by the state.

The two traditional candidates for the moral/political order to be advanced through the coercive power of the criminal law are retributivism and utilitarianism. Retributivism refers to the idea that people should always and only be treated as ends and never as means, and that the actions of government are legitimate only to the degree to which they are consistent with this model of citizenry. The utilitarian ideal is more complicated, in that it posits a desirable consequence of government action and advocates government action that promotes the desirable result (Sen 1979). These views of the moral order to be advanced by the criminal law propose different understandings of harm, especially as they reflect the use of penological harm as an instrument of government.

RETRIBUTIVISM

The predominant tradition of retributive thought has been that "the state of affairs where a wrongdoer suffers punishment is morally better than the state of affairs where he does not" (Rawls 1971: 4). To this end, Kant has given his famous admonition: "Even if a Civil Society resolved to dissolve itself with the consent of all its members . . . the last Murderer lying in prison ought to be executed before the resolution was carried out" (Kant 1887; cited in Braithwaite and Pettit 1990: 198).

The use of harm as a technique of the retributive government is therefore a commandment. It stems from the main function of law, which is to use the state's harming power to identify the prohibited acts in ways that are perfectly clear to the citizenry.

There is some debate among retributivists as to subsidiary elements of the theory. Some have argued that the main object of retribution is "to restore the balance which the offence disturbed" (Ashworth 1983: 16). From this perspective, all society is poised in a delicate balance of the benefits of social living (commerce, aspirations, and so forth) and the burdens it implies (especially, compliance with the law). But this is a precarious balance, for it relies on each person's respect for the rights of the other. Offenders, in choosing to behave criminally, take advantage of the inherent vulnerability of social living and upset the balance. The imposition of penal harms reestablishes the balance by removing the advantage gained by the unlawful act. The original formulation of the "balances-and-burdens" idea of the criminal law (also referred to as benefits-burdens) was provided by Kant (1887), but there are persuasive modern versions of the idea (von Hirsch 1976; Sadurski 1985; Sher 1987).

This formulation has come under some criticism, even by former advocates (von Hirsch 1985), for a variety of reasons. These problems have been well-chronicled (Braithwaite and Pettit 1990) and seem to revolve around the extreme abstractness of the concepts—what constitutes benefits or burdens when applied to the specific circumstance of criminal acts? Moreover, "in any society with gross inequalities of wealth and power, restoring the balance of benefits and burdens is a troubling notion" (Braithwaite and Pettit 1990: 159). In capitalist societies, the benefits of citizenship and the burdens of survival can be unequally distributed, and many of those convicted of crimes are already subjected to the severe burdens of poverty and social disadvantage.

A purer version of retributive thinking is that the state inflicts harm in order to confirm the moral order established by the laws of the state. The threat of the full power of the criminal law is central to the educative function of the law, for it persuades citizens to adopt its moral norms (Gorecki 1979; Murphy 1988; Shafer-Landau 1991). That is one reason why Van den Haag (1975) has argued that any threat made by the criminal law must be carried out against those who ignore it and cannot be waived in the interest of mercy. To make a threat and then not impose what it promises is to break trust with the very moral authority of the law itself, to mock its claims as the moral guide it supposes itself to be.

The moral education basis for retribution need not be so harshly drawn. The main idea is that the offender, by the conduct, demonstrates a kind of moral ignorance. The retributive response serves to educate the offender and the punisher alike as to the forbidden nature of the conduct. It confirms the punisher's commitment to those moral norms, and it calls the lawbreaker's attention to the wrongfulness of the conduct. Thus, the criminal law teaches moral behavior. We will return to the instructive nature of penal harm later in this chapter and also in chapter 4, when we ask the question, "What is learned about the moral order by the person subjected to official harms?" Duff (1986) has offered a retributive answer to this question: the offender should learn from the punishment that he or she is ashamed, feels remorse, and repents of the act; in other words, the offender should change from claiming the right to injure other's legitimate interests to claiming no such right. Using similar logic, Adler (1991) has insisted that the preferable form of a punishment occurs when the wrongdoer admits the error and elects some form of personal loss as a public affirmation of commitment to behave otherwise in the future.

There is also a morally-based pure form of retribution known as "just deserts," which is offered as a basis for understanding the very reason of the criminal law. Deserved punishment is housed in the idea that the conduct it forbids is morally reprehensible (von Hirsch 1985). The instrument of criminal reprobation is inherently moral because it is inherently blaming, and is therefore based upon a claim of moral superiority. The imposition of the penal harm makes tangible the moral evaluation of the criminal's conduct, and it symbolizes the communities' outrage at the crime. This is why the relative reprehensibleness of acts determines the amount of official harm they should evoke (von Hirsch 1985).

From the perspective of the state's use of harm, distinctions among the various schools of retributive thought are generally minor. The moral educator is required to design harms that are most capable of educating, but that difference aside, all retributivists believe harm serves a function both symbolic and real. The symbolic function of harm is to provide visible, public certification of social disapproval of conduct which the society, through whatever processes are used to determine its laws, has defined as unacceptable. This means that the criminal act is exposed as a false social claim that cannot be sustained by the offender (Murphy and Hampton 1988). The more practical function is that by injuring a citizen, the state imposes a cost that denies that citizen the satisfactions which may have accrued from the act.

It is also important to recognize three constraints that a retributive moral theory places on the use of penal harm by government. The first is a set of understandings traditional to Western legal theorists about those acts that the law may forbid: specific behaviors, previously forbidden, which are intentionally chosen when the actor could have behaved otherwise (Hall 1960; Hart 1961; Feinberg 1984). Engaging in such behaviors is a necessary condition of the moral blame of the law. Second, penal harms must be commensurate with (or proportional to) their moral wrongfulness, imposing injury in a way that demonstrates the community's relative disapprobation of the behavior (von Hirsch 1976; Singer 1979). Third, the law must operate within its own procedural and substantive constraints in order to carry the moral authority it claims. Thus the retributivist does not count the official acts of injury against criminal offenders as harm in any meaningful sense. The acts of government may intend (and achieve) pain, loss, and discomfort. Yet the context is the moral high ground of society—the injury is a product of the offender's bankrupt choices and, far from calling the society's morality into question, reflects well upon the seriousness with which the society takes its obligation to publicly defend its legal prohibitions. So long as the pain and suffering of the offender occur within the limits of the law's due process (which can include prohibitions against cruel and unusual inflictions of pain, as does the U.S. Constitution) and is delivered with due regard for proportionality, the existence of well-oiled and effective bureaucracies of penal injury are to be applauded as wise social achievements.

UTILITARIANISM

The discussion of utilitarian moral imperatives in the use of official harm has been made confusing by the common appeal to the types of utilitarian justifications of punishment: rehabilitation,[4] deterrence, and incapacitation (or social defense). The all-too-quick reference to these terms of common usage obscures the argument of utilitarianism in two ways. First, it assumes that crime control is the only utility that a penal harm could be used to achieve. Second, it assumes that this classification of utilities is helpful to understanding the general principles of utilitarianism. Neither assumption is appropriate. Crime control is not the only aim of a utilitarian moral order, and these forms of utilities understate the range of values a utilitarian might use to justify penal harm. The formal basis for a utilitarian argument is straightforward: the use of the intentional harm promotes some larger important benefit. This benefit can accrue to the larger social group (as in reductions in crime) or it can exist for individuals who experience enhanced lives.

There are three main traditions of formal utilitarianism. The first, and perhaps earliest, was Jeremy Bentham's classic treatise, first published in 1789, in which he offered that the purpose of any system of government was to maximize the happiness of its citizens (Bentham 1982) by enhancing their well-being—a formulation that many would find attractive. In doing so, the government should observe closely the rule of social equality that each citizen "counts for one, and only for one."

The utilitarian viewpoint is often interpreted as additively mathematical. If a government act benefits some large number of people at the expense of a smaller number, or if it provides a greater benefit to some, then the costs it places on others are justifiable. The utilitarian ideal is the advance of the common good, as measured by the overall, (sometimes even the average) individual benefits of government action.

There have been two main criticisms of the utilitarian ideal. First, many philosophers are unsettled by an argument that the well-being of some can be sacrificed in order to advance the benefits of others, even when the result is greater social good. Second, critics have argued that happiness is a vague term, likely to have different meaning for different people. Strategies to advance happiness therefore require more detailed ideas about what, exactly, happiness means, and how to get it. Since what makes a person happy varies from individual to individual, it may be impossible to advance the well-being of the larger society—a unitary well-being does not exist. Because of these problems, critics of utilitarianism have argued that the role of government is to ensure that the *means* to happiness are made available to all, but not to choose some individual's well-being as being desirable over others' (Rawls 1971).

Still, there remains a continuing desire for a revised version of the happiness formula which seeks to minimize the experience of pain and harm by offenders. Nils Christie (1981) has written an influential though sympathetic critique of retributive punishment, suggesting that the use of harm as an instrument of government is suspect. David Fogel (1988), a longtime advocate of retributive thinking, has recently sought ways to minimize the harm resulting from correctional policy. Edgardo Rotman (1990) has been more assertive in saying that offenders have a legal right to be rehabilitated rather than merely punished. None of these works seems to take much account of the harms caused by offenders, however, and surely these harms are themselves important aspects of overall happiness in society.

Some critics of traditional utilitarian theory have argued that when one person's interests are sacrificed to increase another's gain, the interests of liberty are offended (Dworkin 1979; 1981). Ironically, this critique has led to a second tradition among utilitarians defining liberty as the main utility to be advanced. In this tradition liberty is often expressed as legitimate *autonomy*. An important refinement of this idea, offered by Braithwaite and Pettit (1990), is the interest in maximizing *dominion*, a term they use to refer to the capacity to elect from among "those options which the normal agent is capable of realizing in normal conditions without the special collaboration of colleagues or circumstances" (61). Since any government use of penal power is an incursion into liberty (or domain), these utilitarians argue that there must be a prior demonstration that such a use of power will, in the long run, promote greater liberty among individuals taken as a whole.

The third tradition of utilitarianism is preventist, in that it seeks to minimize the amount of crime. This approach can be thought of as advancing a kind of negative liberty, or placing a value on government practices that most prevent the criminal behavior which restricts liberty. Here, the traditional forms of utilitarian thinking are considered: general deterrence, rehabilitation (and specific deterrence) and incapacitation. Numerous explanations and defenses of these approaches have been written (see Honderich 1984), which is probably one of the reasons that this tradition of crime prevention has come to be equated (falsely) with the general ideal of utilitarianism.

Recently, a group of Christian reformers has advanced the concept of *restoration* as a utilitarian value (Van Ness 1989). This view is a reformulation of the benefits-burdens model of retribution that incorporates a strong theme of rehabilitation ideas. The utility to be maximized is the reestablishment of harmony between the community (including the victim) and the law violator through a combination of acts of contrition by the offender and behavioral change programs by the state.

Unlike the various forms of retributive models, the choice of a utility to be maximized has substantial implications for the use of harm by the state in service of the utility. The preventionist utilitarian values set the stage for potentially enormous injuries to citizens in pursuit of reductions in crime, for they express no formal limit on the use of official harm to achieve the aims of negative liberty (Braithwaite and Pettit 1990; von Hirsch 1990). This is undoubtedly one reason why populations under all forms of formal government control skyrocketed in the United States during the last 15 years (Austin and Killman 1988; Mauer 1990; see also Chapter 2), because the only apparent policy that has driven the use of official injury during this period has been a kind of frenzied desire to get tough on crime at any cost.

By contrast, other utilitarian models attempt to build in limits to the use of harm. This is true, for example, for harm reduction models that include the experience of harm by the law violator in the overall calculation. They seek to minimize the amount of harm in a society, and they include penal harm to offenders as a part of the equation. Egregious harm to offenders in pursuit of crime reduction would be impermissible under a harm reduction scenario. Equally so, happiness and liberty models are forced to confront the losses incurred in these utilities when offenders are harmed.

Utilitarian models are presented by their advocates as having an advantage over retributive thinking in that they define a target to be achieved rather than a constraint to be obeyed, as is the case for retribution. Under the conditions of uncertainty, which dominate social policy, it is argued that targets provide a rational and empirical basis for choice among policy alternatives, taking into account the inevitable risks of any option. Reliance upon constraints such as desert can only appeal to the original values in choosing policies (Braithwaite and Pettit 1990).

This suggests an important potential limit that may be placed on any utilitarian theory of official harm. Before the harm can be imposed, it must be demonstrated that its invocation will, in fact, tend to advance the valued utility. Otherwise, the harm constitutes gratuitous and indefensible incursion into lives, as well as a misuse of precious governmental resources available in behalf of the utility (Clear and O'Leary 1983).

PUNISHMENT, HARM AND OFFICIAL HARM

A definition of punishment helps identify the circumstances under which harmful acts by government against its citizens might be justified. This is important because of the strong tradition in Western thought that democratic societies are governments of the people, and exist to serve the interests of the people, not to injure those interests. Surely any situation in which a government acts with the full intention of harming one of its members is inherently suspect, and requires explanation and strict limitation.

The need to draw boundaries around the meaning of punishment derives as much from the history of government abuse of power against citizens as it does from philosophical niceties. The standards of punishment in the eighteenth and nineteenth centuries were by any measure extreme. For instance, even in the prerevolutionary Quaker society of Pennsylvania, all felonies except larceny were punishable by death (Barnes and Teeters 1959). In the United States' early development, it was not unusual for penalties to involve hard labor, corporal punishment, and extreme public humiliation. The period of transportation—exile of criminals—had only recently ended. In fact, when the government chose to impose harm on a citizen for an act, the painful result was as obvious as it was injurious.

Drawing restrictions on this power was a concern of the new political order, whose philosophers advanced the idea of representative government (Ford, 1988). They had lived through the experience of brutal despots and indifferent monarchs, and they wanted to create intellectual structures for the use of power by the representatives of the people. They sought a state capable of action in behalf of the interests of the governed, not the government.

Yet they certainly recognized the positive uses of acts of harm. Revolutions against autocratic rulers always required the will to violence. The mechanisms of freedom, then, seemed to demand the aggressive use of injury and its potential to guard liberty, just as the techniques of suppression incorporated pain as a main instrument. Philosophers of freedom thus developed elaborate ideals about how and when to harm citizens officially.

A moment's reflection will reinforce the fact that many kinds of authorities use intentional harm to achieve some desirable aim. Parents spank their children or purposefully withdraw privileges in order to teach them rules. Universities impose fees upon students who fail to register for courses on time or are late in paying their bills. Bosses suspend or even terminate their subordinates when their work performance is inadequate. Intentional, calculated harm as an instrument of the powerful is widespread in modern society.

It would be naive, however, to think of harm as purely an instrument of authorities and power-holders. Unions withhold labor as a means of crippling business owners and equalizing strength of claims over the benefits of commerce. The pains that children impose upon their parents in order to achieve their freedom are legion.

The use of harm and its threat is so fundamental to human interaction that it is important to be clear about the harms specific to punishment if there is to be any sense made of the problem. While there may be a general interest in keeping harm to a minimum in all social transactions, governmental harms against citizens in response to rule-breaking are a special case.

In order to further our understanding of the meaning of penal harm as opposed to other types, we need to consider the several forms that harm may take. As a working definition of harm, let us adopt the following broad statement: harm is the violation of a person's well-being. It should be noted that this definition closely associates the idea of harm with the precepts of utilitarianism. It should be noted as well that the idea of "well-being" is by no means a simple one. But the choice of the definition makes it clear that the injury resulting from an act of harm need not be merely physical; for example, an act of harm may be emotional or economic. The definition also makes it clear that the mere experience of pain may not constitute harm. Medically necessary injections both cause a person pain and, when used correctly, promote that person's well-being.

Well-being, as a concept, is central to the philosophical world of the utilitarian, who assigns to government the responsibility to maximize the well-being of its citizens (Bentham 1982; Mill 1926; 1951). But the problem with the idea of well-being is that, at least initially, it seems so subjective. What makes one person happy makes another bored; what one person desires another disdains, and so forth. With such widely divergent experiences, how can government responsibly take on the duty to maximize well-being without favoring one point of view over another—and thus violating the maxim that "each counts for one and only one?" With all these differences among people, how do we go about making each person count?

In an excellent discussion of this and related problems, Griffin (1986) has proposed that the elements of well-being can be properly conceived as occupying a hierarchical structure that includes needs, informed desires, and "prudential" values (those related to one's self-interest as a social animal), which together connote a "moral notion of well-being" (55). Thus, a person's well-being comprises not simply a person's wants, but includes also the objects of a person's interest, given that the person has an "appreciation of the nature of the objects of his desire." This is an argument for the existence of a higher order of utilities that includes not simply happiness, but also prudential values, which "take a global form: this way of living, all in all, is better than that [way of living]" (323).

Von Hirsch and Jareborg (1991) have suggested a hierarchical model of well-being that can be used to evaluate the degree of harm caused by a criminal act. In effect, they propose using a two-dimensional scale of domains of interest that ranges from temporary physical loss to permanent loss of ability to pursue liberty and happiness. The concept of well-being, according to this scale, infers a pattern of self-interest.

With this kind of understanding of the idea of well-being, it is easier to integrate the views of the traditional legal theorists, who have given such prominence to the idea of autonomy as the appropriate guarantee of the criminal law, with the views of other theorists who see the law as having a more affirmative need to advance specific utilities. People who believe the role of the law is to promote autonomy usually approach their definitions from the standpoint of negative rights; that is, they argue that the law should operate only when there are violations of autonomy. Others, such as Braithwaite and Pettit (1990), argue that the task of the law is to promote "dominion," which is something like the state of equal access to maximum possible liberty (64–5)—a positive version of what they refer to as "autonomy."

These conceptualizations share a common theme: well-being includes the condition of being able to act in one's true self-interest. This is true for the retributivists and the utilitarians alike. While there are numerous subtle and not-so-subtle variations on this theme, they are not important for the purpose of understanding the role of penological harm. Penal harm is that situation when law violators are restricted, hampered or prevented from acting in their own legitimate (or as Griffin would put it, "prudent") self-interest.

Indeed, it is the very existence of the capacity to pursue important and legitimate ends with some reasonable expectation of their achievement that constitutes well-being (Griffin, 1986, 32). As an attack on well-being, then, the correctional sanction takes aim at the self of the law violator, in particular that part of the self that contains aspirations, informed desire, and the pursuit of personal ends.

Because we are discussing the well-being of law violators, it is important to emphasize an aspect of well-being that ordinarily would not be very troublesome. What about the law violator's claim that well-being is dependent upon the capacity to continue to violate the law?

This is not an accurate view of well-being, for it treats any of a person's approaches toward satisfying a desire as equal, no matter how imprudent the approach may be. With the exception of unusual cases (such as civil disobedience), the object of law-violating behavior is seldom simply to violate the law. Rather, the lawbreaking is an instrument toward a larger desire or set of desires that perhaps most people would feel: excitement, the command of material goods, among others (see, for example, Katz 1988). To interfere with crime as the means of meeting those desires is not really an attack on the person's well-being, for it leaves open a variety of other, more prudent, ways to meet the desire. To attack well-being would require interfering with all means of satisfying the desires, regardless of their prudence.

By way of example, a certain person, Tom, may feel a desire for power and may exercise this desire through predatory acts of rape. Neither philosophers nor psychologists would say that Tom's well-being is linked to the ability to rape freely. Rather, they would agree that Tom's personal desire for power had taken an imprudent (to say the least!) manner of expression, and that his true well-being was dependent either upon overcoming his attachment to power or finding other ways of expressing it. They would certainly not feel that in being unable to rape, Tom's well-being would suffer. Nor would they say there is something inherently forbidden about Tom's desire to feel powerful.

This is to say that while the intent of a punishment is to harm well-being, for most law violators, well-being is not tied up in being criminal, per se, but in meeting more or less normal desires which, in fact, the person has chosen to address (abnormally) through crime.[5] It follows that stopping the person from committing a crime is not, in and of itself, a punishment. For instance, we would not say to an offender, "Your punishment is that you are no longer able commit crimes." We would not think that being unable to commit a crime would be a harm—we would not see it as a penal harm or an attack against the person's well-being. Instead, we would expect that as a minimal condition of any reasonable social intervention, the person's ability to harm others would be constrained. The penal intervention that prevented criminality would not be considered "harmful" unless it also injured well-being by attacking the ability to exercise free choice of prudent self-interest to meet desires.

We feel this way because it is never an aspect of legitimate autonomy or dominion to violate the well-being of others. To be specific, no matter how strongly a rapist might believe it so, his prudential well-being is never dependent upon continued raping, for a wholly acceptable level of well-being is conceivable (indeed, perhaps only possible) without raping. To take actions that interfere with his capacity to rape is not to punish; the latter requires a direct reduction of the rapist's well-being. To control his raping may be a socially wise policy, but it is not a punishment.

This discussion suggests three important aspects of penal harm. First, penal harm interferes with a person's pursuit of individual ends that are otherwise legitimate ends. Thus, the claim of the advocates of retributive punishment, that it treats people always as ends and never as means, is a bit overstated—for retributive punishment has repudiated the very ends that give the person well-being. Further, an attack on a person's well-being, in order to promote some negative right (such as autonomy), is only a variant of the circumstance in which human beings are used coercively to promote the interests of others. It would be one thing merely to repudiate illegitimate ends of the law violator, but that is not solely the character of punishment (though that is one of its valuable results). The repudiation is accomplished by damaging the person's own deeply held ends—can it really be said that this is the higher moral position because it is, somehow, respectful of autonomy?

Second, it should be clear that no appeal can be made to objectivity, either in the idea that the criminal law is an instrument, or in the substantial social benefits the law seeks to promote through the use of coercive power. These subjects are patently moral and political. Admittedly, there may be widespread social consensus about much of what the criminal law now protects and how it does so, but social consensus is not the same as sociological objectivity. The central importance of subjective judgments about penal policy, which range from the determining of specific manifestations of negative rights protected by the law (Feinberg 1984; Husak 1987), to deciding which utilities are prudential for citizens (Griffin 1986), is undeniable. Defining harm—either its prevention or its use as a technique—requires making choices about moral and political priorities.

The existence of a proven criminal act, then, does not objectively require a punitive response any more than a heroic act would require a reward. Responding to crime via policies of penal harm is a moral/political act that advances some interests over others. The implications of the policy cannot be relegated to externalized costs of justice. To the contrary, the decision to repay crime with harm produces consequences that must be included in calculations about the wisdom of the decision in the first place. Both retributivists and utilitarians are forced to consider the implications of their moral frameworks when they design penal instruments.

For instance, when retributivists say that the criminal law must be invoked when a citizen harms another because the original harm requires it, they ignore the wide varieties of harm that are not protected by the criminal sanction. They act as though there is some natural hierarchy of harms that is not a product of a given society and a given culture, when a more accurate view is that the construction of law is always an act of political and moral symbolism (Garland 1990). Presenting themselves as the protectors of a legal order, retributivists inevitably find themselves protecting a particular manifestation of social arrangements, one that almost inevitably benefits some groups or individuals more than others (Quinney 1977; Rusche and Kircheimer 1939, among others).

When utilitarians say that the techniques of penal harm are justified by the greater good of the larger society, they ignore the intimate connection between the well-being of any individual citizen in a society and that of all citizens. In order to carry out a penal harm that promotes some utility, utilitarians must engage in acts that damage, at least for the law violator, the very well-being they seek to promote. Holding high the banner of a better world, the utilitarian chooses actions that specifically damage the quality of experience for one member of that world, and this choice is taken even though other actions are possible.

A final point is needed here. The general case of harms that occur to a person's well-being must be differentiated from the specific case of penal harms. All sorts of circumstances, tragic (such as accidents) and intentional (such as gossip), produce deficits in well-being. Often, in fact, the infliction of pain is used as a method of pedagogy—as a technique that teaches the recipient about the social meaning of certain behaviors. What sets penal harms apart is that they are the intentional act of a government, and that they rest upon an appeal to moral rightness. In any case, the intentional choice to use harm as a method of correction sits upon a delicate precipice: it is potentially destructive to the moral order it seeks to promote. In the case of penal sanctions, the paradox of moral authority is complicated by a dilemma of political power.

MODERN FORMS OF PENOLOGICAL HARM

The kinds of harms that government visits upon people convicted of breaking the law have changed. This change contributes to misunderstandings of harm and its meaning in the correctional context.

In one of the most important works ever written on the nature of penology, Foucault (1977) made the point that with the advent of modern government, the nature of the punitive target changed. From recorded history until roughly two centuries ago, punishment was accomplished by harming the body of its target. The emphasis in Hammurabi's code on the calculus of repayments for physical injury, along with the traditional call of the Biblical invocation of "an eye for an eye," represent how deeply corporal pain has been associated with the idea of justice. Thieves were to lose their hands; murderers were to die; liars to lose their tongues.

The use of corporal harm for law violators still has considerable appeal. In many nations, for example, the state may still use techniques of physical mutilation to punish its miscreants (Adler 1983). But the remaining attraction of physically punitive approaches is by no means restricted to the Third World nations. The United States has seen something of a reemergence of the idea in recent years.

The most dramatic example of this rebirth of corporal penology is the renewed call for the death penalty. In the seven years preceding the 1972 Supreme Court decision that declared the extant procedures for imposing the death penalty unconstitutional (*Furman* v. *Georgia*), there were only ten executions in the United States. Indeed, for nearly forty years before that decision, the use of execution as a penalty had been on a steady decline (Zimring, 1991). To those who thought that penal death had been eliminated as an option, its resurgence has been remarkable. Since the Supreme Court's reconsideration of the death penalty (*Gregg* v. *Georgia*, 1976), over 2,500 offenders have been scheduled for execution, and in the last seven years for which we have data, 122 executions have been carried out.

A less extreme example is provided by the enormous popularity of the "boot camp" regimen for young offenders (MacKenzie, 1990; Parent, 1990). The concept combines the idea of penal reform with the subtle suggestion that punishment should hurt. Offenders are awakened at an early hour, as though they live in a military camp, and exposed to a severe fitness regimen and extreme physical strain. They are often humiliated by so-called "guards" who order them around like paternalistic drill sergeants. Discomfort and inconvenience are designed in to make these boot camp experiences unpleasant.

These examples, along with a thousand other familiar examples of the "get tough" movement seen in the United States during the 1980s (Cullen and Gilbert 1982), all testify to the unrelenting appeal of the corporal model of penology. As the new generation of reformative penology developed, the old corporal penology did not disappear. In what appears to be a common pattern in systems of social control (Cohen 1985), the apparatus merely added new manifestations to old ones instead of replacing the old. The idea that penological methods should be physically painful remains a strong theme in corrections.

But it would be a mistake to place too much emphasis on these vestiges of previous eras of punitive harm, for in modern societies they do not play the main theme of punishment. In fact, as Foucault has shown in a major realignment of penological thinking, the target of correctional harm has shifted in the last two centuries from the body of the offender to the mind (Foucault 1977). The rhetoric of this shift often has stressed the need not to injure offenders, but to remake them, to provide a means to adjust to the emerging social order. Harm, at least as an object of the penal act, is downplayed.

There is some disagreement about the precise sociopolitical determinants of this shift. Marxist analysis blames the advent of the industrial state for the change, and argues that capitalism required compliant labor, reformed to meet the needs of the labor-hungry machinery of capitalism (Melossi and Pavarini 1981). Others have found a more complicated explanation, one that reflects the reformist ideologies of the day, the shifts in economic interests, and the developing science of politics (Ignatieff 1978).

In his monumental work on the sociology of punishment, Garland (1990) has shown that none of the most widely acclaimed theories of the function of penal harms is without flaw. He criticizes functionalists and conflict theorists alike for failing to explain adequately the complex apparatus of what he calls "penality". His remarks are aimed at developing a social theory in which the instruments of social control help us to understand better the nature of society.

Garland's analysis makes clear that the products of penal harming processes are neither simple nor unitary. Legislating and punishing systems have impact on societies that is both practical and symbolic; these systems relate to individual, institutional, and community aspects of society. The import of his work is that simple models that seek to explain penal harming activities, such as utilitarian or retributive models, are necessarily too narrow in their focus. His critique corresponds to the limits of harm-justifying arguments summarized above: the advocates of retribution seem hesitant to consider the role of law as a tool of power, especially entrenched governmental power; the proponents of utility seem unwilling to take seriously the fact that law is important as a symbol of social relations, certainly nearly as much as it is a tool to mold individual behavior. The latent uses of law and punishment may be as significant as the formal, visible functions.

The rich literature on the history of penal reform constitutes a powerful comment on the latent functions of criminal law. Many authors (Rothman 1971; Ignatieff 1978; Schlossman 1977, for example) have made the point that various penal reform movements can be thought of as playing fields upon which larger social struggles are carried out. Their work underscores the absurdity of thinking reform is merely an intellectual battle about an abstract idea of how the law should operate. The shift in penal policy, from harming the body to remolding the psyche, should not be seen as an advance in penal thinking, but as a strategic shift in the politics of punishment. In the nineteenth century and again in the early years of the twentieth, it became convenient to portray criminals as needing to be remade, and a coalition of reformers emerged to urge the helping rather than the harming of offenders.

Of course, this turn of events did not really improve the life prospects of offenders caught in the clutches of justice. Critics argued that the helping regimes were often more intrusive, coercive and dehumanizing than the previous approach (Struggle 1971; Kittrie 1971; Mitford 1973). The great experiment of the reformative prison has resulted in an enhanced and newly focussed penal harming apparatus, one that has been reconstituted to defend the system against claims that it is harsh.

The story in the latter half of the twentieth century is straightforward. The arena of penology has shifted to include the community (Cohen 1979). While prison populations have grown dramatically in recent years, the instruments of crime control in the community have also grown. There appears to be no reduction in the importance of the prison as a result of the increase in the importance of community-based social control. As Cohen has put it, in matters of correctional change "the system expands relentlessly while the relative proportions sent to prison rather than community programmes declines" (1985: 49).

Thus, the experience of the latter half of the twentieth century suggests the need for a serious consideration of the comparative harmfulness of prison and non-prison approaches to penology. Has the advent of community-based penal harms resulted in an overall decrease in the actual harmfulness of the penal system?

This is a double-edged question, for the tradition of corporal penology always means that punishment in the community wins when compared to the prison alternative, at least on the criterion of minimal harmfulness. It should be clear that the prison exists in a wholly different category from the community in the ability to deliver harm to the well-being of a citizen. This is mostly a result of the considerably less corporally painful nature of community punishment. The physical deprivations imposed by the prison are well-known (Sykes 1958; Griswold and Misenheimer 1970).

But that does not mean that community penology is harmless; in fact, it promotes harm of several types. The most obvious is a loss of autonomy. The offender is made to report to authorities and is required to answer questions of the most personal nature about aspirations, choices, and needs. Many of the offender's actions must first be approved by an official who stands as a representative of community interests. Ordinary aspects of personal liberty, such as changing homes or jobs, marrying or taking a lover, selecting recreational preferences, and so forth, are subject to review, even prior review, by the community representative. In a way, the law violator is infantilized, made into an incompetent citizen, as a result of the supervision. The loss of autonomy seems appropriate, for by virtue of the crime, the law violator has been exposed as a person who, when allowed autonomy, makes decisions and selects actions that are morally wrong. It seems at least reasonable for the community to take self-protective actions that restrict the types and areas of autonomy the law violator has demonstrated as problematic.

The restrictions imposed are punitive as well self-protective. If agents of the community were scrupulously careful to restrict their incursions into the lives of their clients to only those aspects of autonomy that relate to demonstrated law-violating potential, we could reasonably argue that the community is merely protecting itself. But community agents of social control typically involve themselves in much broader areas of the law violator's life (Stanley 1976).[6] The result is that nearly every aspect of the offender's life becomes public domain, and the loss of autonomy extends deeply into the offender's everyday world. That the law is free to apply its coercive power to the citizen, and the citizen is aware of this reduced status, is a major deficit of well-being.

There are other harms imposed as well. By virtue of being convicted, the law violator suffers a loss of civil rights, including the right to vote, to own firearms, and to work in certain occupations (Burton, Cullen, and Travis 1986). Many law breakers are required to pay fines as a part of their sentence (Cole 1988); others are forced to work on community projects for a number of hours without compensation (Lauen 1990). In several states, law violators who are allowed to remain in the community are also required to pay a monthly fee that supports the state's costs for their supervision (Baird 1986). The combination of fines, fees, and community work can constitute a hardship for lawbreakers who already suffer from marginal financial stability. In Alabama, for example, the typical lawbreaker on probation pays a fine of $500, restitution (an average of about $250), court fees of $250, a penalty fee of $500, a monthly supervision fee of $25, all the while performing unpaid labor of up to 140 hours (Clear 1990). The typical Alabama offender comes from the marginal working class in a state ranked near the bottom in the United States' standard of living. His already vulnerable well-being is made a direct target of these penalties.

Despite their routine means of diminishment of the lawbreaker's autonomy and well-being, community penalties commonly have been criticized as puny. Martinson (1976) once called probation "kind of a standing joke" and a report of the U.S. Comptroller General's Office (1976) evaluated it as "a system in crisis." Wilson (1975) and Van den Haag (1975) dismissed the typical losses imposed by probation as much too harmless to be effective. Petersilia's (1985) study of probation in California described a system seemingly incapable of protecting the community from its lawbreakers or delivering a suitable measure of punishment. These criticisms are perhaps understandable, given the large caseloads and poor performance history of traditional probation (Comptroller General 1977) and parole supervision (von Hirsch and Hanrahan 1979) throughout the 1970s.

But the probation policies of the 1980s, developed in part as a response to those criticisms, cannot be accused of the same inattention to the modern correctional agenda of successful protection and purposeful harming (Morris and Tonry 1991). More than 1000 offenders per month are placed on a program of electronically monitored house arrest in Florida's Community Control program (Baird, 1989). This program, considered a privilege for which offenders must pay a monthly fee, requires that they not leave their places of residence except for preapproved, strictly limited times. The electronic monitor turns the home into a prison—how can this be considered something other than a loss of well-being? Intensive supervision programs impose on offenders a program of surveillance so strict that many law violators offered this option choose instead to remain in prison (Petersilia 1986). The reforms of the 1980s have succeeded in making the harms of the community nearly equal in scale to those of the prison.

How can the authorities condone these losses of well-being imposed upon the law violator who is punished within the community? Three varieties of arguments are made: (1) retributive—by virtue of violating the law, the person deserves the losses of well being; (2) utilitarian—such losses are necessary to promote the overall well-being of the community; (3) pragmatic—these losses are considerably less harmful than what might have occurred by virtue of imprisonment. Let us consider these arguments in reverse order.

THE PRAGMATICS OF HARM

The fact that some offenders would rather be in prison than suffer the loss of autonomy in the community—especially the loss dictated by post-1970s community corrections—is an eloquent statement that these losses are not mediocre, by far. Yet even if every offender preferred to be harmed in the community over being sent to prison, the pragmatic justification of these harms would still be questionable, for it would require that we begin with the prison as the correct unit of analysis for harming offenders.

There is no obvious reason why the harms of the community ought to emulate those of the prison, except that these harms are thought to be cheaper. Studies show that such assessments are not mathematically sound (Tonry 1990). First of all, because these new programs are extremely labor intensive, their operating costs are not always much cheaper than those of prisons (McDonald 1989). Most obviously, in order for a community penalty to cost less than a term served in prison, it must be given to a lawbreaker in place of prison. This is often not the case. The new, intrusively harmful community penalties are typically used instead of lesser versions of community control (Tonry 1990; Austin and Krisberg 1982; Tonry and Will 1988). Thus, they actually result in greater costs, not reduced costs. Even when a community penalty is successful in replacing a threatened prison term, the secondary costs of closely enforcing the community penalty can drive out all the savings of diversion (Clear and Hardyman 1990). The restrictions of the new community control programs are so severe, so difficult for the law violator to abide by, that these programs always incur high rates of failures that have nothing to do with crime (Petersilia 1986; Petersilia 1990). And those offenders who fail the program go to prison, after all.

The pragmatic argument that community controls are cheaper—especially the new, improved versions—is so weak that it is difficult to understand why the argument gets so much coverage. Perhaps the search for cheap penal harms is an irresistible impulse, it is one of the arguments used by Newman (1983) to support his call for electric shocks and other forms of painful punishments. But the search for cheaper punishment seems never to consider the obviously cheapest option: doing nothing.

The other side of the pragmatic argument treats prison as the appropriate referent for the amount and type of harm we should impose on offenders. But there is no obvious reason why these harms ought to be the standard. In fact, it is likely that the use of a term in prison has not been the most commonly imposed criminal sanction for offenders at any time this century (Report, 1988). Certainly, it is not the sanction of choice in other countries (Mathiesson 1990). Thinking that prison is the correct choice of harms and that offenders are fortunate to avoid it ignores the historical reliance on prison as a last-resort sanction, and turns the calculation of correctional harms on its head.

The most obvious flaw in the pragmatic argument is that it lacks a moral basis as a justification. Even if the community penalties were less harmful—and it is plausible that they are so, though not by as much as is often thought—it would not explain why the amount of harm associated with prison is acceptable as a referent for evaluating the harms imposed on citizens. The law, as has been argued, is a moral instrument. To justify its use of harm requires an appeal on moral grounds, not pragmatic ones. For this, we turn to utilitarian and retributive claims.

THE UTILITIES OF HARM

The main argument of utilitarians is that the harms promoted by coercive law produce greater general well-being. It is argued that by allowing these attacks upon an individual's well-being, crime is prevented, and thus the general well-being is improved—either by expanded domain, happiness, or some other benefit. The implication is that without the benefit of improved general well-being, the harms would be indefensible.

The need for an actual benefit from coercive harming is plain from a utilitarian standpoint, in two ways. First, because any instance of penal harming reduces well being, the use of harming is inherently suspect. It can only be justified by a demonstration that the harm is temporary, and is counterbalanced by producing some benefit. There is also a more stringent requirement—the trade-off cannot be merely that by hurting one person, another is helped. To merely exchange one person's well-being for another's would violate the utilitarian principle: "each to count for one and none for more than one." Therefore, each instance of specific penal harming should result in a more widely distributed, general benefit.

We must question whether the harms of corrections survive this test. Two levels of the test need to be distinguished. The first is this: doing some harming increases the level of well-being over what it would be if no harming were done. This justifies harming lawbreakers in the first place. The second level is more complicated: changing the amount of harming—increasing it or decreasing it—will result in a requisite change in well-being. This is the justification for increasing penal harm.

In each of these arguments, the general well-being at stake is what we label "community safety." (A more detailed investigation of this concept is provided in Chapter 5.) Is community safety enhanced by penal harming? The question is extremely complicated, but a general conclusion may be summarized here: the empirical basis for the idea that incremental increases in punitive harming produce greater than incremental increases in community safety is weak or nonexistent. A special report of the National Academy of Sciences on the rehabilitative effects of coercive correctional programs concluded that:

> After 40 years of research and literally hundreds of studies, almost all the conclusions that can be reached have to be formulated in terms of what we do not know. . . . The entire body of research appears to justify only the conclusion that we do not now know of any program or method that could be guaranteed to reduce the criminal activity of released offenders. (Sechrest et. al., 1979: 3)[7]

In a later report, the National Academy of Sciences (Blumstein et. al., 1978) reviewed evidence regarding the incapacitative and deterrent impact of the criminal law. After exhaustive consideration of the research, the writers concluded that the incapacitative and deterrent benefits of current policies can be improved only marginally, and this would require a wholesale increase in the prison population. A similar conclusion is reached by Spelman (1993).

If community protection were the sole issue, then the utilitarian basis for the morality of correctional harms—certainly the proliferation of those harms—could easily be dismissed. Not only is there little scientific basis for increasing the amount of penal harming, the empirical basis for *sustaining* the amount of harm now being imposed is all but missing. In any utilitarian scheme, it would seem that the burden of proof for justifying a specific act of injury would rest upon the agent using the harm to promote the greater good. The harmer would be required to demonstrate the necessity of the harms before they could justifiably be imposed. This would be so because the actual fact of the harm's impact on well-being would be undeniable, but the claim of the benefit would be open to question. Regarding modern penal harms, utilitarians appear to have failed their own moral prerequisite—they cannot demonstrate an empirical case for their proposed harms leading to a better society.

But the betterment of social well-being is a bit more complicated than a series of studies on the effects of sanctions, for social betterment has to do with the use of the criminal justice system as a general social instrument. The claim is that we build the justice process not so much to prevent specifically identifiable criminal events, but to mirror our larger interests in social self-preservation. This was the classic viewpoint of Durkheim (1964). From this point of view, utilitarians need only demonstrate how the application of the harming processes keeps the society from breaking down.

This problem is analogous to the one Isaac Asimov (1954; 1960; 1983) confronted when he wrote his 'robot novel' series. In an introduction to a reprinted version of these novels, he said that his original reason for writing the first three novels in the 1950s was a reaction to the general "robot hysteria" common to the time—people seemed terrified by the very idea of robots. The irony, Asimov felt, was that the robots were built by humans to serve human ends. In his view, robots would have protections built in by their architects.

In his first two novels, written in the 1950s, Asimov envisioned that three design rules (1950: 20) would control robotic decisions:

> *The First Law*: A robot may not injure a human being or, through inaction, allow a human being to come to harm.
> *The Second Law*: A robot must obey the rules given it by human beings, except where such orders would conflict with the First Law.
> *The Third Law*: A robot must protect its own existence, except where such protection conflicts with the First or Second Law.

The point of the rules was to create a scenario in which the robot, as the instrumental creation of people, could only serve the interests of people. But Asimov shows that the narrow interests of individuals cannot support the robots through the series of crises and conflicts he imposes upon them. Robots are continually faced with circumstances in which relative harms must be weighed, especially the long-term well-being of the human group versus the short-term well-being of a specific person. The robots "learn" that the needs of a society of persons are actually different from, and not always sustained by, the needs of particular individuals. The needs of people are not the same as the needs of a single person. By 1983, Asimov is forced to return to his robots and declare a new "law" (1983: 137) inferred by the others and therefore transcendent above them:

> *The Fourth Law*: A robot must always act in the interests of the welfare of the human race.

This law of robots—a law of the social machines of society, illustrates the central problem utilitarians face. The interests of specific people—indeed their very well-being—is not the same as, and in fact is smaller than, their interests as a social unit. What may, at a given moment in time, seem a reasonable sacrifice for the support of human interests, could result in severe human harm, seen from the larger view. As a machine built for human service, a robot can never be limited merely to serving the needs of individual humans and their robots; its work must include serving the needs of humanity.

This example applies to utilitarian thinking about crime control.

It may be that we have no strong factual basis for accelerating penal harms, but what if we did? Should we? If we prevent a few criminal harms and thereby increase the purposeful measure of socially imposed harm by authorities, do we advance the interests of the human order? Is not the definition of the human order more than the collection of the definitions—the additions and subtractions—of individual orders? Is not the well-being of the social group different than a mere sum of the individual levels of well-being on a given day?

There is a larger moral order at stake, not simply a practical need to create community safety or prevent specific crimes. The persons who would advance their social benefits through the careful manipulation of harms to others forget that the definition of the moral order is deeply tied to an understanding of the moral acceptability of the relations between self and others. This is the central moral dilemma of utilitarian concerns: even if harming worked well—and there is little evidence it does—would it enhance the nature of human endeavor to use pain as a means to advancing individual self-interests?

The collective act of harming is not neutral, morally or practically. Much is made of the teaching aspects of the criminal sanction (Gibbs 1975). Indeed, even those who are deeply critical of traditional utilitarian crime control interests are persuaded that penal harm is required for its moral educative value. They agree with the argument that the law serves as an example of social relations, that the law represents the inherent contractual aspect of social living, and that we will obey rules and respect each others' desire for well-being. This argument stands at the intersection of the idea of deterrence and desert—the law works best when it defines the moral boundaries of social relations and then enforces those boundaries.[8]

This is an argument that has been made often in defense of the criminal law: it is the law that defines the society, and its central role is to do so (Durkheim 1964; Erikson 1966; Adler 1983). Critics of this point of view have shown how such a model of a cohesive society is inadequate when applied to modern social relations (Garland 1990). But even if it were an accurate portrayal, would we approve of it? Would we be willing to say that the recent quadrupling of penal harming in the United States (discussed in Chapter 2) presents an appealing view and is a normative expression of our society? Would we be proud of this? (In chapter 6, I return again to these questions about the moral justifiability of the law as it is practiced.)

The view that law is a normative expression of our social conscience is antiseptic and comports only vaguely with modern jurisprudence. To realize the limits of this viewpoint, one need merely spend some time in a busy urban court, or visit a crowded state prison, or sit with an overburdened probation officer. The creators of the law may be trying to teach citizens about the morality of proper social relations, but it stretches credulity to believe that the lesson is being learned. No matter how much we want the lawbreaker to recognize that lawbreaking is wrong, the system seems destined to teach a different truth.

> A further justification of punishment is its being fitting or appropriate. We think it fitting not only that the wrongdoer be unhappy, but that everyone recognize what he did was wrong, and that the strongest form of recognizing this is by making him suffer. But this is pure confusion. It is fitting that he suffer and that what he did be recognized as wrong. But making him suffer does not always, and often will not, make him suffer in the way that he should. (Griffin 1986: 271)

To those who would impose the penalty, the lesson of their imposition is clear and simple: obey the rules or suffer the consequences. This version of the moral message of the law differs from the desired statement, "what I did was wrong." Offenders learn a much less morally valuable alternative when the lesson stresses obedience: they learn that "what I did, I failed to get away with." The everyday occurrence of criminal behavior is eloquent and irrefutable evidence that many people are not getting the desired message, or even its alternative.

Some would say that my analysis confuses two targets of the message of the sanction: the offender and the observer. Yes, they might admit, offenders notoriously distort and misconstrue the meaning of the harms we impose upon them. But the third party observer, watching us as we do our work, most certainly gets the message: laws are reconfirmed and obedience to those laws reestablished. Perhaps this is so. But we saw earlier that the evidence in support of a general deterrent effect of law is ambiguous at best, and it is certainly puny, if one seeks to justify the scale of wholesale increases in harm recently experienced in this country. Third party observers may be getting a message from all this penal harming, but it is not entirely clear what the message is, nor how well it guides their behaviors.

What if the message of punishment—at least the one the recipients and observers hear—is merely that of power? What if the real message of punishment has to do with who has the power and who does not? This is certainly not a new idea (Wright 1973; Quinney 1970; Turk 1969; Taylor 1975), but it raises the most profound of questions for utilitarians. What if a main intention of all these harms is not to make a better society, but rather to make certain that no successful challenge can be mounted to the current one, which benefits the rule-makers and few others?

This idea has been subjected to criticism (Sparks 1980; Garland 1990; Matthews 1992). Perhaps it is an overly zealous view of the law to see it as serving only the entrenched interests of the ruling elites. But it does not require a wildness of imagination to see that a lawbreaker, standing under the relentless forces of the punitive apparatus, might misconstrue the rationale for punishment, much as an employee might perceive a boss to be thoughtlessly authoritarian when this is not so, or a child might likewise misperceive a parent to be arbitrarily cruel. Moreover, the idea that the operations of punishment serve the more narrow interests of the labor marketplace receives considerable empirical support in the literature (Rusche and Kirchheimer 1939; Box 1987; Wilkins 1991; Chiricos and DeLone 1992).

Even assuming the normative message, however, it is one thing to have a message to convey; it is quite another to get it across. The central problem, of course, is the incompatibility of the intended message and the means of its delivery. The agents of penal harm want the lawbreaker and all others who observe the penal process to learn the moral wrongness of choosing to harm others by violating the law. The pedagogical technique they use is to harm, intentionally. Is it any wonder that the lawbreaker, upon experiencing the deliberate harms, fails to get the point that to harm is immoral? "The 'paradox of legal violence' [is that] the essence of penal violence is to enforce inviolability by violence" (Tahtinen 1963: 42). The offender gets the unintended lesson: harm and violence are acceptable if you have the power to get away with it.

Still, the utilitarians could be satisfied if the rest of the citizens—the observers—got the intended message about the moral benefits of obeying the law. Unfortunately, the observers of the penal harm may get the same point as its target does: the law has power. Among the observers, those who already view the law as a moral reason for compliance may stand to learn only of the law's ambivalent relationship to the uses of violence and harm. Those who doubt the moral basis for abstaining from acts of harm are reinforced in their view that the question is merely one of opportunity and logistics.

This problem, more than any other, afflicts the utilitarian pursuit of effectiveness in the use of penal harms. To use the law as an instrument of criminal repression erodes the law's moral force. Perhaps this is one reason why the social benefits of penal harming claimed by utilitarians have failed to materialize.

RETRIBUTION AND HARM

Because the moral claims of the utilitarians have been exposed as too limited, retributivists have entered the breach to make their claims for the moral requirement of harm. They believe it is necessary to impose penal harms without an eye to making society better, but merely to do justice. This approach is not free of problems.

Much has been made of technical difficulties in the retributive justification for harming offenders. It has been pointed out that the necessary scaling of penalties is difficult (Braithwaite and Pettit 1990), though advocates of desert have responded to this problem (von Hirsch 1985). That desert leads to a necessary accelerating of levels of punishment has also been asserted by its detractors (Hudson 1987)— and denied by its advocates (von Hirsch 1990). These criticisms are serious, but they are not the most pressing problems for the retributive point of view of harming offenders.

To understand these problems, let us first restate the central moral claims of the retributivists, that the use of punishment as a symbol has two benefits. First, it respects human dignity by treating individuals as persons of moral significance. Second, it is respectful of humans by treating them as ends, not means. In essence, it is claimed that retribution is simply fair.

Now there is an important twist in the way these claims are made operational, a twist that is illustrated by comparing two perspectives on the idea of what we call "fairness." Nobody would disagree with the goal of being fair. But there are at least two different—nearly opposing—versions of what constitutes a fair action. One calls upon us to treat each other equally, regardless of intrinsic differences from one to another. The other calls upon us to do that which fits the people involved, based on their circumstances—obviously in light of those intrinsic differences. Neither approach has an obviously superior claim to fairness. It seems *prima facie* fair to treat two individuals in the same manner, based on their behavior; it also seems fair on its face to respond to people based upon an understanding of their lives, their histories, experiences, and capabilities. The debate between these possibilities is an old one. Retribution has, in its modern desert form, sided firmly with the former.

The claim that people should be treated with dignity is interesting in light of this distinction, since the moral ideal of retribution requires harm to the well-being of law violators. The famous illustration of Kant, cited earlier, that a society's moral standing is based upon the execution of murderers, illustrates the firm nexus between retributive morality and penal harm. Through punishment (often defined as "censure") and only through punishment, do retributivists separate themselves from the acts they condemn. They also thereby proclaim the dignity of human freedom to choose compliance with the law, and they treat acts in defiance of the law as fully responsible, moral choices.

Is it really respectful of individuals, and especially of their autonomy as fully mature adults capable of judgement and choice, to harm them when they have committed crimes? It may be argued that the requirement of penal harm disregards the dignity of the person in two ways. First, it does not consider the potentially negative effects of being subjected to harm, and ignores even effects that all citizens might agree are undesirable. As Tahtinen (1963) put it, the requirement of penal harm means "that an offender has to be punished painfully even if he then, and only then, becomes a repeated offender beyond all chance of social rehabilitation" (71). In what way can it be respectful of the individual if harms are imposed that benefit nobody and lead inexorably to even more harms?

The requirement of retribution degrades people in another way as well. In a persuasive argument about desert, Griffin (1986) points out that a respectful understanding of the person as a moral agent recognizes the possibility of remorse and change. It is not that reproach is an inadequate response to crime, but rather that it is incomplete:

> Your response [to my crime] would be: resentment, anger, sometimes also fear, avoidance self-defence, retaliation. . . . But when I do repent and change, a lot in your response loses appropriateness. Certainly fear and self-defence do. So, I think, would anger and retaliation. (268–9)

The problem with retribution as a requirement rather than merely as an option is that it degrades, rather than respects the individual. It requires that people experience harm for their acts regardless of their circumstances, regardless of changes in their circumstances. Once convicted of a crime, the only (or at least primary) characteristic to be considered is the newly achieved status as a wrongdoer. Everything else about a person's life disappears into insignificance in comparison to the single criminal act. Retribution discounts real properties of humans—that they have pasts and futures; that they change and grow from their experience. Retribution says: "Regardless of who you are now and how you got here, I will now harm you for one action you have taken in the past." Ackerman's widely quoted derision of utilitarian trade-offs seems to apply equally to retribution: "Nobody in his right mind would consent to such degradation" (Ackerman

1982: 343). Far from confirming human dignity, retribution degrades the dignity of the person to whom it is applied. The idea of the detached punisher, disinterested in the well-being of the so-called "client," is not acceptable on its face. In the quotation that opened this chapter, Wolfe tellingly illustrates the depravity of pure desert, which refuses to take the person into account. To act as though the person being punished is a nondescript "object," a non-person—that is, to refuse to consider the unique aspects that come together to make that person's feelings and reactions—repudiates the core ideal of retribution, that everyone be treated as an end and not a means.

Once we admit that to treat people with dignity, to deal with them as ends in themselves, requires taking into account who they are and giving consideration to the response that best fits their lives, we are faced with a dilemma. The longstanding tradition of retributive thought is equal treatment based upon the crime. Yet in harming two burglars identically, we must recognize that they are not affected identically by our punishment. A host of factors can influence the degree of harm a punishment entails, ranging from the age and experience of the lawbreaker to mental and physical health. To act as though these characteristics do not matter is to ignore the dignity of the offender as a unique person. To set the abstract interests of justice above the need to deal with the law breaker in ways that fit the lawbreaker's circumstances is to use the lawbreaker as an instrument of some abstraction called justice—as a means, not an end.[9] To act as though the lawbreaker cannot repent or overcome the forces that led to crime is to dress ourselves in a severe habit of pessimism; to act as though such issues are unimportant is to ignore the reality of offenders' lives and their struggles.

On the other hand, should we wish to ally ourselves with these good objectives, and punish each person as fits the crime and the human circumstances surrounding it, we must admit to a woefully inadequate technology for doing so. For instance, let us assume we were willing to take seriously the obligation to design a punishment that effectively takes into account the way damaging childhood experiences such as poverty, loss of a parent, sexual victimization, or even *in utero* transmission of disease and defect might contribute to a person's criminality. How would we do so? To what science would we turn? What proportion of the deserved penal harm is excused by the permanent disability of multiple personalty disorder, which results from the experience of childhood assaults by parents and tends to contribute to patterns of adult violence? How much self-satisfied redemption are we entitled to feel for blaming such people, and how much of our blame are we obligated to excuse?

The dilemma of the retributivist is that in order to penally harm for the law violation, these characteristics must be ignored as irrelevant, though a moment's reflection tells us this is surely not fair. If the retributivist cannot find a way to take these aspects of the law violator into account, then the claim that the harm affirms the dignity of the person is exposed as hollow. In fact, the retributivist says, "Everything about you that leads up to who you are and explains your life as you have lived it and experienced it counts for naught; the only relevant fact in your life is this one act for which you stand convicted." It is hard to see how such a stance promotes dignity and treats the person as an end, not a means.

What is fair for a person who breaks the law extends well beyond merely harming that person. The person who has been fairly harmed by a set of retributive rules does not feel treated fairly (Goodstein and Hepburn, 1985). The facts of a human life are much more complicated. To treat people as people requires understanding them as individuals, not merely harming them and being done with it.

CONCLUSION

The purpose of this chapter has been to introduce the idea of penal harm and to explore its justifications. The term refers to the attack upon the law violator's well-being that is the essence of punishment. The question was then asked: How can we justify this harming of the well-being of fellow citizens?

In exploring the answer to this question, several points were made about penal harm that might undercut our confidence in this social practice.

First, I argued that there is something inherently suspicious about organized harming bureaucracies that are run by government for the purpose of coercively injuring citizens. We have grown comfortable with being the nation with the largest incarcerated population in the world, but perhaps this is a fact we should not so easily accept.

My second point was that the classic retributive justifications for harming ultimately come down to approving undesirable means to achieve desirable ends. Yet this is precisely the moral quandary that retributivists find repulsive in their utilitarian counterparts, and avoiding the moral dilemma is one of the supposed advantages of being retributive.

Third, I argued that utilitarians find their case for penal harming hard to sustain on both scientific and logical grounds. This is especially problematic for them, since the utilitarian case is clothed in the robes of science.

Fourth, penal harming's recent shifts to the community setting do not materially change the nature of the arguments about its use. There are some ways, in fact, in which the community can be a more opprobrious setting for penal harm than is the prison.

Fifth, the core message conveyed by acts of penal harm is more about power relations in society than it is about moral living in society.

The practice of penal harming is not purely advantageous to society—not by far. Instances of penal harming have obvious detriments for the object of the harm, of course. There are also detriments for the society doing the harming and for the relations among citizens who live in that society. The detriments are not solely symbolic, either. Instances of penal harm commonly lower the threshold of well-being within a society, and examples of this dynamic are provided in the chapters that follow.

Does this mean we have no reason for penal harm? Does this mean that offenders, once caught and convicted, should not be harmed?

It is one thing to argue, as I have above, that the practice of penal harm lacks a fully successful justification. It is quite another to argue that the practice should be abandoned. Having encountered law violators in our midst, the question is, "What should we do?" My point is a small one, perhaps laboriously developed: the urge to harm the criminal, however deeply felt, carries with it certain irrationalities and inconsistencies.

With these limitations to penal harming, it would seem there would be a strong reaction against penal harms, especially in a nation that prides itself on being "free." As is shown in Chapter 2, nothing could be further from the truth. Instead, there has been a stupendous growth in penal harming of all types and forms in the last 20 years.

This growth has been justified, not by the broad philosophical arguments discussed in this chapter, but by much more narrow claims; in particular, that (1) the growth in crime has caused the growth in penal harm, and/or (2) in order to suppress crime, we have been forced to harm more. These two claims are explored in the following chapter.[10]

2

The Punishment Experiment

> *The choice is clear: more prison space or more crime.*
>> —William Barr, United States Attorney General, 1991–92

> *Few ideas are more utopian than the belief that we can stop crime by changing the way it is handled within the formal criminal justice system.*
>> —Elliot Currie, *Confronting Crime* (p. 229)

Since the middle part of the 1970s, the United States has engaged in what might be thought of as a social experiment in punishment.[11] By the end of this experiment, the reach of the corrections system had nearly quadrupled over levels that had been constant throughout the twentieth century. My purpose in this chapter is threefold: (1) to document the nature of the growth in the penal system; (2) to compare competing paradigms about the causes of this growth; and (3) to assess the changes in crime and justice resulting from this grand experiment. I will argue a fairly simple conclusion: the growth in penal harms, as well as the impact of that growth, was due more to social and political forces than it was to levels of crime. To construct this simple argument requires a detailed excursion through the social machinery of our penal system.

THE PENAL SYSTEM

It is not fully accurate to describe the changes of the last 20 years as an experiment, of course, because if it were, there would be an explicit statement of the experiment's central hypotheses, there would be a control, and the nation's criminologists would anxiously be awaiting its results.

Yet it is not entirely wrong to think of recent penal policy as a type of experiment. First, there is something of an experimental condition, in that the practices of recent years constitute a radical departure from prior policy. Second, the formal justification for this wholesale change was a new vision of reducing crime through penal policy. Third, the results of this unprecedented change are now becoming apparent. Thus we have at least three of the elements of a decent social experiment: an idea about a better way to do things, changes that are consistent with that idea, and results of those changes.

As is shown in the statistics which follow, the results of this 20-year experiment are not entirely clear. To be sure, our system of corrections has never been more crowded, never faced a more debilitating crisis of resources. On the other hand, the impact on crime of a burgeoning corrections system is not at all apparent: crime rates have certainly continued to rise along with the correctional population, but no one can say with confidence what *would* have happened to crime if the explosion in punishment had not occurred.

In this chapter, I develop a working model of the punishment system in the United States—a model of the punitive machine. At the system's core are the penal harms inflicted upon the lawbreaker, the panoply of ways in which the dignity and self-worth of offenders are assaulted by deliberate penal action. This part of the punishment system is analyzed first, to show the remarkable extent to which the punitive capacity of corrections has increased in recent years.

If the system's *materiel* is penal harm, its domain is crime, which is itself a function of certain social forces, among them age, gender, and disadvantage. An investigation of the social forces that coincide with criminality indicates the potential of the punitive net—the size of its playing field. Since 1970, for example, the number of males aged 15–34 has increased by over one-third, while the number living below the poverty line increased by over one-fourth (U.S. Census 1990). With such an increase in the pool of eligible offenders, it would be expected—absent some important intervention—that crime would increase.

Indeed, since 1973, Part I felonies reported to the police have increased a whopping 63% (U.S. Department of Justice, 1973 and 1990). It is possible, however, that perhaps crime has not increased: surveys of households conducted annually since 1973 have shown a fluctuation, but have estimated an extraordinarily modest overall increase in crimes of .003% (U.S. Department of Justice, 1991). This statistical discrepancy demonstrates starkly the grossly speculative nature of our knowledge about crime. Having embarked on this stupendous experiment in punishment, we lack even rudimentary statistical bases for concluding what changes have accompanied it, much less what changes it caused.[12]

It is possible to analyze criminality as the energy that sustains the corrections system—after all, without crimes there is no punishment. The energy that sustains corrections can be measured in two ways. The first is the substance flowing through the system, composed of felony arrests and convictions. The second energy source is the law, which acts as a kind of punishment calibration system specifying degrees of harm that are thought reasonable for particular offenses.

Drawing the distinction between these two types of system energy is important. Crime is labelled a "natural" energy source, in that its fluctuations are products of the powerful ebb and flow of social forces, and the system can do little but respond. Law is considered an "artificial" energy source, in the sense that the calibration of penal harms is a creation of decision-makers who, at least theoretically, could have decided otherwise.

Below, we analyze these two energy sources for punishment, and find evidence that both have contributed to the major escalation of punishment in the United States. This means that the expansion of corrections is based both upon natural phenomena and upon artificial policy decisions.

Oddly, crime, or at least crime rates, may also be seen as the machine's *product*. At first blush, some people may think this a controversial idea, because they believe the corrections system is built as a response to crime. But in fact, crime is thought to be a product of the machine by nearly all advocates of expanded punitiveness. Even retributivists believe that the deterrent effect of punishment justifies the suffering it imposes (von Hirsch, 1975). Utilitarians, of course, argue that the central purpose of all punishments is to reduce crime. The view that crime is an *output* of the punishment system, then, is an important component of advocacy for the wisdom of penal harm.

Once again, however, we are caught in a vexing contradiction about how the system works: we have made crime both a cause and a result of the punishment level. This is one of the classic sleights of hand performed by penal growth advocates—when crime goes up, they see a need for more increasing punishment, but when crime goes down, they believe punishment increases have been vindicated.

In our usage, however, two different measures of crime are intended. The penal system is fueled by *persons*—actual offenders who have been accused and convicted. The belief—and this is pivotal to the entire "experiment" of the last 20 years—is that by being more punitive, fewer crime incidents occur. Thus, in order to understand the corrections system, we need to draw a distinction between crimes reported (either to police or in surveys) and offenders arrested and processed.

Two Caveats in System Models

Before moving to a statistical description of the system in operation, it is important to stress caution in the interpretation of our data: in general, the measures are poor and the patterns are ambivalent. Caution is especially warranted in attempting to understand the results of a so-called "experiment." In evaluating aspects of crime, as with nearly any social problem, it is virtually impossible to prove that one set of changes over time has been caused by another. The technique for demonstrating a statistical relationship consistent with causes using time series data is complicated (McCleary 1980) and is based on a stringent set of assumptions about the nature of the data. Traditional time series analyses require lengthy observations over time that can be made stationary for level and variance. Multivariate time series analyses are based upon an assumption that the forces causing the various time series are themselves stable in the way they determine the series over time. A simple inspection of the incarceration rates (see below) indicates that whatever stability was apparent in the first part of this century has all but disappeared in the years since 1970. This suggests that to lump these time series together into a single string of data would be inadvisable, because there is a sense in which the pre-1970 string is made of 'apples,' while the post-1970 data are 'oranges.' Yet to analyze the post-1970 data separately provides only 20 data points, not nearly enough to construct reliable univariate models, much less multivariate models, even though some analysts (Zedlewski 1987) have erroneously tried this approach.

Therefore, it is most accurate to understand the following analyses as *describing* a system of penal harm rather than *proving,* necessarily, how its elements relate to one another. Indeed, criminologists are in heated disagreement about the implications of the patterns described below (compare DiIulio 1991, to Baird 1993). The main forces of the system are, in fact, mutually causational, and therefore it is possible to speculate about a variety of explanations of how they intersect to produce the pattern described.

A second caveat regarding analysis of system data has to do with the decision to focus on national data rather than, say, state-level data or county data. Justice systems, for the most part, operate on smaller levels of government, and patterns of crime and punishment vary—often quite dramatically—across these levels. Zimring and Hawkins (1991) have made the point that nearly every pattern of crime and punishment that a person would choose to emphasize can be found when comparing the states of the United States. By choosing to portray national-level data, we are almost certainly obscuring important patterns which exist in some states but not in others.

Thus, we are faced with a considerable problem of science as we try to understand how the mechanism of the crime-punishment system worked during this experiment. The relationships among the key variables are almost certainly reciprocal and multiple, yet there are insufficient observations to allow confident multivariate analysis. We lack a useful control group. The main dependent variable, crime, is also a major independent variable—and as if that were not enough, it has been measured both as increasing and as decreasing during the years of the experiment. Finally, the gross national figures are not always representative of patterns existing within the various states and urban counties.

Given these problems of science, it should surprise no one that statistical bases may be found to argue virtually any position regarding what precisely has been learned from this experiment. The politics of punishment being what they are, nearly every plausible position has been argued by one or another advocate. From the standpoint of science, we must begin our own analysis with a frank admission that it is unlikely any research strategy will tell us, with certainty, the experiment's bottom line. The strategic choice of particular measures and how to array them often determines the eventual result, and so we are left to choose a series of broad analyses and to be circumspect in trying to understand their meaning.

Yet the reader need not be completely paralyzed by these issues. Instead of the conundrum, we can focus on the central patterns that overwhelm the numbers reported below: The number of citizens harmed by penal action has more than tripled in a mere 20 years. During that same period, arrests did not even double, nor did all crime reported to police. Violent crime reported to the police barely doubled (though if you have some confidence in victimization studies, violent crime actually decreased slightly). In the face of these numbers, those who would argue that the experiment has been socially beneficial—that the escalation of penal harming has (1) resulted naturally from a similar increase in criminal behavior, or (2) resulted in a reduction in the level of crime—have a difficult case to make. Perhaps the fact that even the most supportive credible studies find only marginal effects (see Chapter 3; see also Mathiesen 1990) is understandable, in light of these patterns.

A final point should be made before moving into the data about penal harming systems, and that has to do with the quality, availability, and interpretability of various measures. Much has been written on this topic (see, for example, Maltz 1977). For the purposes of the discussion that follows, three observations are important. First, since 1970, the centralized collection of data on punishment has been uneven. For some years, counts of offenders living on probation, in jail, or under other forms of control are unavailable. Therefore, where there are gaps in data, estimates have been made in order to fill them in.[13] Second, fluctuations in measures from year to year are often dramatic, and may obscure the underlying trends in the data. Sometimes, by smoothing the data (displaying the averages of three consecutive observations, called the "moving average") it is easier to see the trends that have been sustained over long periods. Third, it must be constantly remembered that measures of phenomena such as crime and punishment are actually approximations of the true phenomena, and some variation (basically of unknown level) exists between the official measure and the true phenomenon it represents.

THE PUNISHMENT EXPERIMENT

There are two main ways to present data about the extent of punitiveness in the United States: raw numbers and rates. Each is a measure of levels of harm inflicted as a result of social policy.

The raw numbers are the grossest measure; they tell the true extent of punishment experienced by citizens of this country. Figure 2–1 shows the numbers of offenders under any form of correctional control, from 1970 to 1990. This number includes offenders incarcerated and those under community supervision during that period.

The figures are astounding. Since 1975 and 1990, the number of offenders under any form of correctional supervision has increased by 188%. Prisoners increased by 332% between 1973 and 1992; between 1975 and 1990, probationers increased by 203%; parolees by 270%. Not only have the numbers changed, but the rates have changed, as well. Figure 2–2 shows that incarceration rates (per 100,000 citizens) increased 205% between 1973 and 1990.

The changes indicated in figures 2–1 and 2–2 are astounding by any measure. A person would be hard pressed to identify any other social measure that is so closely tied to lethargic demographic indicators, yet which has changed so substantially and inexorably. Even these data may understate the degree of change that has taken place in

Figure 2-1

Growth in total number of offenders under correctional control

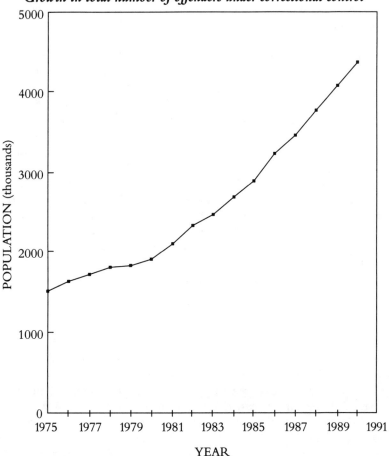

YEAR

recent years. Blumstein and Cohen (1973) demonstrated that from 1925 through 1970, punishment levels in the United States were relatively stable, ranging between about 90 and 110 (per 100,000), with major fluctuations occurring during times of world war and world depression. What has happened during the last two decades of this century has been a destabilization of the heretofore semi-stable rates of punishment characterizing the nation since the turn of the century.

If the analysis incorporates prior changes in levels and rates of

Figure 2–2

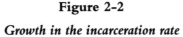

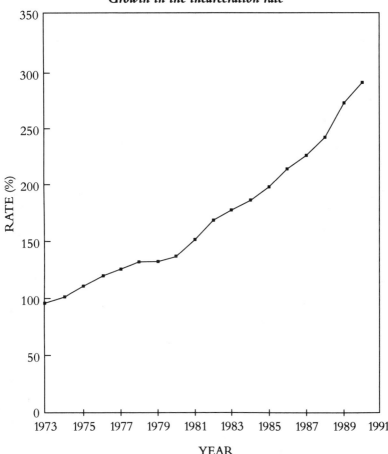

penal harming into the equation, and presents the percentage change from one year to the next, a sense of the unprecedented degree of change in punishment during the experiment of the last 20 years is provided. This is shown in figure 2–3 (and is smoothed as a three-year moving average of change rates), and indicates that not only have the levels and rates of penal harming increased, but that these changes have accelerated during the time period. In other words, the levels, rates and levels of rates showed consistent increases in the period from 1970 to 1990.

What do these changes in penal harm indicate? The answer is

Figure 2-3

*Three-year moving average of the annual rate of change in total
correctional population*

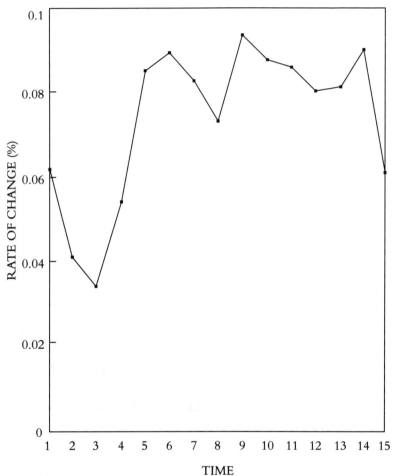

more obvious than the answer to virtually any other question one
might ask about this complicated field of corrections: in the United
States, when it comes to the issue of harming its own citizens through
the penal process, a quite unprecedented and dramatic escalation
occurred during the 1970s and 1980s. The penal system achieved a
completely new level of capacity in the last quarter of the twentieth
century. This is especially the case when it comes to incarceration,

which, since 1973, has increased more rapidly than any other form of punishment.

THE SOCIAL CONDITIONS OF CRIME

Some people have argued that the increase in punishment is a natural result of increases in crime proneness in the United States, especially with respect to the age and gender of the citizenry and the general social circumstances they experience (Braithwaite 1980; 1989). Each of these is a powerful correlate of criminal behavior and deserves investigation.

Age and Gender

The relationships among age, gender, and criminal behavior are among the strongest of all in criminology (Gottfredson and Hirschi 1990). Criminal behavior is associated with adolescent and young adult males, and the number of persons in this age group will help to determine the total amount of crime. Figure 2–4 displays the number of U.S. citizens in this age and gender group from 1970 to 1990 and the ratio of the total punishment rate to the size of this group. This figure demonstrates that while the crime-prone age and gender group increased significantly during the experiment, this is not the entire explanation of the growth in punishment. If it had been, the ratio of penalty growth to age-gender group growth would be stable for the period. In fact, the corrections system housed an increasing proportion of this group during the punishment experiment.

Social Conditions

There are, of course, many social measures associated with crime. Unemployment (Box, 1987; Farrington, et. al., 1986; Sampson and Wooldredge; 1987), relative economic disadvantage (Braithwaite, 1980), minorities living in urban environments (Laub, 1983; Archer and Gartner, 1984), and drug use (Ball, Shaffer and Nurco, 1983) are but a few of them. Recent research in England has shown that property crime is closely associated with patterns of economic well-being (Field, 1990), as is punishment itself (Box, 1987). It is also the case that these measures of deprived social conditions are themselves highly intercorrelated.

Two of the best measures of crime-relevant social conditions are unemployment and number of citizens living below the poverty line. The first is a standard measure of "surplus labor," and is commonly found as a factor in fluctuations in crimes as measured by the UCR

Figure 2-4

U.S. male population age 14–24 and ratio to numbers incarcerated

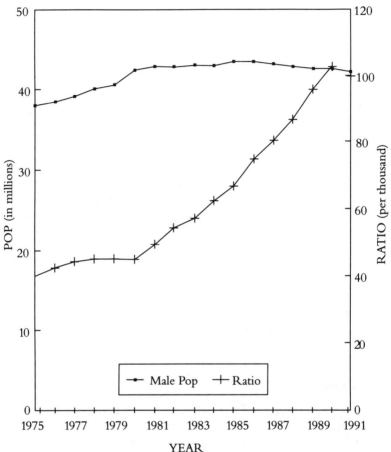

(DeLone and Chiricos 1991). The second is a more general measure of the health of the social system; it estimates the size of the under-class, the pool who stand to gain little by compliance with traditional laws and who most heavily populate our penal process (Irwin and Austin, 1993).

Figure 2–5 displays changes in these measures from 1973 until 1992. The table shows that these social indicators fluctuated during the time period. Poverty increased slightly, and unemployment did not increase or decrease in any particular pattern. Indeed, during the last years of this time period, the two measures of disadvantage were

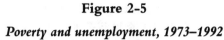

Figure 2-5

Poverty and unemployment, 1973–1992

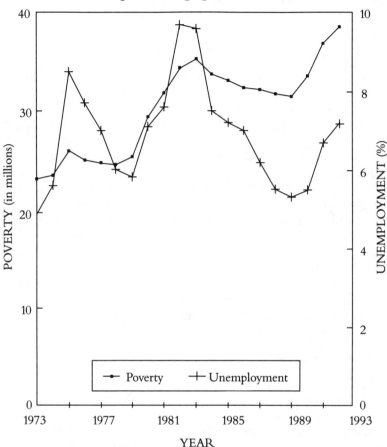

in consistent decline. This pattern was matched by another social correlate of crime, drug use (not in the table), which also declined toward the end of the two decades (Johnston, 1988). Relative income disparity also grew; between 1980 and 1990, the average income of the highest 20% of Americans grew 32.5% (the highest 1% grew 87.1%), while the lowest 20% actually *declined* by 5.2% (cited in Baird 1993: 5).

In order to visualize how changes in these crime-generating factors relate to changes in punishment, the graph also shows the number of offenders under correctional control. By the end of the decade, the number being harmed by penal authorities was greater than 10% of those living in poverty. From figures such as these, it is implausible to argue that trends in ingrained social forces compelled an increase in crime that, itself, forced a requisite increase in rates of punishment.

THE CALIBRATION OF PENAL HARMS

Getting an exact measure of the number and type of changes in the law of punishment is difficult, for several reasons. There are 50 state jurisdictions in addition to the federal courts and the District of Columbia. Each has its own penal code. In all these systems, the power to punish is balanced among the legislative branch (making laws), the judicial branch (imposing sentences), and the executive branch (determining release eligibility). Each jurisdiction distributes differently the amount of discretion to be exercised by these parties. To get an idea about the complexities involved, we might take the index crimes, multiply them by 50 penal statutes, 50 sentencing practices and 50 release practices—the result is a daunting 875,000 possible combinations of means to determine how even this subsample of lawbreakers has been handled.

This may explain why good statistics about punishment practice are nearly impossible to obtain. The discussion below, therefore, is but a guide to understanding what has happened in recent years to the legal calibration of penal harm.

The Legislative Branch

Table 2-1 is a listing of states that passed parole restrictions, probation restrictions, or sentence enhancements during the height of the experiment in punishment, the years 1972–1982. Half the states placed restrictions on parole, and another eight abolished parole altogether. Nearly every state legislature passed a law restricting the availability of probation (mandatory sentencing) and two-thirds enacted enhanced maximum terms for at least some offenses. In effect, legislatures voted about participation in the experiment, and there was unanimity: in one way or another, every state altered its penal policy in the direction of greater punitive severity.

Pennsylvania and Colorado provide excellent examples of the punitiveness common to the legislative branch. In Pennsylvania, the legislature established a Sentencing Commission and assigned it the task of devising a new sentencing code. After months of work, the Commission proposed to the legislature a tough new set of sentencing guidelines that, once implemented, would, according to conservative estimates, require the Commonwealth to construct two new maxi-

Table 2-1   States with Altered Penalties for Certain Offenses

	Increased Penalties		Decreased Penalties
1972	Maryland		
1973	Delaware Nevada New York		
1974	Massachusetts		
1975	New Hampshire South Carolina		
1976	Colorado Hawaii Kansas Maine Oklahoma		
1977	California Indiana Michigan New Mexico Oregan	1977	Maine
1978	Arizona Idaho Illinois Louisiana South Dakota		
1979	Alabama Missouri Nebraska New Jersey Tennessee	1979	New Jersey
1980	Georgia		
1981	Arkansas Connecticut North Carolina Pennsylvania	1981	North Carolina South Carolina
1982	District of Columbia Kentucky	1982	Tennessee

	Parole Restricted		Parole Abolished
1974	Alaska Massachusetts		
1975	Arkansas		

Table 2-1 (*continued*)

	Parole Restricted		Parole Abolished
1977	Idaho Michigan Missouri Oregon Texas	1977	California Indiana Maine
1978	Arizona Iowa	1978	Illinois Minnesota
1979	Maryland Montana Nevada New Jersey New Mexico Oklahoma Utah Virginia	1979	Colorado
1980	Alabama Georgia Hawaii	1981	Connecticut Washington
1981	North Carolina Pennsylvania New Hampshire		
1982	Kansas Tennessee		

mum-security prisons. Not to be outdone, the legislature rejected the proposal as too lenient, and instructed the Commission to redraft the proposal to make it even tougher. Pennsylvania's prison population grew 149% in the 1980s (Pennsylvania Commission on Crime and Delinquency 1990).

In Colorado, the legislature took the simple step of doubling all sentences for felonies. When correctional professionals pointed out the likely impact of the legislation on Colorado's already overcrowded prisons, sponsors of the law responded that the tougher sentences would scare so many criminals out of crime that the impact on prison populations would be canceled by the drop in crime. Colorado's prison population grew 137% in the 1980s (Colorado Department of Corrections 1980 and 1989).

None of the states can match what appears to be happening in the Federal penal system as a result of the Sentencing Reform Act of 1984, which took effect on November 1, 1987—the waning years of the statewide experiment. In its first four years of operation, the new law has (1) increased the proportion of sentences to prison from 52% to 60%, (2) decreased sentences to probation from 63% to 44%, and (3)

Table 2-2   States with Mandatory Terms for Certain Offenses

1972	Maryland	illegal wearing of handgun
1973	Delaware	robbery, drug offenses
	Nevada	use of firearm in crime
	New York	drug offenses, habitual offender laws
	Tennessee	habitual offender laws
1974	Massachusetts	violent offenses against elderly
1975	Kentucky	repeat offender laws
	South Carolina	armed robbery
1976	Hawaii	firearm use in felony, repeat offenders
	Kansas	firearm use, sex offenses
	Maryland	repeater violence
	Mississippi	repeat offender laws
	Oklahoma	offense w/ deadly weapon
1977	Maine	firearm use
	Michigan	firearm use in felony
	Missouri	dangerous weapon use in felony persistent sexual offender
	North Carolina	burglary, armed robbery
1978	Iowa	firearm use in forcible felony, habitual offender, drug offenses
	Michigan	drug offenses
	Nebraska	firearm use, repeat sex offender
1979	Idaho	firearm use
1980	Alabama	repeat offender laws
	Georgia	drug trafficking laws
	Massachusetts	second car theft offense, drug trafficking carrying a handgun
	North Carolina	drug offenses
1981	Arkansas	firearm laws
	Delaware	rape
	Idaho	repeat offenders
	New Hampshire	firearm laws
	Vermont	motor vehicle offenses
	West Virginia	firearm use
1982	District of Columbia	handgun use
	Maryland	handgun use in crime
	Pennsylvania	firearm laws
	South Dakota	drug offenses
	Virginia	firearm use

increased the expected time served by an estimated 37% for violent crimes and 123% for drug crimes[14] (McDonald and Carlson, 1992).

The Judicial Branch

Several studies have shown that during the 1970s and 1980s, judges increased the harshness of their sentences (see for example, Casper,

Table 2-2 (*continued*)

year		
unknown	Alaska	drug offenses
	Florida	firearm use, drug offenses
	Georgia	vehicular homicide w/ revoked license
	Kentucky	firearm laws
	Montana	firearm use in crime
	New Mexico	use of firearm
	New York	firearm laws
	Ohio	drug, sex offenses
	Oregon	firearm use
	Rhode Island	firearm use

Brerton and Neal 1981; Committee on Corrections 1991). In 1965, felons entering prison for the first time served sentences averaging about 33 months, and this number increased by only two months over the next nine years. Sentence lengths started to increase by the middle of the 1970s, however, and by 1985, the average sentence for first admissions had nearly doubled to 67 months (Clear and Cole 1994: 197).

Judges are not the sole source of increased punishment. They operate within the laws that establish the penal code, and this accounts for some of the increases in sentence severity. Moreover, in many trials, the jury has the responsibility to impose the sentence, though jury trials make up less than 10% of the convictions in felony cases (Boland, 1990). There are other indications of increasing judicial toughness, as borne out by tougher sentences. In 1970, there were 608 persons on death row; as of April 1991, the number had increased to nearly 2500 (U. S. Department of Justice 1991). California, a bell-wether state in the so-called "get tough" movement, is perhaps typical. Changes in California's sentencing practices meant that by 1988, nearly one in five offenders in prison had been there five years or longer, compared to less than one in ten in 1982—a mere six years earlier (Branham 1992). It may be that legislatures make the severe punishments possible, but judges and juries seem willing to impose them. Nationwide, between 1981 and 1987, the probability that a conviction for a serious offense would lead to a prison sentence increased dramatically (for example, 41% for burglary; 166% for rape) while actual time served by these offenders also increased (53% for burglary; 129% for rape), demonstrating a double blow of toughness (Farrington and Langan 1992).[15] Boggess and Bound (1993) inspected the rates of crime and incarceration in the 1980s, and concluded that "the large increase in the incarceration rate in the 1980s seems primarily attributable to . . . an increase in the probability of incarceration conditional upon arrest for all offense categories [and] a large increase in new commitments for drug offenses" (16).

Studies of sentencing practices in the federal system found a general, gradual, upward trend in the length of sentences imposed by judges: from an average of 25 months in 1984 to 31 months in 1988 (Meierhoefer 1992: 3). This shift was accelerated by the new federal sentencing guidelines, which increased average sentences by over four months between 1988–1990. Much of the increase was due to judges imposing mandatory minimum terms, which eliminate early release possibilities.

The Executive Branch

It is most difficult to know with certainty what has happened to executive branch powers, especially parole, because it is this branch of government that is asked to solve the problem of prison crowding. When the federal courts begin taking managerial control over correctional systems, as has happened in over 40 States during the punishment experiment, the executive branch of government loses much of its authority. Thus, the executive branch seeks ways to manage crises in correctional resources, often inventing creative ways to release inmates (Weisburd and Chayet 1989). As an example, at one time there were 13 ways to rearrange release in South Carolina, including one called "Christmas parole," which applied to anyone whose parole date was within 30 days after December 25.

There is some indication that the aggressive work of the executive branch of government has counteracted some of the increases in punishments imposed by the other two branches. The average time served of first-time prison releases was 20 months in 1965, 18 months in 1973, 21 months in 1985, and 22 months in 1989 (Clear and Cole 1994: 197; Irwin and Austin 1993: 115) Yet these data may distort the true nature of the problem. Many of the sentence enhancements enacted in recent years are targeted on recidivist offenders, and therefore are not reflected in figures for first-time releasees. Moreover, the figures do not count unreleased offenders, who are stacking up in the prisons and jails in unprecedented numbers. Finally, the time-served estimates are slanted by the large number of nonviolent offenders contained in the calculation; when only violent offenders are considered, total time served tripled since 1975 (Reiss and Roth 1993). When recidivists, long-termers and violent offenders are included in overall estimates, one study has estimated that time served nearly doubles (Austin 1993). A recent federal report estimates that prisoners in 1991 will serve an average of 66 months before release (BJS 1991: 7).

For the executive branch of government, the cold realities of politics must also be balanced against the need to responsibly manage correctional resources. Perhaps the best example is provided by the improbable advent of the George Bush drug war, as embodied in the Anti-Drug Abuse Act of 1988. Despite severe institutional overcrowding throughout the United States—and despite evidence that drug use was actually declining at the time—the federal policies stressed the use of new toughness with criminals who distributed drugs and with drug users as well. To pay for this, the Bush Administration proposed a 75% increase in federal prison capacity (The White House 1991).

Around the United States, leaders responded to the clarion call from our Chief Executive for a War on Drugs. State-elected officials, often with strong support from governors and their staff, sponsored a spate of legislation that sought tougher penalties. A powerful example is Delaware, where the mere possession of five grams of any illegal substance called for an astounding three years in prison without possibility of parole. Similar laws made mere possession of any drug while inside a designated "school zone" a three-year penalty in New Jersey. The legislation had a predictable result: between 1978 and 1990, the percentage of prisoners incarcerated in New Jersey whose crime was the possession or sale of drugs had increased from 5% to 25% (California Blue Ribbon Commission 1990). At the level of federal government, the drug laws and their more aggressive enforcement increased the proportion of drug offenders included in the federal system from less than a quarter in 1980 to more than half in 1992 (U.S. Bureau of Prisons 1993). The National Council on Crime and Delinquency originally estimated that these new laws, if fully enforced, would result in a 60% increase in prison populations in only five years (Austin, Jones and McVey 1991). Largely due to lack of police and correctional resources, however, it appears the impact will not be that great, as more recent data project prison populations will rise by only about 33% (Austin, Jones, and McVey 1991).

In the collective work of these officials—judges, elected executives, legislators, and line criminal justice workers—to increase punitiveness, no single actor stands out as primary. At times, the punishment experiment seemed to take on the appearance of a kind of contest—who can advocate the most severe punitiveness? With all three forces adamantly in pursuit of toughness, something of a cycle of toughness occurred, in which each official agency sought a way to top the punitiveness of the other. Each newly adopted punitiveness upped the ante for the next round of toughness.

The drug war, the most recent example of the contemporary penal harm movement, is an ominous contribution to the experiment. Mere possession of drugs now generates a presumption of a severely punitive sentence, often more severe than sentences incurred for rape, burglary, or even child sexual abuse. In the federal system, drug offenders get sentences nearly three times as long; robbers' sentences were "only" doubled. We are left to wonder how long it will be before the imbalance of penalties created by the drug war will lead to a call for even more draconian penalties for offenders not involved with drugs.

CRIME

One justification of increases in punishment is the existence of crime. The need to respond to growing crime (or, alternatively, growing concern about crime) is taken to justify growth in penal harm as a policy. This may be referred to as the "demand" argument: the amount of punishment required is determined by the amount of crime; we have increasing punishment because we have increasing crime.

The need to prevent crime is also used to justify increases in punishment. This argument, which might be called the "suppression" thesis, is deeply encased in the utilitarian reasoning explored in the preceding chapter: increased levels of penal harm are useful because of the reduced level of crime that results.

Thus, according to a double-pronged argument, crime is both an input and output of the punitive system: increases in crime have caused the resultant increases in punishment, and increases in punishment are needed to cause the suppression of crime.

The anomaly is so apparent that the argument seems at first to be incredible. It appears obviously contradictory to use the same measure—crime—to justify the need for expansions in penal harm because crime is growing, and in the same breath to justify the use of penal harm because crime is shrinking. How can crime be growing and shrinking at the same time?

The argument becomes a little less troublesome if it is changed slightly, to claim that an increase in the number and seriousness of apprehended offenders has justified an increase in the levels of punishment; this increased punishment has, in turn, resulted in a reduction in crime, especially serious crime. This revised version of the argument takes account of the well-known fact that a small percentage of crimes result in an arrest (BJS 1990), and it is therefore plausible that a more efficient system could apprehend more offenders and treat them more harshly, with crime going down as a result.

This reformulated version of the crime control argument can be investigated by reviewing numbers of arrests and crimes since 1970.

Numbers of arrests are used because these represent the actual number of persons available to be punished—the system 'inputs.' Rates of crime are used because they better represent thresholds of crime in the society—the system 'outputs.'

Figure 2–6 displays the number of persons arrested for felonies and violent felonies[16] from 1970 to 1990, showing that both types of arrests have gradually and persistently increased since 1970. Whether this gradual increase is fully responsible for the sharp increase in

Figure 2-6

Arrests for felonies and violent felonies, 1973–1991

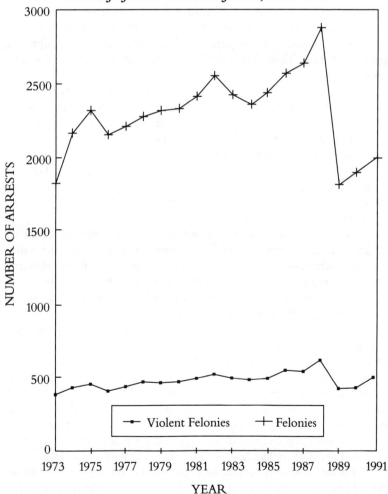

punitiveness is not clear from this graph alone. A comparison of the growth in arrests to the growth in punishments will help clarify the importance of arrests as a demand for punishment.

In the case of this comparison, it is helpful to smooth the data and to use selected patterns to test the importance of the demand hypothesis. A three-year moving average helps to smooth out the trends, and use of violent arrests and imprisonment levels gives the most direct test of the "demand" hypothesis. After all, the apprehension of a violent offender would seem clearly to "demand" a prison or jail response, according to the elemental sense of the demand thesis. In order to better represent the impact of an arrest on incarceration, we lag arrests by three years in order to incorporate the delay in the courts process and the additive effect of the long sentence that occurs for violent offenders. The results of this comparison are shown in Figure 2–7.

This figure shows that while the general drift of arrests was upward, the upward trend in imprisonment was considerably more marked. There were more than two (averaged and lagged) violent arrests for every 1974 prisoner. Barely 14 years later, the ratios were approximately 1:1. The demand hypothesis receives some support—after all, both levels of serious arrests and serious punishments increase markedly throughout the so-called "experiment" with punishment. But as a sole explanation of the increase in punitiveness, the demand hypothesis fails. The rate of growth in serious penal harm has far outstripped the rate of growth in serious arrests. That this growth is true for all crimes, not merely the most serious ones, is shown in figure 2–8, which displays the percentage change over the previous year in total felony arrests and total offenders under correctional control (again, lagged). While the growth in arrest rate fluctuates slightly above zero growth, or homeostasis, the punishment rate growth is consistently higher, and exceeds arrests in almost every year of the time series. In other words, the rate of growth in penal harming was on a different order than the rate of growth in arrests. As Zimring and Hawkins have put it, "fluctuating rates of criminality do not provide a short cut to understanding the fundamental changes in rates of imprisonment that occurred in the United States from 1950 to 1990" (Zimring and Hawkins 1991: 124).

If the demand hypothesis is clearly inadequate to explain the increase in punitiveness over the last 20 years, then perhaps its opposite side, the suppression thesis, will do so. This is the argument that the growth in punishment is well justified in terms of its benefits in commensurate reductions in crime.

Again we use violent crimes to investigate the impact of punish-

Figure 2-7

Impact of violent arrests (lagged three years) on numbers incarcerated

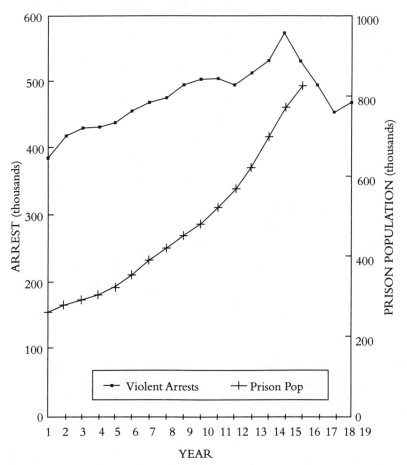

ment upon crime, and we lag the crime rates a year in the interest of causation. Figure 2–9 displays the number of violent crimes— measured by Uniform Crime Reports (UCR) data and by victimization surveys (transformed by multiplication by a constant)—and the level of imprisonment from 1970 to 1990.

There is, of course, considerable debate about whether victimization data or official police reports are a better indicator of actual crime. UCR data underestimate the crime rate because so much of crime is unreported, and changes in the UCR are highly correlated to changes in reporting practices. By contrast, the problems of error in

Figure 2-8

Average annual change in arrests and (lagged) average change in prison population, 1973–1991

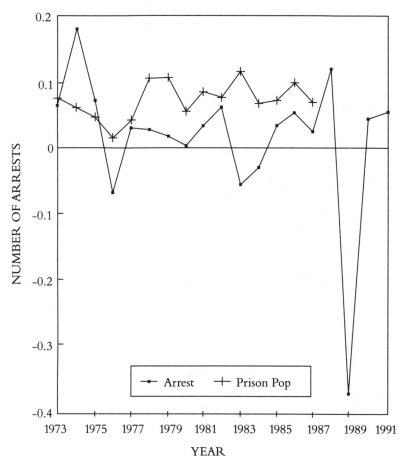

victim surveys are products of inaccuracies in victim memory and crime reporting, although standardization in the techniques of sampling and measurement suggest to some that changes over time in victimization statistics may be less a result of measurement bias than similar changes in UCR data (Maltz 1977).

Indeed, the statistics are quite different in their patterns. UCR data show an escalating rate of violent crime, while victimization data show a basic stability in violent crime, with slight reductions in the latter half of the measurement period. It is clear, however, that

Figure 2-9

Impact of incarceration (lagged one year) on crime (UCR and NCS)

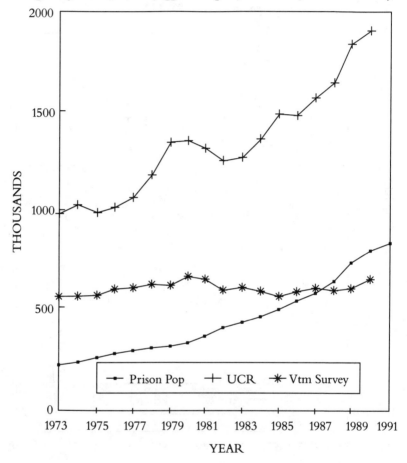

YEAR

neither measure provides a very strong argument for the suppression hypothesis. The inexorable increase in penal harm is either accompanied by an equivalent (lagged) increase in crime, or no essential change in crime. The argument that punishment changes produce crime changes is not supported by these data.

Taken together, the data in figures 2–6 though 2–9 do not support the demand-suppression model of punishment. The system increased the number of offenders it apprehended and subjected to harm, but not to the extent it increased its capacity for harming them, once apprehended. The increase in harm did not produce a commensurate reduction in the amount of crime. The increase in penal harm may have been in part due to what we might call "natural" manifestations of demand and suppression, but this is not a sufficient explanation.

The more plausible case appears to be that some external force is causing, or at least contributing to, the patterns of harming and of crime—that crime and punishment are not linked in the form of a crime control system. Perhaps we should rethink the models we use to explain the workings of the punitive machinery of society.

COMPARING TWO MODELS OF PENAL HARM

More than scientific validity is at stake in the argument about what drives the apparatus of punishment. Central to the debate are the politics of punishment, especially as they regard the breadth of options to deal with crime.

The demand-suppression model treats punishment as something of a natural necessity. This model says, on the one hand, that the amount of penal harm is caused by the number of criminals who deserve it. It posits, on the other hand, that a given amount of punitiveness is therefore needed in order to prevent the social ills that result from crime. The understood implication of this is that societies have few choices but to punish offenders at levels that keep up with demand and sustain the suppressive effects of penal harm. Increases in punishment derive from (a) increases in crime, and (b) increased need for harsher techniques of suppressing crime. The evils resulting from punishments are a regrettable but unavoidable consequence of the irresistible pressures of crime and the need to control its growth. Advocates of the demand-suppression model include some of the most influential criminologists writing today, among them Wilson (1983), Van den Haag (1975) and Blumstein and his colleagues (see for example, Blumstein, Cohen, and Nagin 1978).

A second model might be called a "policy" model, in which it is asserted that the level of punishment is a product of the collective policies that prescribe it. Among these policies are the contents of the penal law, the resources devoted to apprehension of criminals, and the distribution of resources among correctional agencies. The inherent point of the policy model is that the level of penal harm is more or less arbitrary, a product of decisions and political priorities. Its advocates maintain that the evils associated with penal harm are not inevitable, but rather result from deliberate choices that could (presumably) be made otherwise. The proponents of this model have been less visible and less influential than their counterparts, but no less strong in their advocacy (Sherman and Hawkins 1981; Currie 1985; Mathiesen 1990; Gordon 1990).

These models need not be mutually exclusive, of course. Recently, Blumstein—who has long been an advocate of the demand-suppression model—has presented data that support a more direct policy interpretation of punishment practice in the United States—especially as regards drug laws (Blumstein 1993). But the nature of the political debate has meant that these two models are presented as though they are incompatible. One reason may be basic economics. The cost of the expansion in corrections has been extraordinary, and the most recent increases have occurred in the midst of governmental hard times. Since 1975, government expenditures on corrections have grown by 989%—more than doubling, in constant dollars (U.S. Department of Justice 1992). State expenditures on education, highways and, welfare actually have decreased since 1980, and expenditures on health and hospitals have not grown (Steve Gold, cited in Austin 1990:5). A shift of this magnitude in public spending priorities is hard to imagine, unless it is somehow understood as irresistible. Therefore, political leaders who advanced this expensive agenda found it useful to represent the policy as unavoidable and necessary.

Those who dispute the demand-suppression model are nearly as adamant about the irrelevance of crime to punishment, and theirs is an equally demanding political problem. If we consider the vociferous and unrelenting public concern about crime that dominates political discourse on the topic, it is difficult to see how any reductions in punishment could be accomplished without first achieving the conceptual necessity of separating the amount of crime from the amount of punishment. The task of those who dispute the demand-suppression model is to make a case that crime can be confronted without the need for massive expansion of the machinery of penal harm. More directly, their problem is to refute "the absurdity of thinking about punishment as if it had nothing to do with crime" (Garland 1990, 20).

Data suggest that neither of these two simple models is fully satisfactory as an explanation of the penal harm machine, and that neither stands alone as a description of the basis for the punishment experiment of the 1970s and 1980s. Even the most optimistic construction of the demand thesis must recognize that the scope of punishment grew more rapidly than either crimes or arrests. The most damaging problem for the advocates of this model is that hardly any case at all can be made that the unprecedented explosion in the penal machinery has reduced crime. By the same token, policy model advocates find it difficult to incorporate into their arguments the increase in the crime-prone age group of males and the resulting increase in their arrests.

Other writers have reached similar conclusions about the complexity of the crime-punishment relationship. Zimring and Hawkins (1991) provide a thorough analysis demonstrating that patterns of crime and punishment in the United States in this century conform to no existing theory. They suggest that a multidimensional model of punishment processes is needed. Similarly, in their analysis of age-specific arrest rates, Steffensmeier and Harer (1991) show that the amount of crime and the rate of criminality of youth are not identical phenomena. Criminality rates estimated from arrest rates explain neither rates of crime nor rates of punishment, though associations among those rates may be drawn.

The failure of the traditional models to fit the data adequately suggests the need to search for ways to integrate those models. At first, we could posit a very simple model, beginning with the fact, argued elsewhere (National Research Council, 1978), that any crime suppression impact of punishment is small in size and lagged over time. Crime itself, though, is a direct (immediate) product of certain criminogenic variables (referred to here as "Factor X," which may be thought of as a demand-generating measure) determining the number of offenders eligible for punishment. The eventual amount of punishment results from the percentage of eligible criminals apprehended for a crime. (See figure 2-10.)

Eventually, we will need to integrate the policy variables into this model—we will call them "Factor Y"—but it is worth pausing for a moment to recognize that this model is already complex enough. Even if it were to be used without the policy variables, the model components would need to be specified with precision: the length of the suppression lag would have to be known, along with the precise content of Factor X variables. The relative strength of the relationships must be estimated, especially the key relationships influencing the level of crime. For example, if the relationship between penal harm and crime were formed to be small compared to that between Factor X and crime, it may be possible simultaneously to observe increases in crime and increases in punishment level, even though the model is correct. The reason would be that the lagged suppression effect of punishment is small compared to the immediate impact of Factor X.

There are considerable technical problems in testing such a model. Some of these problems—sample size and assumptions of temporal stability in the model's causal structure—were mentioned earlier in the chapter. In addition, there is the overwhelming importance of

Figure 2-10

Simple Model with "Factor X"

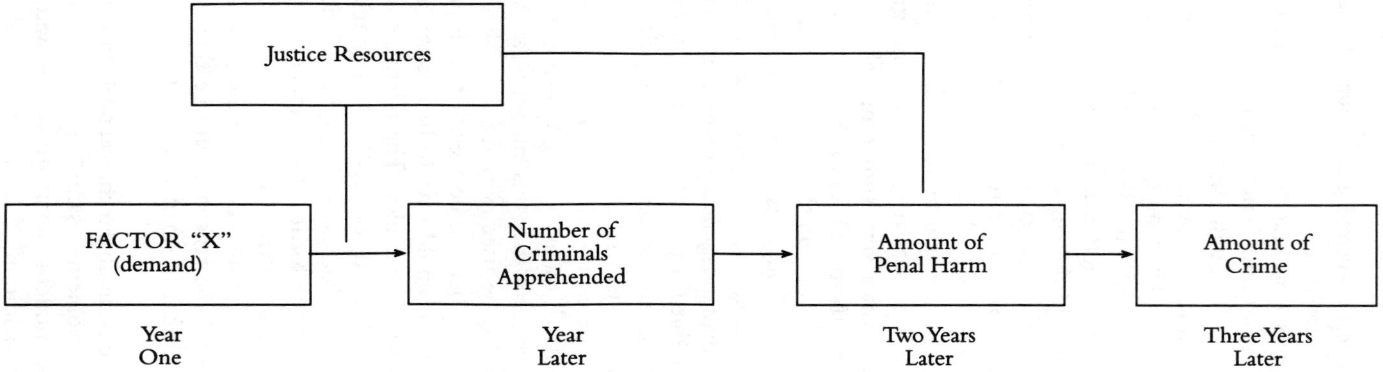

accurate measurement, particularly of Factor X. While much is known about the social correlates of crime (see Gottfredson and Hirschi 1990, for example, for a summary and discussion) most of what is known provokes controversy. Debates ensue about the relative importance of measures such as employment, absolute and relative deprivation, social disorganization, and so forth (see, for example, Cohen, 1988). Moreover, these are merely social attributes, and they exclude the kinds of personal characteristics, such as antisocial attitudes, that might influence numbers of criminals (see Andrews et. al., 1990). There is also the problem of how crime is measured—self report or UCR data—as well as which crimes are measured—violent, property or combinations. Finally, there is the problem of how to evaluate "harming" by using various penal indices, incarceration, or other measures. All these problems of specification make it infeasible to arrange a full-blown test of our model on data from the short time period of 1970–1990 (for a similar conclusion, see Box and Hale 1982 and Hale and Sabbagh 1991).

It is possible, however, to get a feeling for the model's usefulness by using a more or less arbitrary selection of measures and lags and investigating how they work together. This is done in tables 2–10 and 2–11, which show the pattern of certain measures of model components that include arrests for violent crime, prison population, violent crimes reported to the police, and Factor X; violent crime and imprisonment rates are used because of the greater plausibility of the interconnectedness of these trends. Factor X provides a constructed measure of numbers of unemployed and numbers living in poverty. The factor measures the criminogenic impact of these social forces as "multiplicative," in that as each force grows, it exacerbates the impact of the other force on violent crime.

The number of offenders arrested for violence is the input. The prisoner population is lagged two years (as above) to reflect system delays, the number of violent crimes (using UCR data) as an output is lagged three years, to reflect so-called "learning delays" in deterrence. Figure 2–11 illustrates the actual measures, while figure 2–12 marks the percent change in the various measures over the previous year. Because of the lags, the years shown occur during the height of the punishment experiment—1973 to 1988—with the associated values of lagged variables incorporating the lags.

From figure 2–11, we can see that the simple, first-stage model has some plausibility. All measures increase during the period, as we would expect. However, the way that our constructed Factor X variable behaves—which is certainly no better than a rough approximation of criminogenic forces—is roughly similar to the way violent

Figure 2-11

Demand-suppression time series model with "Factor X"

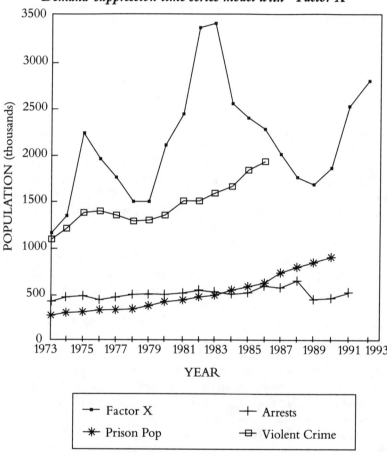

crime rates behave, and especially similar to violent crime arrests. In addition, throughout the period, the slope of the increase in imprisonment remains greater than any of the other measures, suggesting that the measure of prison population is not caused by the same factors as the other measures.

This hypothesis is borne out by figure 2–12, which displays the changes in *rates* of change. It is clear that these variables have changed in similar pattern over time, and with the arbitrary lags incorporated, they seem to ebb and flow together. Except, once again, imprisonment behaves differently: while the other measures occasionally dip below zero, indicating a negative change, the drop in rate of change

Figure 2-12

Annual change in demand–suppression model time series

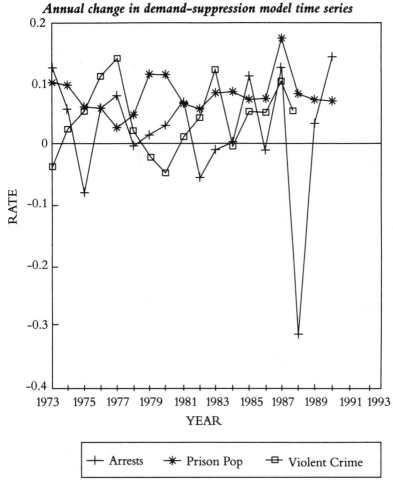

never falls as far for imprisonment. This trend is *always* positive, again suggesting that while it is influenced in the same ways as the other variables in our model, it is determined by a different set of rules that prohibit negative changes. This suggests that we would do well to expand the basic model by adding what I call "Factor Y", which serves as a policy filter. (See figure 2-13.) This filter accepts the number of arrested persons entering (as demand) and then transforms them into the amount of penal harm. Since 1970, it appears that the effect of the policy filter (Factor Y) is to establish a floor, below which the punishment changes from year to year may not fall.

Figure 2-13

Complex Model with "Factors X and Y"

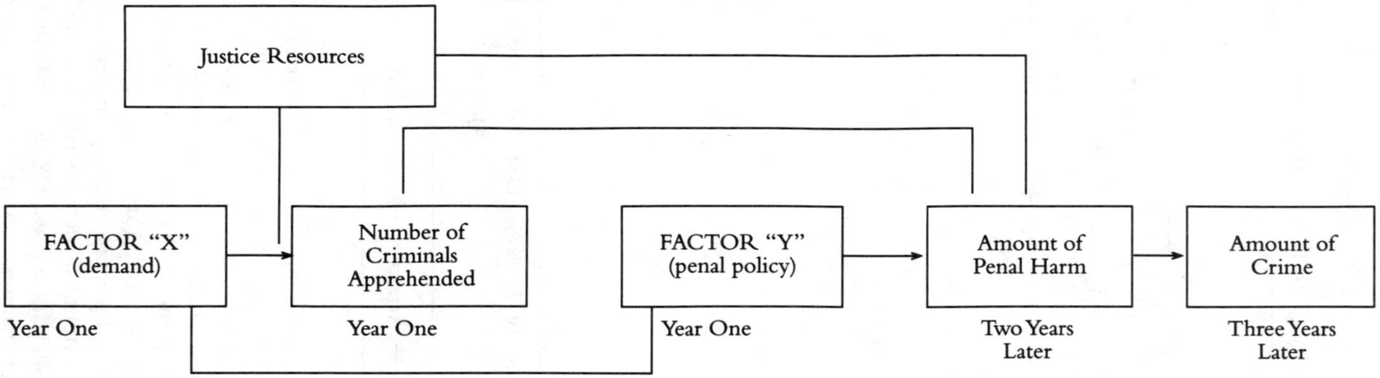

These tables do not represent a complete test of either model, of course, but they promote some interesting speculation. Forces such as arrests, punishment, social malady, and crime are indeed connected. They have been on a upswing during the punishment experiment, and they have covaried as well. But punishment, the topic of our great social experiment, has been able to live under a different set of parameters, buffeted by these other forces but not controlled by them.

Thus the so-called "natural" model, as indicated by the demand-suppression hypothesis, is inadequate, though not wholly without merit. It is true to say that the amount of punishment comes from the number of criminals; it is correct to say that punishing them will have something to do with the amount of crime. What is incorrect is to presume that this is the entire story. The level of penal harm has a different set of determinants that have little to do with these forces, though they are not antagonistic to them.

A variation in this model—a higher order version of it—posits that both crime and penal harm are products of social forces. Because the factors causing crime and those causing penal harms are themselves related—and perhaps include some common factors—they suggest a relationship between crime rates and harm rates that is, in fact, spurious.

This model has been popular among sociologists for many years, particularly those who are interested in the role of punishment in social conflict. One of the best reviews of these various viewpoints is provided by Garland's (1990) excellent *Punishment in Modern Society*. While this review offers a complex summary of existing theory about the social functions of punishment, it presents as well a common theme within its critical review of the theories.

> It is clear enough that criminal conduct does not determine the kind of penal action that a society adopts. . . . [T]o the extent that penal systems adapt their practices to the problems of crime control, they do so in ways which are heavily mediated by independent considerations such as cultural conventions, economic resources, institutional dynamics, and political arguments. (Garland 1990, 20)

A systems model of penal harm that incorporates policy measures is necessary. But if measurement poses a problem for the basic model, it is doubly so for this elaboration of it. In addition to the problem of the measuring Factor X, there is now the problem of specifying Factor Y—the policy pressures that control levels of penal harm. Obtaining adequate quantitative measures of what Garland calls "cultural conventions" or "political arguments" is quite difficult. Even more troubling would be the effort to include crime rate as both resulting from one component (Factor X) and contributing to another (Factor Y) to which the former is correlated. Obtaining a quantitative version of this model seems quite unlikely, due to problems in specification (Kennedy 1992).

Then again, both factors represent constructs that might be labeled "soft," in that they are not easily subjected to measurement. In the case of Factor X, for example, it is possible to generate a number of different indicators of deprivation, disorganization, disadvantage, and so on—it is even possible to control for ethnic, gender, and age distributions. But whether even these measures, carefully constructed, would represent the kinds of criminogenic forces that influence the Factor Y cultural/political forces is a problematic question, at best.

Further, when it comes to Factor Y, the problems of measurement are even more troubling. Foucault (1977), for instance, makes a highly persuasive argument for the impact of power-knowledge spirals in the nature of punishment, but how would someone credibly boil his argument down to a series of numerical measures? When the argument is that punishment levels stem from problems in advanced capitalism (Pashukanis 1978), how does one disentangle the measures of this idea that relate to crime from those that relate to punishment? Measures of relative deprivation and spending patterns have been used (Field 1990), but this is surely a simplified beginning to the idea. Contained within Factor Y might also be such variables as income inequality and predominance of minorities in a population, since these are known to be associated with rates of imprisonment (Chiricos and DeLone 1992). Our own analysis shows a strong, unitary movement among lawmaking bodies to increase the punitive character of the penal law in the 1970s and 1980s, but this is not a direct measure of Factor Y—rather, it is indirect demonstration that the factor exists and therefore ought to be incorporated into our model.

Interestingly, one promising lead in identifying the nature of the social forces has been demonstrated by the work of two British criminologists, Stephen Box and Chris Hale (1982; 1985; Box 1987; Hale 1989). Upon investigating the impact of various justice system rates and unemployment rates on prison admissions (which do not always translate directly into measures of population), they found

> the major factor affecting changes in admissions is . . . changes in convictions. Changes in the per capita recorded arrest rate has no significant effect. . . . Changes in the unemployment rate, after controlling for these and other relevant factors, do have a statistically significant effect. . . . (Hale 1989:183)

Unemployment, then, which is normally thought of as a crime-generating factor, turns out to have an impact on punishment that is independent of its impact on crime. Critical social theorists have long argued that this relationship is important, because the same degradations that make life less satisfying for marginal members in society tend to make them more likely to engage in crime *and* make more necessary the state's use of penal harm to suppress that impulse. Some of what is contained in Factor X will also, then, most likely be found in Factor Y as a result of how the politics of punishment work. This further complicates our desire to build a full model of the penal harm system. Wilkins (1991) makes a similar point, when he argues "that crime and punishment are best seen as separate variables, and that it is the demand for punishment which reveals much of the nature of the culture and quality of life of a country" (84).

In an earlier study, Wilkins and Pease (1988) found that "the proportion of income earned by the highest 5% correlates +.81 with average detention length"(16), suggesting another instance in which a variable driving crime (in Factor X) also drives punishment.

In U.S. culture, the growth in penal harms has remained steady even as crime rises and falls. Punishment is far from a natural consequence of crime. It is a deeply ingrained aspect of our culture, and it is one that has experienced a radical reformulation during the punishment experiment.

No complete analysis of the social reasons for this exists, although there has been speculation about the causes (Cohen 1985; Walker 1989; Pepinsky and Jesilow 1984). The symbolic uses of the crime issue have become, in the last 15 years, an important element of election campaigns, both local and national (Finckenauer 1978; Johnson 1990). The attitudes a person has toward what is known as "the crime issue" tend to correspond with attitudes toward race relations, urban politics and beliefs about social entitlements. To be against crime is to stand for core American values of hard work, initiative, and honest living. The anti-crime appeal harkens back to a simpler model of American society, prior to the emergence of inner city poverty as an intractable public problem and race relations as a volatile public social issue.

Thus, the issue of punishment is a symbol for culture conflict in a variety of its battlegrounds. As popular and one-time dominant social values, along with the associated social arrangements they stand for, have been threatened by recent changes in our culture, political leaders have adopted the crime issue as a sort of shorthand for the disintegration of these values. In this way, crime and punishment become stand-ins for a more generalized public ethos against social change. The capacity to deliver ever-increasing levels of penal harm is a statement about the ascendant power of the majorities and the constraints within which minorities must live.

Compelling as this political imagery must seem, after two decades of accelerating punitiveness this type of analysis seems shallow. Standing next to a discussion of the solid and forceful notions of crime and criminals, concepts such as racism and class struggle come off as soft and tenuous. The problem is more than one of quantification; it is that we have grown used to seeing our public policy world through a pragmatic lens: if there is a problem, let us name it and then solve it. Factor Y in our model, suggests that the pragmatism itself may be a part of the problem, and that instead of viewing crime as an alien part of our culture, something to be fought through brutal but necessary penal harms, that crime is instead better understood as deeply linked to the symbols and mechanisms of our cultural identity. Factor Y is about much more basic stuff than mere political expedience.

It is important to recognize that the elaborated model is not merely an anti-capitalist paradigm, even though its most ardent advocates tend to be critical of post-modern capitalism. After all, punishment—penal harming—exists in all modern societies, regardless of economic arrangements. In American society, the apparent value placed on freedom of expression may support a tension between stability and change that gets caught up in the uses of punishment as social and political statements. In understanding how we get a punishment apparatus, it is important to consider both the realities of hard factors, such as poverty, unemployment and crime, as well as soft factors, such as racism, class conflict, and the symbolic politics of political self-interest (Wilkins 1991).

It is important to understand the way in which we mix the reality of crime and its popularized representation to determine the level and nature of penal harming we will sustain. In America, it is well established that inaccurate perceptions of both crime and the workings of the system responding to it dominate the popular opinion on the topic (Walker 1989). If changes in the inaccurate public opinion seem to contribute to changes in support for penal harming (that is, they reside as a part of Factor Y) then this provides evidence in support of our elaborated model.

It must be recognized that punishment in the United States has been driven by forces that can be separated from pragmatic concerns, such as the need to respond to crime or the need to prevent it. Punishment has been a social barometer of public disquiet about social change, but it has also been a manifestation of our most firmly entrenched beliefs about 'the order of things.'

Seen in this way, the great experiment in punishment of the 1970s and 1980s is not merely a policy test; it is also a fundamental political and social self-inquiry. We ask ourselves, "What is our culture about, when it comes to those who do wrong within it?" (This is, the reader will note, a very different question from its alternative, suggested in earlier models: "What do we want to do about crime?") The answer has been, in part, the grand experiment: We are about being tough and tolerating no more nonsense.

DISCUSSION

What does it mean that the penal harming machine has operated as it has in the last 20 years? Equally important, what does it mean that no obvious explanation exists for the relationships among crime levels, social change, societal/political characteristics, and punishment?

There are those, criminologists among them, who would disagree vehemently with the conclusions of the analysis above. They believe deeply in the demand-suppression model of penal harming—though many are more enamored of the suppression side of the formula than the demand side. Attempts not just to demonstrate, but to measure precisely, the exact nature of punishment's suppressive impact on crime, have become commonplace in American criminology—almost as much of a tradition as what is known as "policy" alternative in European sociology. In the next chapter, these studies are discussed in more detail, and their importance in sustaining the punishment agenda is assessed.

But given the basic statistics of the penal harm experiment of the 1970s and 1980s, there cannot be much optimism that the secret to crime control will be found within the precise calibrations of penal harm. Punishment has increased inexorably over the past two decades, but it must be fully faced that from year to year, crime rates have sometimes increased, sometimes decreased, and sometimes have not changed much.

For some, this is very bad news. The vast bulk of the research on criminal justice has been based on an unstated axiom that the best way to organize justice practices so that we may decrease the crime is knowable. If there is no such relationship, or if the relationship is small, compared to others, then this strategy of inquiry becomes unpromising, at best, and fruitless, at worst.

In a way, however, the result is liberating. A government might well view as a duty the need to construct penal policy in ways that prevent crime. If so, then it is bound to try whatever methods it can afford to suppress crime. What we have referred to as Factor Y contains, to a great extent, this very idea of government's role in crime prevention. Yet, as was argued in the opening chapter of this book, this is inevitably a self-injurious process, for controlling crime by using penal harm means we control crime by harming citizens. If crime cannot be suppressed to any meaningful extent by penal harms, then the extremes to which governments often go in trying to do so are unnecessary.

But to say this is to mix metaphors—it is to use the limitations of a social system model of the penal harming machine to answer the wishes of the so-called "crime control" version of the same phenomenon. If both models, standing alone, are inadequate—if what we really need is an integration of them—then how do we proceed to analyze the need for punishment and, in particular, the great growth in punishment seen in the last two decades?

Three main arguments have been made to support the value of growth in punishment: (1) studies of criminals demand penal harming; (2) the plight of victims demands penal harming; and (3) community protection demands penal harming.

In the three chapters that follow, each of these arguments is considered, in turn. In the final chapter, I will begin with a summary of these arguments, then explore options for a way out of the dilemma of accelerating penal harm.

3

Penal Science

> The history of crime control is seen as a
> record of inexorable progress: a triumph of
> enlightened humanism over barbarity, and of
> rationality and scientific knowledge over
> irrationality and prejudice.
> —Stanley Cohen, *Against Criminology*

Since the mid 1970s, the conceptual underpinning of punishment policy in the United States has been that crime is reduced by suppressing the criminality of individual offenders. The great expansion in penal harm described in the preceding chapter was in part, as we saw, a realization of this idea. Throughout these years, the offender-suppression strategy was often justified on the basis of scientific knowledge: studies showed (a) such strategies would work, and (b) other strategies would not work. One purpose of this chapter is to explore those arguments; I will contend that the scientific case for escalation in punishment was never as strong or unambiguous as its advocates maintained.

A second purpose of this chapter is to explore the role of science in the making of penal policy. I will argue an almost obvious point, that penal policy makers use science selectively to advance their agendas. I will also argue that policy scientists tend to design their research in ways that follow the contemporary policy agenda. The result is quite similar to what Foucault (1977) has described as "power-knowledge spirals" in the formation of social policy.

Perspectives on Crime and Criminals

The idea that crime is fought by targeting individuals who commit them is, in the United States, an uncontroversial idea with a long tradition that arose long before the last quarter of the twentieth century. It is an equally well-established notion that scientists who study crime provide the best and least biased view of how to respond to criminals. These two companion thoughts—we should deal with crime through attacking criminals and invoke science when doing so—have been the mainstays of thinking about penal harm for nearly two centuries.

Until recently, every version of penal harms stressed that the proper mode of correctional policy should emphasize changing, rather than controlling, the proclivities of offenders. If citizens who showed the willingness to commit crimes could somehow be turned away from that behavior, communities would then experience a reduction in crime. For at least a century, penological thinking in the United States and Europe emphasized various strategies for changing individual offenders (Garland 1990), though the ideologies supporting offender change have themselves shifted to reflect scientific and social thought of the day.

The traditional emphasis on offender change underwent a revision in the last quarter of the twentieth century. Considerable ferment existed among penologists about the best means to deal with offenders. Despite eloquent arguments in support of retributive penology—partly because it turns away from offender-focused crime reduction strategies—policy makers held onto the seminal idea that the task of penology is to organize punishment so as to prevent crime. For the most part, changes in penal policy were little more than shifts in technical ideas about crime prevention and control. The most recent thinking included a detailed examination of exactly the amount of harm needed to achieve correctional aims and to hold offenders accountable for their conduct.

A brief review of penal thought prior to the 1970s shows how the stage was set for the punitive penology of the 1980s.

THREE VIEWS ON CHANGING OFFENDERS

There exist several good reviews of evolution in penological thinking about offender change (Cullen and Gilbert 1982; Rotman 1990; Hudson 1987; O'Leary and Duffee 1971). These studies demonstrate how correctional paradigms relate to management strategies applied in this century to individual offenders. Three such paradigms are worth comment, for they imply different uses of harm in correctional practice.

Reform

The earliest models of offender change emphasized what has been referred to as the *reform* paradigm of penology. This paradigm viewed offenders as imbued with free will, which they have used to choose their lives of crime. The writing that informed this thinking was best represented by European penologists who thought people chose crime, and is often referred to as the "classical school" of penology. According to this perspective, people made criminal choices for a number of reasons, but the foremost cause was their confused morality, which so often resulted from growing up in the dense urban centers of the day. The city, seen as a main culprit, promoted values inconsistent with the ideals of modern life. People learned shiftlessness and were bombarded with the temptation to engage in shady dealings. The story of Pinnochio was something of a reformist morality play, illustrating the importance of industriousness and fidelity in contrast to the kind of self-indulgence that turns a person into a jackass.

The reformist task of corrections, then, was to instruct offenders in the right ways to live. This correction normally required removal of offenders from the environment that promoted their criminality. As the United States entered the twentieth century, a large number of new prisons were built, mostly in rural settings, many of them linked to farming industry (O'Leary and Duffee, 1971). The prisons' task was to inculcate new values into the offender through regimes of discipline that would promote a model of 'the good life' within the prison.

Critics of this reformist zeal have shown how closely linked its ideas were to the needs of an urbanizing, industrialized capitalist state (Foucault 1977). Reform enthusiasts were less interested in the quality of life they offered their charges than they were in being able to "produce the right thinking citizen ready for work" (Hudson 1987: 5). Indeed, establishment of ticket-of-leave and parole were based largely on the idea that offenders' behaviors improved when they could earn their freedom by demonstrating their readiness for responsible labor. Yet even these high-minded ideals were often subverted, as prison labor was used "to defray the expenses of the institution and possibly earn a profit for the state" (Conley 1980: 270).

Harming the offender was central to the reform technique. In order to teach the offender how to behave appropriately, some aspect or another of the offender's well-being was held hostage by the authorities, who would await his compliance. The explicit intention of reformative penology was to use the apparatus of corrections, especially the prison, to make wrongful living so painfully undesirable that the offender elected to change his or her ways. (The recent promise by the Governor of Massachusetts, to make terms served in that state's prisons "worse than life in hell," is vintage reformist logic.) Parole was invented as a reformist technique: only those who comply with the parole board's vision of right living will be released early (von Hirsch and Hanrahan 1979). That reformist zeal is a direct attack on the personal integrity of offenders has been a common criticism of the concept of parole and was one of the major complaints of the parole abolition movement of the 1970s (Allen 1964).

Rehabilitation

Behavioral science forced a rethinking of the reform model by positing a more determinist understanding of criminal behavior, often called "positivist" penology. Soon after the founding by Freud of the practice of psychanalysis, it became an accepted dogma that human maladjustment was the product of the human psyche. The most traditional view held that crime evolved as a result of early childhood experiences. Less doctrinaire views attributed criminal behavior to a host of social, educational, and intellectual ineptitudes.

Whichever the school of thought, the idea that offenders committed crimes due to psycho-emotional deficits, which they themselves had not caused, and over which they had little control, dominated penological thinking for nearly a generation. The theory of offender behavior change, under this rehabilitation paradigm, held that to treat offenders as though they were actively electing to be criminal was seen as worse than wrong; it was foolish.

The best presentation of this viewpoint was Menninger's *The Crime of Punishment*, published in 1968. He put into writing a view that had already gained widespread acceptance among professional penologists—that dealing with offenders was the proper province of trained specialists who could help them sort out the bases for their difficulties in order to overcome them.

The rehabilitation model of penology was popular among actors in the field for several reasons. First, it asserted that the work of penology had reached the elevated level of science. This meant that the career professionals could reclaim the field from philanthropic reformers who had dominated the penological scene for so many years. Second, adoption of a professionalized view of the offender change problem called for an infusion of new roles into the correctional workplace—psychiatrists, psychologists, therapeutic counselors, and so forth. These new professionals expanded the correctional infrastructure in a classic example of organizational domain management (Thompson 1967). Third, the ideal of rehabilitation and its promise of crime control justified increased expenditures on corrections.

To implement the idea, better educated staff were asked to provide a variety of treatments within a variety of settings. Individual treatment approaches sought to promote personal insight into criminal desires; group approaches were used to eradicate inadequacies in interpersonal behavior; behavioral approaches were thought helpful in retraining offenders who suffered from learned criminal adaptive behaviors. The varied use of programs was thought essential to an effective policy of rehabilitation (Barnes and Teeters 1959).

The rhetoric of the rehabilitation movement treated harm as an anathema. According to its leading advocates, harming offenders was counterproductive to the rehabilitative task (Menninger 1968). Instead, the professional rehabilitative agenda was to create within the offender the ability to live a fuller life, one devoid of the internal conflicts and emotional distress that produces crime. This was best done, it was argued, by providing both emotional and material support, something that intentional acts of harm could only make more difficult—thus came about the title of Menninger's classic defense of this position, *The Crime of Punishment*. More recent advocates of rehabilitation have reiterated the point that the desire to change offenders establishes a natural barrier to the penal use of gratuitous harm (Cullen and Gilbert 1982; Rotman 1990).

It would not be accurate, however, to think that the rehabilitative technique was successful in removing harm from the penal arsenal. There may well be dispute about the question of whether the idea was ever really tried, especially in the United States, but there can be no dispute that in the name of rehabilitation, much abuse was poured upon the heads of lawbreakers (Allen 1964; American Friends Service Committee 1971).

Perhaps the most extreme example of the abuses attributed to this ideology was the advent of the indeterminate sentence. In its purest form, indeterminacy embraced the romantic idea that all offenders could be rehabilitated, and that the appropriate prison sentence was the one that lasted just long enough to enable rehabilitation to occur. This meant that judges should impose a prison penalty encompassing a wide range of time—perhaps zero to life—and allow the expert penologists to determine the best release date, based on their knowledge of the offender's rehabilitative progress.

By the 1960s, the indeterminate sentence had come to represent everything that was wrong with penology: rampant discretion in the hands of insulated 'experts' who were virtually unaccountable for the excesses they imposed upon offenders (not to mention the mistakes they imposed on the community). In fact, the most extreme version of indeterminacy was quite an uncommon occurrence. Only a few states allowed it at all in their penal codes, and only California made it a standard part of the sentencing apparatus. Nevertheless, the indeterminate sentence, while perhaps not so commonly imposed, became the focal point of much of the heated criticism of the excesses inherent in the rehabilitation idea.

Whether or not indeterminacy was ever in reality the awful, widespread practice its detractors accused it of being, it is best seen as a metaphor for what was really wrong with the paradigm it came from. Liberals and dismayed conservatives alike were frightened by the idea that the welfare of an offender could be determined by an expert without much accountability for decisions. The rehabilitation field was plagued by excessive technical uncertainty. Decision errors—often made without third-party review—caused the carefully built structure of professional expertise to crumble. By their often grandiose and repeatedly incorrect claims to knowledge of offenders, the technicians of rehabilitation assisted their own downfall.

The innate harmfulness of both reform and rehabilitation approaches to offender change lies in the way these approaches use coercion. The painfulness of coercive change is so salient that prisoners themselves organized to try to eliminate the most obvious institutional manifestation of coercion—parole (Goodstein and Hepburn, 1985, 315).

In some ways, the use of coercion to change offenders is technically quite odd. Virtually all schools of thought about individual behavior change recognize that the involvement and commitment of the target of the change effort are centrally important to success (Kelman 1961). Yet, in corrections, the offender typically receives little choice about whether to be placed in a program or which type of program to receive. The apparent incompatibility of coercion and change is so important that some have blamed the reliance on coercion for the failure of prior offender change approaches (Rotman 1990). Certainly, the coercive methods of these programs came under attack as violations of basic human dignity (American Friends Service Committee 1971; Stanley 1976; Mitford 1973), and these criticisms, combined with summary studies exposing their apparent ineffectuality (Bailey 1966, Wilkins 1969; Martinson 1976), led to a wholesale retreat from the coercive change agenda, though other forms of penal coercion were not questioned to the same extent.

Reintegration[17]

A third view of the offender change task has recently emerged, attributing criminal behavior to the problems in urban neighborhoods. These problems promote crime not because of the bad attitudes they encourage (as reformists argued) but because of the way they isolate young males from legitimate social opportunities to make money and achieve status. Studies seemed to support this view (Merton 1957; Cloward and Ohlin 1960; Becker 1963; Lemert 1967).

This type of thinking led scholars to believe that the key to crime prevention lay in community change. The reintegration paradigm of offender change held the seemingly self-evident idea that until communities become places where disadvantaged inhabitants were able to succeed without breaking the law, then law breaking would continue to be common in those communities. The idea was most forcefully presented by an official commission appointed by President Johnson (President's Commission 1967).

The reintegration idea was attractive on several grounds. First, it was entirely consonant with the American dream—the only thing wrong with America was that not enough citizens had yet benefited from its economic promise. Second, it drew moral power from the Civil Rights movement emerging in the United States (Clear and Cole 1990). The same evils that blocked minorities and the poor from full participation in society were also portrayed as producers of its crime. Third, the focus of the offender change enterprise could be moved from the prison to the community, something that pleased correctional administrators and academics alike—both groups having grown tired of the obvious failure of the earlier rehabilitation model.

The reintegrative strategies of correctional intervention were different from their predecessors in two other important respects. The coercive element of treatment was deemphasized, as experts recognized that to invade personal rights and integrity only interfered with the offender's citizenship. More important, the target of change was not only the individual offender, but also the community.

> There is, within this model, a major concern with reducing the stigma attached to criminality because that stigma is a block to entrance to the community. Stress on community . . . mean[s] . . . promoting changes as well within its institutional structure to provide opportunities for offenders and reduce systemic discrimination because of economic or cultural variances. (O'Leary and Duffee 1970: 5)

The emphasis on change within the community gave the correctional agenda a distinctly moral overtone—its leaders were not simply trying to control the errant citizen, but were in fact bonded with them, charged with the responsibility for enriching the quality of their lives and their community. Not only was coercion unnecessary, it was counterproductive. Correctional change would build upon the energy those communities already maintained; it would use communities' resources to make them better places.

The programs using the reintegration model were not numerous. The few that were tried received widespread attention, especially for their disappointing results (Moynihan 1969). Of the three models of offender change, the reintegration one has been the most short-lived, born and abandoned in the 1960s.

In fact, some might well observe that the reintegration model, in its full regalia, was never really allowed to flourish. In theory, the approach called for the remaking of inner-city communities. This is a pretty remarkable expectation—that the government would, in its wisdom, seek to activate a marginal class of politically and economically disenfranchised poor. The very idea flies in the face of what we know about modern governing, and it requires an entrenched confusion about the term *community* (Cohen 1979; 1985). In practice, the strategy devolved into a fairly basic emphasis upon creating or providing jobs and job training in lower-end economic enterprise.

There may also have been a fundamental conflict between the idea of *empowerment*, which underlies the reintegrative idea, and the penal system's historical reliance on harm to well-being as its core moral message. There is, of course, no inherent incompatibility between the idea of reprobation and the idea of the integrative community, as Brathwaite has recognized in his argument for "reintegrative shaming" (1989). But there is no chance that the correctional approaches of the 1970s could be thought of as reintegrative in the main. The dramatic restructuring—or as Cohen (1985) calls it, destructuring—of penal harm systems required by the model simply never occurred (Austin and Krisberg 1982).

A single thread has run through this century's ideas about offender change: the way to deal with crime is to find a way to change individual criminal offenders. For reformists, offenders needed to be taught moral living; for rehabilitionists, the aim was to rebuild damaged psyches and revamp incompetent social behavior; for reintegrationists, the solution required offering meaningful jobs and realistic opportunities for marginal economic success. By the early 1970s, the energy had gone out of the offender change paradigms, and they were replaced with a paradigm of punishment and control.

THE DEMISE OF OFFENDER CHANGE

Hudson (1987) has attributed the decline of the individual change agenda in corrections to the coincidence of attacks from three interest groups: civil libertarians, due process lawyers, and 'get tough' politicians. A chorus of criticism (see Table 3–1) from these otherwise diverse groups occurred in the middle of the 1970s, contributing to

Table 3–1.   Selected Critiques of Offender Change

Year	Author	Title
1972	George Jackson	*Soledad Brother*
1973	Marvin Frankl	*Criminal Sentencing: Law Without Order*
	Nicholas Kittrie	*The Right to be Different*
	Jessica Mitford	*Kind and Usual Punishment*
1974		
1975	American Friends Service Committee	*Struggle for Justice*
1975	David Fogel	*"We Are the Living Proof:" The Justice Model for Corrections*
1976	Andrew von Hirsch	*Doing Justice: The Choice of Punishments*
1975	Ernest Van Den Haag	*Punishing Criminals: On an Old and Painful Question*
1977	James Q. Wilson	*Thinking About Crime*

the demise of offender change ideologies. It is instructive to list some noteworthy examples of this line of argument in temporal order, and then to recite their main claims.

George Jackson's (1972) spirited and effective critique of California corrections was effective due to his life as a prisoner and his controversial death at the hands of corrections officers, and it presaged a sustained attack on the penal logic of the day. In 1973, the scholarly debate was begun, perhaps, by Judge Marvin Frankel's (1973) famous charge that criminal sentencing had become "law without order." Also that year, Kittrie's (1971) unrelenting criticism of the coercive mental health practice was published. In 1974, two books were published that proved extremely important because of their impact on specific audiences. Mitford's (1973) acerbic analysis of the U.S. corrections system, which paid special attention to the indeterminate sentence in California, was widely acclaimed among intellectuals and made prison reform a topic of public discourse. The Quakers' report, *Struggle for Justice*, performed the same role for the scholarly community. In 1975, Fogel published his advocacy of the "justice model" for corrections, a book widely read by professionals in the field and noteworthy by virtue of his long experience as a respected corrections professional. The next year, von Hirsch published his classic treatise on "desert." Perhaps as much as any other work, this book established the reasoned basis for a retreat from the rehabilitationist approach.

That same year, the Twentieth Century Fund published a report that demonstrated how principles of commensurate desert could be used to create sentencing reform, and Stanley (1976) exposed the U.S. parole system as technically and philosophically flawed. Van den Haag (1975) wrote an influential argument in favor of the desert-deterrence formulation of the criminal law. In 1977, Wilson published his conservative critique of crime prevention policy, which included a strong attack against the joint ideas of rehabilitation and reintegration.

Three points about this list deserve emphasis. First, it represents a remarkable consensus of opinion from a collection of otherwise sometimes strident opponents. Van den Haag, for instance, is a right-wing political scientist; Wilson is a neo-conservative policy researcher. By contrast, Fogel and the Quakers are sewn from classic liberal cloth, and write from a sense of obligation for society's least fortunate members, while Jackson was a self proclaimed "revolutionary." Fogel, former director of corrections in Illinois, was known as a system "insider," as was (in a slightly different respect) Jackson; Mitford, a journalist specializing in government exposé, was a true "outsider." Second, the audiences of these works are considerably diverse, ranging from the popular readership of Mitford and the Quakers to the highly specialized audiences of the Twentieth Century Fund and von Hirsch, to the wide scholarly audiences of Wilson, Van den Haag, and Frankl. Nearly all these books were reviewed in the *New York Times Review of Books*; two—those by Mitford and Jackson—reached bestseller lists. Third, and perhaps most remarkable of all, there was not a single original study contained in these documents. Every book was in essence an argument about social policy that was based on previous studies and debates, not on new or previously unavailable data.

This listing of ten important books published in a half-decade period is impressive, yet it excludes the scores of articles, papers and talks written or given during the same period—all critical of the general idea of offender change, whatever the paradigm. That such a collection should be produced in such a short period of time illustrates that in the middle of the 1970s, those opposed to offender change practices in corrections were trumpeting an idea already in good currency. By 1977, there were virtually no effective advocates of treatment left among the influential writers of the day.[18]

Although criminological argument was central to the demise of offender change approaches in punishment, an important role was also played by criminological research. The most important work was Martinson's (1976) overview of the general effectiveness of treatment, published in *The Public Interest*, a journal aimed for a nonspecialist, informed readership. His work, which was confirmed by later studies

(Greenberg 1975; Klein 1979; Sechrest, et al. 1979), had been preceded by other critiques of the effectiveness of coercive treatment in corrections (Bailey 1966; Wilkins 1969; Robison and Smith 1971), but was particularly important because it pounded the final scientific nail into the coffin of offender change, at a time when the thinking public policy community had determined to abandon that model anyway.

The juggernaut against offender change was so overwhelming, however, scientific evidence played only a tangential, confirmatory role in the debates surrounding it, and certainly would not turn the tide against it. A more important social science story is revealed in the way the research community responded to the change in policy.

The Rise of the Punish-and-Control Paradigm

The offender punishment and control paradigm that has been the dominant idea of penology since the early 1980s takes as unchallenged the same two ideas that dominated criminological thinking during this century: (1) the proper response to crime requires a focus on coercively doing things to individuals caught by the criminal justice system, and (2) scientific experts can know what is best to do to those offenders. The departure from previous strategies was caused by a third truism which, as we saw, came to be widely accepted: the various strategies of offender change have all proven wildly incapable of reducing crime.

The central assertion of what I refer to as the offender punishment and control movement was the logical result of these three ideas. The assertion holds that the proper role of corrections is to prevent crime by incapacitating active criminals and deterring potential ones. Thus, the paradigm called for a two-pronged penal agenda: enough punishment to deter potential lawbreakers; enough incarceration to control current ones. Most observers would agree that this is the ascendant paradigm in the United States, today.

Science played an important part in the rise of offender punishment and control policies, though its role differed from the one played in the rise and subsequent fall of the rehabilitationist policies. In the latter case, criminologists produced considerable speculation about the causes of crime and the appropriate strategies for dealing with offenders, but by comparison to hyperbole, there was little in the way of "hard" research studies (Wilson 1975). There was, of course, a longstanding practice of program evaluation among those who have been called "the California researchers" (Martinson, 1976). But few of these studies were formally published, and their practical impact upon correctional policy was limited and indirect. By the end of the

1970s, influential criminologists were in agreement with Wilson (1982), who wondered why "we persist in our view that we can find and alleviate the 'causes' of crime [and] that serious criminals can be rehabilitated" (11).

The books and articles that attacked offender change in the 1970s made more of a conceptual or philosophical argument than an empirical one. Studies showing the ineffectiveness of treatment were often tacked on to the central arguments of justice and basic logic. By contrast, the role of criminological studies (as opposed to jargonistic argumentation) was crucial to—and in many respects formative of—the offender punishment and control movement that caught on in the 1980s. The scientist's new task was to carry out carefully-executed studies of criminal behavior designed to elucidate the best strategies of control. Two areas of inquiry dominated: the study of criminal careers and the improvement of prediction.

Criminal careers

As the offender change paradigm was losing its steam, the scientific precursors of the offender punish-and-control agenda were already being published. The initial thinking was presented in a pair of papers about the distribution over time of the criminal behavior of active offenders. The first paper (Avi-Itzhak and Shinnar 1973) was primarily mathematical, demonstrating how different specifications of criminal activity can be used to estimate the crime control impact (through incapacitation) of specific sentencing policies. A second paper (Shinnar and Shinnar 1975) applied these models to crime and punishment data gathered from the State of New York, and concluded that an increase in the frequency and length of prison sentences for certain offenders could reduce violent crime by 25%. For New Yorkers, whose lives seemed increasingly besieged by crime, any estimate such as this must have seemed to offer a powerful respite.

This estimate seemed inordinately optimistic to many scholars, for it ran counter to the commonly accepted idea that criminal behavior was difficult to predict (Monahan 1981) and nearly impossible to control through preventive detention (Wilkins 1969). But it was not surprising to criminologists who had been following a wide variety of studies on criminal careers. Despite criticism of the famous studies of Glueck and Glueck (1930, 1934), which claimed that early intervention and suppression could reduce criminal activity (Farrington and Tarling 1985), later cohort studies continued to demonstrate the important fact that a minority of active offenders produced the majority of crimes (Farrington and West 1984; Wolfgang,

Figlio and, Sellin 1972). The problem was to distinguish these offenders from the others, early in their lawbreaking careers.

The breakthrough study was conducted by a team of Rand researchers. They administered a self-completion questionnaire to a sample of inmates in California, Michigan, and Texas, to determine their rates of criminality in the two years prior to their incarceration. Although the data were subjected to a variety of analyses and reported in a series of documents, two were the most important: Chaiken and Chaiken's (1982) "typology" of criminal careers and Greenwood's (1982) estimate of the incapacitative effects of selective mandatory sentences.

Even though prior studies had hinted that the rates of criminal behavior among active offenders were quite high, the results of the Rand survey produced numbers that were startling. Two findings were particularly powerful. First, the offenders in their survey admitted to an average of nearly 200 crimes per year. Second, the distribution of offending behavior was extraordinarily skewed—the "high rate," or 10% most criminally active of what Chaiken and Chaiken call "violent predators," admitted to an average of over 500 burglaries and 150 robberies per year.

Numbers such as these could not help but draw attention of social scientists and public officials alike. Even though there were fewer than 40 "high-rate, violent predator" cases in the Rand sample of nearly 2200 offenders, the feeling a person got from reading popular references to the work was that of a menacing core of offenders were nearly single-handedly destroying the safety of the community.

It was natural, in the face of such powerful data, that people would want to figure out a way to identify those "high rate predators" so they could be isolated. This was the contribution of Peter Greenwood's (1982) analysis. Through multivariate statistical methods, he determined that having at least three of a set of seven personal characteristics identified correctly a large percentage of the high rate cases, and he projected that a policy of mandatory, eight-year prison terms would reduce the rate of robbery in California by up to 20 percent. To the New Yorkers whose attention might have been attracted by the earlier work of the Shinnars must now be added the heartfelt hope of Californians who read the Greenwood research.

Greenwood's analysis received a great deal of attention. The political uses of the study, which were considerable, are discussed below. The impact on social science research was substantial as well. A spate of analyses followed, both supporting and criticizing Greenwood's view of "selective incapacitation." Criminal career research became a national priority.

In fact, research on criminal careers had been of long-standing interest to federal funding agencies from as early as 1970. In its fiscal plan for 1971 (LEAA, 1970), the Law Enforcement Assistance Administration listed "intervention in criminal careers" as a research funding topic. The nature of the interest was quite different from what we now see under the label of "criminal career," however. The 1970 solicitation sought information "designed to prevent an individual from entering a criminal career or to induce an offender to terminate that career" (10).

The prevention focus of the criminal career research agenda continued through the 1970s, and was strengthened in 1976 when the first special research agreement was established on the topic. In 1978, the National Institute of Law Enforcement and Criminal Justice was "guided by recommendations that emerged from a colloquium it sponsored in March, 1978. The meeting assembled experts from a cross section of the disciplines involved in behavioral research" (NILECJ, 1978: 5) and led to a call for longitudinal studies of criminal careers. Seven percent of the budget for post-conviction research was devoted to the topic (apparently less than $200,000: 1978: 4).

In 1982, both the scope and the focus of criminal career research sponsored by federal funds changed. The National Institute of Justice revamped its grant solicitations in order "to support . . . the mandates of the Attorney General's Task Force on Violent Crime [whose] major themes . . . are interwoven throughout the research agenda for 1982" (1982: iii). The scope of funding grew steadility to reach $750,000 in 1985 and 1986, and reached $700,000 in 1987,[19] when $1.5 million was shifted to drug research (NIJ, 1985, 1986, 1987). The focus shifted to fit the 'get tough' rhetoric of the Attorney General's report, and included selective prosecution and the modeling of incapacitation effects. From 1982 on, the offender control model received primary funding importance in all NIJ research solicitations on crime and corrections.

A new vocabulary developed during this period, and is illustrated by the criminal career paradigm shown in Figure 3–1. Elaborate statistical models were developed to analyze "participation rates," "age of onset," "career length," "desistence," and the all-important "lambda" (the average rate of offending for an active offender). Borrowing from the fields of economics and statistics, researchers busied themselves with fine-tuning the models of criminal careers, clarifying the assumptions underlying the models, and estimating the effects of various policies.

The research on criminal careers has added a great deal to our knowledge base in criminology. Two important practical results also

Figure 3-1

Incapacitation, rehabilitation and criminogenic effects in an individual criminal career

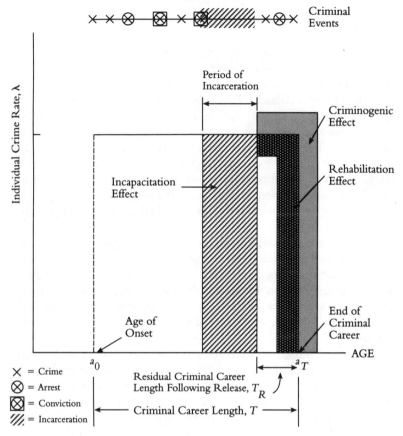

grew from this line of inquiry. First, the elements of the career criminal paradigm, with its elaborate array of interrelated variables, spawned an abundance of statistical journeys. Every parameter of the paradigm was a candidate for testing on the multitude of new databases compiled under the 1960s sponsorship of the LEAA and its progeny. Each new statistical procedure, underlying assumption, or posited relationship could be tested on each component of the criminal career paradigm, and this could be done for successive databases. The result was a seemingly unending explosion of theoretical models and statistical processes for testing them, all of which seemed to deserve official interest.

Second, nearly every such study found the same result: a policy basing itself upon incarceration would reduce crime, often by substantial levels. The clarion call for incapacitation had found its scientific basis.

Prediction

As a companion to the research on criminal careers, there was a renewed interest in methods and results of prediction. Since the 1950s, prediction methods had remained a choice between rather crude statistical devices (Glaser 1955; Wilkins 1969) and ineffectual clinical approaches (Monahan 1981; Steadman 1985). It seemed that regardless of the method selected, the result was always an extremely high rate of "false positives"—inaccurate predictions that the offender is bound to recidivate (Gottfredson and Gottfredson 1986)—and a relatively moderate rate of "true positives"—accurate predictions of recidivism. Yet the results reported by Greenwood resuscitated the hope that improvements in statistical technique could enable more accurate predictions.

In 1982, Rhodes and his colleagues proposed a prediction scale to identify career criminals with a reported false positive rate of only 15%. A year later, Fischer (1983; 1984) reported a prediction device developed for the Iowa Parole Board that was over 80% accurate in its classifications of risk. In both cases, the researchers argued that use of their scale could (or in the case of Fischer, did) result in reductions in crime.

The proliferation of databases also made possible the widespread use of actuarial methods for classifications by risk. These are classification methods that place individuals into risk groups based on prior criminal history and other personal characteristics (Clear 1988). The use of actuarial risk scales has become commonplace in correctional practice (Baird 1984). The National Institute of Justice took a strong interest in prediction, with a special interest in developing new techniques for reducing errors in prediction. In the mid 1980s, the amounts devoted to this topic were approximately equal to those devoted to the criminal career research, described above (NIJ 1985; 1986; 1987).

The dual strategies of measuring criminal careers and improving predictions became a dominant aspect of criminological research enterprise. The National Science Foundation funded a series referred to as "panel reports," in which the estimation of incapacitation and deterrence was the topic in 1978 (Blumstein et. al.), and criminal careers was the topic in 1986 (Blumstein et. al.). The National Institute of Justice supported an edited volume on prediction and classification (Gottfredson and Tonry 1987), which presented the "state-of-the-art" techniques and limitations to this approach.

CRITICS OF OFFENDER PUNISHMENT-AND-CONTROL SCIENCE

Even though the incapacitation/prediction/criminal career agenda dominated criminological research from 1975–1990, the approach was not without its critics. Gottfredson and Hirschi (1986) poked fun at what might be called the "search for lambda" by writing a summary of current research whose title tells the story: "The True Value of Lambda Would Appear to be Zero." Their point was that current data, combined with reasonable assumptions about the results of possible studies, could not suggest using any other estimate of lambda except "zero," and if this was the case, why spend so much time and money on the quest? More serious were the studies of actual effects of incapacitation in Denver (Petersilia and Greenwood 1978) and Columbus, Ohio (Van Dine, Conrad, and Dinitz 1979), which found negligible crime reduction effects produced at the cost of considerable increases in imprisonment.

Prediction techniques were also criticized. Gottfredson and Gottfredson (1986) reviewed recent prediction studies, including those of Rhodes and Fischer. In view of limitations in quality of data and statistical methods, they concluded that significant improvements in prediction strategies were unlikely. Because of the high rate of false positives, they argued that prediction was better used as a device to identify the low-risk offender rather than the high-rate offender.

Perhaps the most damaging critique of the research spawning the offender punishment-and-control movement was produced by Visher (1986), who reanalyzed the Rand data. She found that the estimate of crime reduction through eight-year sentences was at best only 13% for California offenders, and could be much lower. If the same prediction scale were applied to Michigan or Texas cases, "the crime rate would probably increase" (205). Realizing the accuracy of these and other criticisms, Greenwood later recanted many of his original claims (1987).

POLITICS AND OFFENDER PUNISHMENT/CONTROL

None of this stopped the Federal Government from using the results of the research it spawned for advancing its political aims. In a widely disseminated national plan to combat violent crime (1981), President Reagan's first Attorney General, William French Smith, produced an agenda including a shift in sentencing away from the current sentencing approach, which is "outmoded and unfair" since it is "based on an outmoded rehabilitation model" (56). The new approach would abolish parole and put in its place a determinate sentencing system with guidelines based on

> The need to afford adequate deterrence to criminal conduct. The need to protect the public from further crimes of the defendant. The need to reflect the seriousness of the offense, to promote respect for the law, and to provide just punishment. (57)

The Smith report, as it was called, thus defined the offender punishment and control agenda, insofar as sentencing was concerned. The Greenwood research, to be published the following year, would supply the approving stamp of science to support the political agenda.

Once it appeared, Greenwood's study was disseminated widely among elected state legislators and executives, thereby building impetus for a new idea: social science says, "lock 'em up." It may have seemed an innocent act to have disseminated so widely an important, groundbreaking study, but it was not. Other studies paid for by the National Institute of Justice, whose findings did not support the 'get tough' approach, were never given this kind of public acclaim.

The best example is provided by the treatment given to the research of Greenwood's Rand colleague, Joan Petersilia. Petersilia (who participated in producing the selective incapacitation database) followed up a sample of California probationers and found that a shocking 61% were rearrested within three years. The study proved so popular with the U.S. Department of Justice that they paid for its reproduction and mailing to a large audience in state and local government, and made it a "highlight" study in their monthly newsletter (Petersilia 1985). When Petersilia (1986) reanalyzed the same database, she found that, when compared to a matched prison sample, the probationers in her study actually had lower arrest rates than the prisoners, and that with time, even the incapacitation differences might wash out. The Department of Justice reaction to this reanalysis was quite different. Faced with a set of findings that refuted the punishment-and-control agenda, in that the findings suggested that the incapacitative effect of imprisonment may be washed out, over time, by its criminogenic effects, the Department refused to support further dissemination. Instead, the National Institute of Justice, which funded the study (expecting, no doubt, a different result) refused to allow it to be published under federal dollars and attempted to stop Rand from publishing the revised analysis with its own money, claiming that the research was "flawed."

There is a notable sense of paranoia that attaches to the idea that the government's scientific institutes support flawed research when the results are kind to its agenda, but suppress it otherwise. Claims of official suppression of research are rightly to be received with considerable skepticism, especially when they are directed at an official government institute charged with knowing the difference between good and bad research. Scholars notoriously disagree on the quality of studies—perhaps the findings were not the main problem with the second Petersilia study.

Yet the extremely cautious handling of the second Petersilia study must be compared to the lavish acceptance of an internally commissioned paper by Zedlewski (1987). The study argued the implausible line that locking up convicted offenders is cheaper than leaving them on the streets, and that higher national incarceration rates are associated with reduced rates of serious crime. Not sent out for review by independent social scientists, the study was instead immediately circulated free of charge, to elected officials throughout the nation—to state legislators, governor's staff, law enforcement personnel, and so forth.[20]

Why send out such a study without first reviewing it carefully? The idea, undoubtedly, was to continue to fuel an official Federal agenda for building prisons that was already beginning to face heavy criticism, even from political conservatives, due to the heavy costs of prison overcrowding (McGuinan and Pascale 1986). The fact that the study, which relied on the controversial results of the Rand self-report surveys, was itself seriously flawed, seemed unimportant to the Federal leadership in criminal justice. The claims of the paper made its way into numerous editorials of local news media, legislative debates and even official publications of the justice department.

Yet the study's flaws were extremely basic. It used a causal time series approach to argue that high incarceration causes low crime—yet there were so few observations over time (less than 25) that any causal attribution is extremely unreliable (McCleary 1980). In failing to lag the crime prevention effect, the study may have been obscuring what is actually a positive relationship between crime rates and incarceration. The study argued that criminality is more expensive than incarceration by including in its cost estimates the price tag of private security—three times the amount of money spent on government criminal justice—as a cost of crime, even though nearly all of these costs would be borne by employers to prevent employee crime, regardless of the number of drug sales, rapes, murders, and other crimes that occur on the streets. The study included all crime, minor and felonious, in the calculation of crime prevented by incarceration, and estimated that the "average" apprehended street criminal engages in an astonishing 171 crimes per year—using the highly skewed "average" California robber and burglar self-reported crime rate from the Rand studies cited earlier.

The flaws in the study were so serious, the claims so preposterous, that a response was rapidly produced by two prominent criminologists (Zimring and Hawkins 1988), showing that if the numbers in the paper were accurate, the threefold increase in imprisonment since 1978 should have led to a *negative* crime rate in 1988. The Zimring/ Hawkins paper made the rounds of criminologists, who privately chuckled at the excessive zeal of the powers that be. Yet the widespread emphasis on the Zedlewski work continued, as legislators and local media used the study's claims to argue for increasingly tough sentencing of offenders. One of the Rand researchers (Petersilia 1989) was sufficiently troubled by Zedlewski's use of the Rand data that she wrote to Assistant Attorney General Richard Abell to say that "several individuals and organizations have used information from the Rand Inmate Surveys out of context" in ways that overestimate potential crime prevention effects of imprisonment. The Justice Department continued to use the Zedlewski report, despite the disclaimers of the original Rand researchers.

Policy makers certainly paid attention to studies such as Zedlewski's, but it would be unfair to characterize the social sciences as somehow causing the offender control movement. The opposite is more plausible: the unrelenting investment of federal and local political agendas in tough measures of control led criminologists to consider these policies in order to keep their research relevant to the policy debate. By 1980, the determinate sentencing movement had already peaked, as summarized in chapter 2 (see also Shane-DuBow, Brown, and Olson 1985). What had begun as a reform movement to eliminate (or structure) parole release decisions in order to treat prisoners with greater humaneness transformed into a juggernaut for tough measures in sentencing (Greenberg and Humphries 1980). The call for "toughness" seemed irresistible and it distorted almost any attempt to reform sentencing practice—Pennsylvania's inability to implement innocuous guidelines (described earlier) is an excellent example of the call's powerful impact upon sentencing reform (Kramer and Lubitz 1985).

Studies of the effects of sentencing reform suggest that the experience in Pennsylvania, while public and visible, was not unusual. A report by the National Academy of Sciences Panel on Sentencing Reform and its Effects (1983) concluded that "the substantial increases in prison populations in jurisdictions that have adopted sentencing reforms continue preexisting trends in sentencing and do not appear to be substantially caused by these sentencing reforms."

The most powerful example of this was Casper's (Casper, Brerton and Neal: 1982: 133) finding that the tough sentences in California were less a product of the new determinate sentencing law than they were a longstanding trend in the behavior of the California judiciary. It was not that the sentencing reforms were irrelevant to the offender punishment-and-control movement; rather, they codified (and thereby solidified) a trend already in place.

Criminologists and Offender Control[21]

In the offender control movement of the 1970's and 1980's, the criminological research community played three distinct roles. The first role has already been described—criminologists were responsive to already existing political trends. Evidence for the responsive role of criminology is provided by Table 3–2, which shows the overlap in time of major sentencing reform and major criminological writing.

Criminologists were also responsive to the financial marketplace for research. It is a bit of an overstatement, but not much of one, to say that any American criminologist desiring to write about penal policy—especially anyone trying to obtain research funding and to establish a reputation in the field—had to be interested in the punishment-and-control agenda. Those who disputed the agenda had to find ways to incorporate their research into its general call, since these were the primary studies being funded, at least by government.

The second role played by criminologists was advisory. The agencies funding crime research, the Federal Government and private foundations, operate with advisory boards. Prominent criminologists occupied key roles on those boards, and they advised the direction of funds toward the questions in which they, and others like them, were

Table 3–2   Criminological Writing and Penal Code Reform

Date of Publication	Date of Law Reform
1973 Frankl, *Law Without Order*	1974 Maine Parole Abolition
1974 AFSC, Struggle	
1975 Fogel, *"We are the Living Proof"*	1975 Indiana Code Passed
1976 von Hirsch, *Justice*	1976 California Code Passed
1976 Van Den Haag, *Punishing*	
1977 Wilson, *Thinking*	1977 New Jersey, Determinate Sentencing Passed
	1978 Connecticut Parole Abolished

interested. Because the intellectual consensus of the 1970s was that rehabilitation was no longer a viable policy, program evaluation emphases waned in favor of criminal-career/sentencing impact studies. Because different advisory boards often share members, the spread of the new criminological gospel was extremely rapid.

The criminologists also advised on legislation that was currently in process. As Fogel was reviewing his "justice model" book galleys, he was advising the Indiana State Legislature on its pending sentencing reform (Clear, Hewitt and Regoli, 1978). Similarly, as von Hirsch was making revisions in the Committee Report (1975) that preceded his book, he was also advising legislative reformers in Oregon and Minnesota. The publication of the ideas did not precede the sentence reform movement; rather, they were coterminous.

It would be too simple to picture the U.S. criminological community as merely responsive to and advisory of public policy, for they played a third role as well. Their work legitimated policy by placing the exalted mantle of scientific approval upon it. This role was central to the political agenda of the key elected officials, for it gave them a two-punch ability to counteract the longstanding liberal tradition that held sway among so-called "experts." The litany of studies showing the skewed distribution of individual offending rates allowed the pro-incarceration lobby to ask of its opponents, "What do you propose to do about these very bad people who hurt innocent citizens?" The collection of studies promising (via statistical models) crime prevention effects of various levels of tough, incarceration-based policies allowed the proponents of prison to challenge their detractors by saying, "Whatever your ideas, you must beat this!"

Those who would argue against the escalation of punishment in the United States therefore faced a dilemma. The rhetoric supporting escalation was impossibly simple and common-sensical: "Find the bad guys and get them off the streets." The empirical backup to the strategy was impossibly encased in complex and inaccessible statistical formulae, stochastic models, and alternative operating assumptions. The political elite promised a take-no-prisoners war against crime; the scientific community seemed to promise highly technical pinpoint accuracy. Even though critics of the criminal career research agree that its founders were "extremely responsible in acknowledging the limits [of the methods] . . . laypersons' misunderstandings . . . can themselves become a political reality . . ." (Greenberg 1991: 40). It is difficult to deny this assessment.

The years from 1970 to 1990 became a time of spectacular growth in all forms of correctional control. The socio-political groundwork for these changes was already in place by the time criminologists began writing their critiques of rehabilitation in the 1970s (Cohen 1985; Cohen 1988). The legislative products of these forces were, for the most part, already in place as criminologists produced, during the 1980s, the writing that justified them.

This second thrust of criminological work was different in form from the first. The writing that fed what Cohen has called the 1970s "deconstruction" movement in social control was largely argument, with doses of empirical grounding. The work of the 1980s was solidly empirical, impeccably driven by numbers. At times it seemed as though debate was secondary to the processes of measurement. The uses of science would be left to the makers of public policy.

This is an old idea: scientists search for 'truth' by the mere act of following evidentiary paths; it is for politicians to turn the truth into action. This would be a fair argument if not for the fact that the 'evidentiary paths' to be traversed were increasingly defined by political interests as represented by the rhetoric of 'getting tough.' The scientific search for truth was funneled into a series of key ideas about individual offense patterns, because this was the framework most consistent with the elected leadership's agenda of offender punishment and control.

Some of the more recent research has been directly gauged to affect public policy. Three studies in particular illustrate this type of work: DiIulio's (1990) reworking of the Rand analysis on a sample of Wisconsin inmates, Reynolds' (1991) time series analysis of changes in punishment probabilities in Texas; and Methvin's (1992) analysis of crime and punishment trends in Michigan. Each study concludes its analysis with a "what if?" section, in which claims are made that more prisons would result in less crime in the state being studied. And each study, distributed among state elected officials, immediately translated into legislative interest and calls for tougher sentencing.[22]

Political leaders, especially the federal leadership, have used this type of research to support the get-tough agenda with a vengeance. The monthly newsletter of the National Institute of Justice, formerly a rather ordinary summary of NIJ-supported research activity, sent primarily to an academic audience, was transformed under the Reagan administration into an upscale, glossy advertisement for its social control agenda, and distributed widely within the criminal justice and political systems across the country. The careful management of this report was an important aspect of the political agenda. For instance, when the NIJ Reports presented a description of the "intermediate sanctions" work going on around the country (1990), the Director of the Institute, James "Chips" Stewart, felt obligated to write an introduction to the piece making clear that the official attitude of the government toward such strategies was one of great doubt and begrudging acceptance, to be reluctantly embraced only in the face of extensive problems of overcrowding across the nation.[23]

The role of researchers described here is consistent with what Foucault has described as the "knowledge-power" spiral. It is a mutually reinforcing pattern of social change in which the sources of power help to define what is "known," and the sources of knowledge take their intellectual cue from arenas of power. Given the way that research is funded and its results disseminated in the United States, it is difficult to imagine any other possible circumstance. In practice, empirical scholarship in the area of crime is closely linked, perhaps inevitably, to social agendas occurring in the political arena.

A CRITICAL LOOK AT OFFENDER CONTROL CRIMINOLOGY

There has been a close association between the kind of crime research being conducted and the types of penal policies pursued. Table 3–3 shows three post-war eras of criminological research, each associated with a policy orientation. During the heyday of "causes" research, correctional programs emphasized prevention of juvenile crime; during the "evaluation" era, the emphasis shifted to treatment of adult offenders. Each of these eras of research ended coterminously with a shifting public belief that the correctional methods associated with them were not working.

To the surprise of few but its truest believers, the 'patterns' era, with its associated emphasis on punishment and control, joins it forbears in minuscule success. Having claimed to be the means for crime control, the punishment-and-control movement finds itself faced with discouraging statistics about its impact. The reasons lie in both theoretical and practical weaknesses in the movement's approach.

Problems of Theory

The main trouble with the punish-and-control approach is that among its many assumptions, two are extremely problematic: first, that the

Table 3–3   Eras of Penological Research

1950–1965	*The 'causes' era*: Research focus on the relationship of delinquency and criminality to social structure and social process
1965–1975	*The 'evaluation' era*: Research focus on correctional programs and how well they work
1975–1990	*The 'patterns' era*: Research focus on individual offending rates and patterns

amounts of crime in a society are best understood as a product of decisions made by individuals; and second, that actions taken with regard to those individuals will have effects only on them and not on others.

There is a string of studies demonstrating the social patterns of crime: it is associated with young, disadvantaged males, especially from urban centers. (summarized in Braithwaite 1989; Nettler 1984; Gottfredson and Hirschi 1990). Of course, there is considerable debate about whether and to what extent crime is caused by these forces, and so the causation question has proven exceedingly difficult to answer with authority. Yet lack of concern about the precise causes of criminality does not make it wise to ignore the possible ways that the correlates of crime may actually be producing crime, especially when the main interest is in preventing crime.

The punishment-and-control strategy is based upon an idea that crimes are individual decisions of individual actors, and that these decisions can be prevented by restricting the individual's access to criminal opportunities. The most common method is the crude technique of incarcerative incapacitation, but other methods also exist. Some are now under use—electronic monitoring, chemical castration—while other methods, such as sensory implants, are only ideas. The combined impact of these methods is to ensure that the willing criminal cannot commit a crime.

One of the attractions of the control movement is its claim to be unconcerned with 'causes of crime.' It is instead concerned merely with targeting and restraining those who would commit crimes. Since criminal acts are nearly always the result of individual behaviors, the strategy has powerful intuitive appeal.

What happens to the control model, though, if the decision to engage in a criminal act only *resides* within the criminal actor, but is *generated* by interactions with the surrounding circumstances? What is the importance of all these correlates of criminal behavior for the offender control model? What does it mean when the criminal sanction ends up continuously dealing with the products of criminal processes, not their antecedents?

Let us assume, for the moment, the accuracy of a plausible circumstance—that crime is caused in large part by a combination of youth, with its search for personal thrills and challenge to authority (Gottfredson & Hirschi 1990; Katz 1988), relative poverty, with its constant appeal to youth to "get what everyone else has" (Taylor and Young 1973; Braithwaite 1979), and the decayed urban center, with the persistent alienation it creates via its disorganization and what are known as its "broken windows" (Shaw and McKay 1942; Wilson and

Kelling 1982). Let us further assume that these factors and others, taken as a whole, constitute something of a generating milieu of crime, which is further stimulated by forces taking place in the larger marketplace (Field 1990). Even though this is a simplistic formulation, it is not outrageously so.[24] Any realistic model of crime causation in the United States will have to include these ideas.

What does a policy of punishment-and-control do about these crime-generating factors? Nearly nothing. This is what the cliché that we are "dealing the symptoms and not the causes" really means in practice. Although it is a phrase in wide disrepute among criminologists, its importance, when used as a critique of punishment-and-control policies, is nonetheless difficult to ignore. The strategy of offender control—locking up an active offender, or placing an electronic monitor around his wrist—cannot stop other young boys from growing into adolescence and young adulthood. Nor does this strategy make the poor, young, minority male more wealthy relative to the rest of society. Nor does this stragety make the disorganized and filthy inner-city environment more pleasant. It cannot. It is not designed to do any of these things. *The offender control strategy is not designed to do anything at all about the forces that lead young, inner city, poor, minority males to engage in crime.*

Defenders of the offender control movement have asserted that the drop in crime will occur by removing the active offender (and thus eliminating those potential offenses) and deterring likely ones. But if the causes making more or less ordinary youth into active offenders remain undisturbed, this seriously reduces the potential impact of either effect intended by offender control.

The offender control model makes the most sense when crime is seen as (1) a rational choice of offenders who accurately assess their criminal opportunities and benefits; or (2) an uncontrollable act of an offender whose mental state is deranged. When crime is seen as a social process, in which certain contextual factors promote it and certain widely distributed human traits make it possible for the majority of males to engage in criminal acts (Farrington 1985), then removing a handful of active criminals to try to control crime is bound to disappoint.

This raises a fundamental concern about the punishment-and-control model as a theory. If disorganized urban communities keep producing disadvantaged male youth, then locking a few of them up after they reach adulthood is likely to be relevant to only a small portion of the social machinery of crime. Locking up all or most of them is patently unthinkable.

The punishment-and-control model, as now practiced, is not so much wrong theoretically as it is incomplete. The simple idea that the offender who is locked up cannot be committing a crime is correct, but as is usual in life, this is only part of the story. It is precisely because the model eschews any intent to struggle with complicated forces producing crime that it leaves so much to be desired as a crime control strategy.

The model also misunderstands the reasons people obey the law. It is based on an idea that that the threat and experience of penal harm motivates law-abiding behavior. A recent study by Tyler (1990) suggests these are minor causes of legal compliance. Of much greater importance is the *legitimacy* of the law, and this depends on how people experience the law in practice. In the end,

> people obey the law because they believe that it is proper to do so, they react to their experiences by evaluating their justice or injustice, and in evaluating the justice of their experiences they consider factors . . . such as whether they have had a chance to state their case and whether they were treated with dignity and respect. (Tyler 1990: 178)

It is hard to see how the penal harm movement—particularly as constituted in the recent growth in harms—achieves an increase in any person's experience of justice at the hands of the system.

Problems of Practice

There are three main problems hampering the practice of offender control: strategy backfire, system capacity, and technical capacity.

Incapacitation may fail to prevent crime because it backfires. Much of urban crime is a group economic phenomenon, and when active offenders are removed and imprisoned they are often quickly replaced by new recruits (Reiss 1988). This is almost certainly true of drug crime (DiNardo 1993; Caulkins, Crawford, and Reuter 1993), and drug offenders have been one of the driving forces of the prison population in the last 10 years (Austin and Killman 1990). Also, the vast majority of prison sentences amount to less than two years time served. Recent research suggests that "the estimated overall termination rate from serious offending is 14% per year for offenders on the streets" (Golub 1990), but during incarceration, the rate is zero (Golub 1992). Incarceration may actually interrupt the natural process toward desistence of criminal careers.

Incarceration also interferes with natural processes that would reduce the intensity of criminal activity. Sampson and Laub (1992; Laub and Sampson 1993) have described the "turning points" that may promote an end to the criminal career, primary among them jobs and family responsibilities. But turning points such as employment or family duty are not aided by incarceration; indeed, they are made less likely by removal from the community.

Nor does there appear to be much promise of a large deterrent effect of imprisonment. Ethnographies of street crime showing the realities of the street criminal's world (Rosenbaum 1981) explain why megastudies of deterrence (Blumstien et. al., 1978) consistently find that the effects of deterrence are at best small and are certainly not easily increased merely by imposing harsher penalties. Moreover, some have speculated that the removal of so-called "active offenders" has negative impact on inner city communities, in that removal undermines sources of the economic base those communities enjoy and eliminates male role models (Currie 1985).

The programs of control, especially those in the community, are sufficiently tough that they often backfire (Clear and Hardyman 1990). The best example of this phenomenon is the intensive supervision movement of the 1980s, which promised close surveillance and stiff enforcement of rules. The result of these programs has been high rates of program failure, despite arrest rates that are not abnormally high (Morris and Tonry 1990; Petersilia 1987; Erwin 1984; Pearson 1987). In fact, experiments indicate that although program failure rates are increased by intensity of supervision, arrest rates stay the same (Petersilia and Turner 1990). Instead of improving law-abiding behavior by offenders, these programs impose rules of compliance that produce failure and result in the offender's return to prison. It has been argued that control itself does not reduce crime. In a meta-analysis of several hundred correctional evaluations, Andrews (1990) found that what he terms "sanction" approaches—increases in the severity of punishment or control—had no evidence of impact on offender behavior.

The problem of system capacity is so obvious that it can be easily summarized. About one offender is arrested for every eight crimes reported to the police, but only about 36% of crimes known to victims are reported to police—and even these disappointing figures overestimate the efficiency of the system, since most arrests are for drug possession or sales, and these crimes are not counted in either UCR data or victimization surveys. Assuming that every offender arrested for a non-drug offense was responsible for four non-drug crimes, the most optimistic construction of the argument would be that the system currently processes about two percent of the available business. This is a system that already is overstrained to the point of chaos.

It is inconceivable that government could afford to increase its expenditures on corrections—or find enough prison, probation, and legal staff—to allow capacity to meet potential demand. Even if the system were to try to cover one-third this total, it would suggest the need for an increase of more than 1000% in judges, prosecutors, prisons and so forth. By comparison, the 277% increase in prison capacity actually experienced since 1973 seems puny.

But even if this pricetag were acceptable, there are formidable technical constraints. For reasons of efficiency, offender control is based upon an ability to determine the most active criminal offenders. This incorporates two ideas: apprehension and prediction. Each has technical limits.

The police have made strides in improving their ability to catch criminals in recent years, but it is unreasonable to think that there is no ceiling to these improvements, especially in the near future. The fact is that the apprehension probability for each criminal act is quite low—recent estimates in California place it as low as three percent of all robberies and burglaries (Greenwood and Turner 1987). To a certain extent, the more criminally active offenders have the greater chance of being caught, as the odds begin to stack up against them— although there are certainly some exceedingly effective criminals (Chaiken and Chaiken 1982).

But the general case is that offenders get caught sometime after their criminal career has commenced, depending on their criminality level, with the more active criminal more likely to be caught. Thus, as apprehension rates start to increase, the efficiency of the crime-prevention apprehension begins to decrease—since it is into the pool of less active offenders that the police dip to achieve their increase in arrest efficiency. Thus, there are decreasing marginal gains in crime prevention of each additional arrest. The only way to improve the system's effectiveness through apprehension of criminals is to catch the high-rate offenders earlier in their career.

This strategy raises the second problem of limits in the effectiveness of prediction. There are, of course, various kinds of errors in prediction (Clear 1988; Monahan 1981), but that is not even the main problem. More troublesome is the factual accuracy of the old adage that "the best predictor of the future is the past" (see Nagin and Farrington 1991). In order to know which offenders are likely to be highly active, the system must wait for them to demonstrate some of their high activity. The system must also have some capacity to reliably estimate the activity level, and this is not an inconsiderable problem, since some of the best predictors are not represented in official databases (Chaiken and Chaiken, 1982).

It is not likely we will soon achieve a breakthrough in the ability to predict criminal behavior, at least one significant enough to enable us to prevent much crime through selective punishment. This is a serious problem for the offender control model, because it means that the use of control sanctions will be fraught with error—namely, errors of overcontrol and undercontrol. As if the theoretical problems were not enough, the problems of practice are nearly insurmountable. Gottfredson and Gottfredson (1992) identified three assumptions of the selective incapacitation model of punishment. They are:

1. Criminal activity is patterned with respect to types of behaviors,
2. The seriousness of offending changes in meaningful ways throughout the career,
3. The rate of offending changes in meaningful ways throughout the career.

Studying detailed data on two California samples of offenders, the Gottfredsons concluded that these assumptions are not supported, and that "the state of nature . . . does not appear conducive to the effective development of [incapacitation] strategies" (6).

Taken together, these limitations of theory and practice explain the reasons why, when the National Research Council of the National Academy of Sciences asked, "What effect has increasing the prison population had on levels of violent crime?" the answer was, "Apparently, very little." (Reiss and Roth 1993: 4). A study commissioned by the Council (Cohen and Canelo-Cacho 1993) estimated that the tripling of time served for violent offenders resulted in a modest 10–15% decrease in violent crimes through incapacitation alone.[25] They also estimate that increases in the probability of incarceration are considerably more effective than increases in the length of time served.

Problems of Science

So much research has exhaustively detailed the projected benefits of greater punishment and control; how can it be that these studies have missed the mark? The answer lies partly in the fact that they are merely models, and they poorly represent reality.[26]

Almost all of the models make the flaw of comparing the effects of imposing prison sentences to what we might call the act of "doing nothing," when "doing nothing" is almost never a real option or the most accurate comparison. This error is true of Zedlewski (1987), DiIulio (1990) and Methvin (1992). Each uses an estimate of crimes committed during a pre-incarceration period spent "on the street" as the number of crimes prevented by the prison sentence. But if the offender were not in prison, he or she would be under some form of correctional control. It is reasonable to assume some crime suppression effect due to correctional methods such as probation or parole.

In modeling, it is important to make the distinction between prevalence and incidence. Studies that show small differences in arrest rates by comparing two forms of non-prison penal methods (see Petersilia and Turner 1994) estimate prevalence, not incidence, and they compare one correctional form to another. It should by now not be surprising that correctional forms, especially those that are based upon controls, are so unsuccessful at changing offender arrest rates.

A more informative study would compare correctional supervision to its absence. Few such studies have been done, but the routine finding of prison release studies is that over long periods, rates of arrest for those released to parole are not significantly different than for those released outright, but the former stay arrest-free for a significantly longer period after release (Raab 1976; Saks and Logan 1984). The fact that the supervised group is under greater official scrutiny and survives longer without arrest is strongly suggestive that the underlying incidence rates have been affected by supervision. Thus, incapacitation models need to be built by comparing prison to *something*. The qualities of this *something* are themselves likely to influence the degree of crime suppression (Andrews and Bonta 1993).

Incapacitation rate studies also fail to build in a factor for deterioration in criminal career over time. With each new year in prison, the aging process discounts the rate of crimes the person might have committed had he or she been free. When this statistical modeling problem is combined with the idea (stated earlier) that incarceration seems to retard rates of desistence among those who are locked up, while potentially increasing their criminality upon release, this suggests the need to build into the models displacement and acceleration components that become active after release. Thus, the crime prevention effect, which is temporary, is at least somewhat washed out over time by these components, the effects of which are observed upon release.

The evidence mounts that earlier methodologies vastly overestimated the incapacitative effects of incarceration. A major culprit in overstating incapacitation effects of imprisonment was the original Rand surveys (described above), which supported a belief that active offenders commit over 200 crimes per year while on the streets. Spelman (1993) has reanalyzed the Rand surveys to develop estimates of likely incapacitation effects under various assumptions. He corrected the Rand data to reduce the impact of untrustworthy respondents, and he developed statistical models that take into account such problems as selection bias, co-offending, replacement, and deterioration of criminal careers.

His conclusions are not promising for proponents of incapacitation policies. As a best case scenario, selective incapacitation policies could "reduce crime by 4 to 8 percent" (Spelman 1994: 289), but only after having based the modeling on assumptions that are "not even close" to being correct, and whose violation may "effect the results in important but unpredictable ways" (289). One of the assumptions, for example, is that the only alternative to incapacitating an offender is to do nothing. Another such assumption is that the policy of removing young males from the community has no impact on the criminal potential of their children.

Deterrence models have some of the same flaws that plague incapacitation studies; most of these models compare the effect of prison to that of doing nothing, beginning with Erlich's famous pioneering work using econometric methods. These studies fail to account for deterrent potentials of some non-prison methods, as indicated by offender's preferences to stay in prison rather than enter them (Petersilia and Turner, 1993). Finally, deterrence models face a reality-check problem, in that "the flat trend in violent crimes between 1975 and 1989 in the face of a tripling of average prison time served per crime is not compatible with any substantial deterrent effect" (Reiss and Roth 1993: 293).

Deterrence models can also misrepresent the way deterrence works. Reynolds (1991), for example, calculated that on the average, very little time is served in Texas by any offender for each crime committed. The numbers were rather startling—for each burglary committed in Texas, a figure measured in weeks is served by some prisoner for a burglary. Reynolds then builds his deterrence model to say that each burglar "calculates" his or her potential loss based on that averaged penalty, and concludes that a few days in prison are unlikely to deter a person from committing burglary.

This is surely fuzzy scientific modeling. Deterrence theorists agree that the main ingredient in deterrence modeling is the probability of getting caught; the degree of punishment is secondary. Reynold's model fits active offenders who calculate thus: "I will go ahead and commit one burglary, for on the average my penalty will be a few days, and that is not so bad. But I will forego committing ten burglaries, since my loss would be ten times that number of days, and that sounds undesirable." It is more plausible to imagine a burglar who exhibits two-stage thinking: "What are my chances of getting caught, and if caught, what is likely to happen to me?"[27] One would model apprehension probabilities coupled with median penalty levels (not their product).

So the punishment-and-control strategy, so widely believed and energetically advanced, confronts serious problems of theory, practice, and science. Yet these problems may not represent the major inadequacy of the offender control model. Its main problem may be that it operates via an insatiable appetite for harming lawbreakers. It has no self-limiting capacity (Braithwaite and Pettit 1990). When crime rates go down, enthusiasts of offender control can point to the obvious success of their methods, and use that success as an appeal for more of the same. When crime rates go up, the proponents of control can point with alarm to the large number of people escaping the system's clutches and call triumphantly for "tough measures."[28] The answer is always the same, regardless of the amount of crime or its impact—society must exert more control over the law violators.

HARM AND OFFENDER CONTROL

The punishment-and-control movement receives such lengthy analysis not only because it is the current ideology in force, but also because it has such a direct relationship with the nature of and especially the amount of penal harm imposed on offenders. More so than perhaps any other model of the system, its currency is direct and intentional pain.

This fact comes through in several ways. To the degree that the aim of the penal sanction is to serve as a deterrent, it calls for law violators to experience visible and obvious pains at the hands of the law. The view, always, is that the penal sanctions need constantly to be toughened, made more opprobrious. In this vein, the so-called "boot camp" owes some of its popularity to the way it portrays the experience as difficult and unpleasant. Likewise, the new intensive supervision movement often represents itself as a "no nonsense" method, one that is tough and firm. The attractiveness of electronic monitoring and other such new community programs is tied up in imagery of nastiness, to the point that several programs promote themselves on their records that some prisoners would rather be in prison than be in the community program alternative.

The escalation of harmfulness of community punishments, at least in rhetoric if not always in fact, poses a challenge to the traditional punitive ascendancy of the prison. In recent years, the proliferation of what are called "shock" sentencing programs advances the claim that a little bit of pain is a good thing, and works ever so much better than no pain at all. That evaluations continually find these programs fail to reduce recidivism (Latessa and Gennaro 1988; Finckenauer 1982; MacKenzie 1990; Andrews, Bonta and Hoge 1990) never seems to have much impact on the deeply ingrained ideology of penal harm. The ineffectiveness of harm is thought to reside in the hope offenders have for lenience, and so the solution is to legislate it away, with a litany of mandatory penalties for all manner of evil acts, from drug use to gun possession. The overriding idea is that we must convince offenders of the monumental power of the law by using it to hurt them in as many ways as seems feasible.

The ideology of harm as it stems from offender control is an accelerating spiral of threats and disappointments. The government draws a line in the dirt, citizens cross the line, and this leads government to draw new, more threatening lines, in a charade that has changed the face of penal methods in the last 20 years.

The harm-acceleration cycle has a self-contained, addictive quality to it. Believing that the solution to crime involves being nasty to criminals, the nation finds itself in a cycle of escalation. A nasty idea is proposed to respond to crime. Once imposed, it has almost no relationship to actual crime. In frustration, observers of this impotence quickly accept that the reason must be that the idea was not nasty enough, and so its painfulness is again increased in tone and substance, only to once again fail. And so on. Any other symbolism, certainly a symbolism that the currency in harm is at best irrelevant to the problem, and at worst one of its sources, seems impossible. In the first year after the passage of the Indiana penal code in 1976, over 100 bills were proposed to amend penalties—all but one provided for an increase in sentence length. In New Jersey, legislators have proposed a law to place automatic liens on the income and property of felons at the time of their conviction, up to the amount of the cost of their incarceration. The unsubtle idea is to deter drug dealers and white collar criminals; the open justification is a remarkable one, in that it suggests that users of public services ought to pay for their costs, as if the user were the inmate and the service were the penal harm. Federal civil statutes allow property to be seized if law enforcement officials believe they are being used to facilitate drug distribution—they need not even make an arrest![29]

These are but examples of the quantum leap in harm that has accompanied the punishment-and-control movement. In a way, this new ideology has changed nothing, for it still is based on the belief that the way to deal with crime is to focus on apprehended offenders, using the suggestions of scientific research. In a way, the ideology has changed everything, by elevating penal harm to a level of primary social utility.

POLITICS, AGAIN, BUT WITH SCIENCE

The focus on offenders as the means to confront crime is so central to policy thinking that it is difficult to describe an alternative model. Similarly, the close connection between this idea and the research and theory interests of criminologists is apparent from both historical studies and in a review of contemporary argument. The general belief has been that the steady progress of science will open doors toward strategies that will help reduce crime. For its part, science has not been reticent to advance this claim in its own behalf.

If anything, the view continues today with even greater fervor than ever. A recent study by Langan (1991) analyzing crime and punishment since the mid-1970s found that increases in the size of the prison population were driven primarily by policy considerations such as law enforcement, sentencing and parole, and to a much lesser extent resulted from changes in crime rates. Langan also argued that the increases were associated with a modest decrease in crime rates. United States Attorney General Thornburg embraced the latter findings to the exclusion of the former, in that he made the claim that prison prevented crime a standard part of his speeches as he traveled the country. A few months later, the FBI announced its crime figures for the year, which showed a dramatic increase—over 10%, especially in the cities—of violent crime.[30] In the following year, a new administration arrived at the White House; its first crime bill called for more of the same: police, prisons, boot camps, and death penalties.

Does anyone really expect policy makers to drop the mention of scientific studies that promise results, just because the results never seem to arrive? Hardly. One need only hear how would-be-president Joseph Biden (Senator from Delaware) reacted to one year's announcement of increases in crime. He said: "The President and Congress must pass tough measures to fight crime" ("Seven Cities," 1991: 1). In a similar vein, the scientific reliability of three "more prisons" studies mentioned above—those from Wisconsin, Texas, and Michigan—has been subjected to a wide range of criticism (for a summary, see Baird 1993) along the lines of that received by the original Zedlewski study. Yet another would-be president, Phil Gramm (Senator from Texas), routinely mentions these studies in speeches and editorials that call for more prisons and tougher sentencing. It is safe to say that the critiques of science receive far less play in political circles than the original research.

As one of his last acts in office—called, by some, "General Barr's last stand" (Tonry, 1993)—Attorney General William Barr published a report entitled *The Case for More Incarceration* (1992). It was exactly that—advocacy of a point of view. It cited none of the research listed here, which criticized the punishment-and-control model, even though some of the studies I have listed were funded by the Justice Department. It cited uncritically a long list of studies supporting the punishment-and-control agenda, even though some of them have been discredited (as we have seen).[31] It opens with an appeal, stating that

> there is no better way to reduce crime than to identify, target, and incapacitate those hardened criminals who commit staggering numbers of violent crimes whenever they are on the streets. Of course, we cannot incapacitate these criminals unless we build suffi- cient prison and jail space to house them. (ii)

This appeal in itself is not remarkable. By 1992, the penal policy of the Federal leadership had become baldly punitive. What makes the report interesting is that it had originally been an internal working paper of the Justice Department's Office of Policy and Communica- tions, and Barr decided to publish it because it "discusses in detail the reasoning behind some of the most important recommendations in *Combatting Violent Crime*" (ii). Not surprisingly, the recommendations in *Combatting* (1992) include preventive detention, restrictions on parole, mandatory minimum sentences, growth in prison and jail capacity, expansion of the death penalty, and tougher juvenile sanc- tions (6).

Thus, we are left to conclude with some astonishment that, when the Justice Department set about to make a series of recommendations for reform of the penal system, it began by reviewing internal working documents that selectively reviewed the literature, and then reported only studies supporting its preconceived position.

It is as though everyone has forgotten precisely what has been happening at the punishment front for 20 years—with little apprecia- ble impact on crime. For the world of politics, however, the uses of science are plain. No matter what happens with crime, the political response will be that we must "get tougher". And scientists will continue to produce studies to support the political agenda—studies that always begin by calling attention to the flaws of past research.

4

Victims and Punishment

> *Legend tells us that one day man spoke to God in this wise:*
>
> *"Let us change about. You be man, and I will be God. For only one second."*
>
> *God smiled gently and asked him, "Aren't you afraid?"*
>
> *"No. and you?"*
>
> *"Yes, I am," God said.*
>
> *Nevertheless he granted man's desire. He became a man, and the man took his place and immediately availed himself of his omnipotence: he refused to revert to his previous state. So neither God nor man was ever again what he seemed to be.*
>
> *Years passed, centuries, perhaps eternities. And suddenly the drama quickened. The past for one, and the present for the other, were too heavy to be borne.*
>
> *As the liberation of the one was bound to the liberation of the other, they renewed the ancient dialogue whose echoes come to us in the night, charged with hatred, with remorse, and most of all, with infinite yearning.*
>
> —Elie Weisel, *The Town Beyond the Wall*

In the early 1970s, it became popular to ask, "What about the victim?" The question was usually posed as an accusation, and it nearly always meant something like this: "How can you justify treating the offender with such leniency? Don't you care about the feelings of the victim?"

This chapter is about the feelings and needs of victims of crime. It is also about the extent to which those feelings and needs are met by the amount of penal harm imposed upon the offender. In addressing these ideas, I will develop a fairly complex argument: in the short run, victims need offenders to be punished as an affirmation that the crime was wrong; but in the long run, they need much more, and may even need to be able to forgive the offender—as difficult as that may be for non-victims to believe or for victims to do. I will also argue that linking the needs of victims to the degree of punishment serves certain political interests as much as it serves the actual needs of victims.

Convinced though I am that my position is correct, I make this argument with a certain uneasiness. While we have developed in recent years a remarkable literature on victims, little of it is relevant to my discussion here. The bulk of the research on victims is designed to document their loss, and most of the remainder measures victims' feelings toward the offender and/or the justice system. These feelings are usually quite angry. In this chapter, I want to consider victims and their experiences in a different light: to what degree has the penal harm movement, spawned partly in behalf of victims, served their interests either individually or collectively? In carrying out this analysis, I have had few research resources upon which to rely.[32] Instead, I have been forced to think critically about what it means to be a victim, and about the relationship of varying levels of penal harm to that experience. This chapter, then, is less empirical than it is analytical.

There are two additional caveats. First, though I have personally suffered as the victim of several crimes—thefts, burglaries, vandalism, among them—I have never been a victim of what I would consider a serious personal crime. Much of what I say on this topic is drawn from secondary experience—friends, family and a few studies. Certainly, if I were to experience such a crime, it would shape my views in unknown ways—perhaps strengthen some and shake others. Second, I count among my friends several who have suffered very serious crimes. I know how important it is to them that their feelings about the crime be taken seriously. I hope that what I have written here in no way denigrates the undeniable experience of victims of crime and the often impassioned feelings this experience provokes. I hope, instead, to speak with sensitivity about how we might better take victims seriously.

DEFINING VICTIMS

We begin with a discussion of the meaning of the phrase *crime victim*, because in its common usage, the term is more an overarching expression than a precise concept. The most obvious usage of the word refers to specific persons who have been subjected to specific crimes. There is also a way in which the word is commonly used to refer to collectives and to processes. Each of these usages makes a different inference about the role of punishment. Before entering into a larger discussion of the relationship existing between victims and punishment, the different meanings of the phrase must first be sorted out.

Even these three usages are narrow, because they are based on a definition of criminal victimization. There are numerous other kinds of victimizing experiences that for one reason or another do not amount to crimes (Feinberg 1984). Some might result from routine social relations, and as a result the state may not wish to treat them as crimes (for example, the emotional injuries that so often result from ordinary adolescent dating experiences). Others, such as damaging business practices or misallocations of public wealth, are more controversial, because to not criminalize certain acts tends to protect the interests of powerful social subgroups (Michael Parenti 1983). For instance, medical doctors are free to charge very high fees for their services, even though this may mean that many citizens cannot afford medical care.

Some of the harms people experience as a result of acts not typically thought of in criminal terms may be of considerable magnitude. As Robert Elias has pointed out: "While we deplore our homicide rate, which kills one person every 26 minutes, we virtually ignore our loss of one person every 4½ minutes from a workplace disease or accident (1986: 32)." Perhaps a useful case could be made for a definition of victimization that includes more than the so-called "crime victim," especially if one is concerned about all harms done to ordinary citizens. Yet these forms of victimization, however important they may be, are not related to punishment in the United States. When it comes to the penal process, we normally define the victim as one who suffers from traditional notions of personal street crime. In the state prisons of the United States, 85% of prisoners are there for crimes against persons or their property (BJS 1986). The experiences of their victims shape correctional policy.

In recent years the term *crime victim* has become an inseparable part of modern penal policy in the United States. This is a major change from earlier attitudes, and is seen perhaps as recently as the early 1970s (see McDonald 1976), when victim's opinions were thought to be essentially irrelevant to the justice system. The advent of a number of victims groups, together with a Federal Government leadership inclined to urge a "victim's agenda," led to a revolution in thinking about the role of the victim in the criminal justice process.

There have been several excellent discussions of the rise of the so-called "victimization movement" (see, for example, Flowers 1986; Rock 1990), and there is no need to restate this literature here. For our purposes, we note that the new interest in the victim began with a "concern about the lack of cooperation by witnesses" (Maguire 1992: 169) to a crime, and evolved into advocacy of a wide range of victim's interests. In its later stages, the victim's movement has coincided with the modern 'get tough' movement (see Elias 1986), and the two movements, which theoretically could have been separate, instead have been closely linked.

Today, there are three ways in which the term *crime victim* is used, each referring to different aspects of traditional street crime: the person, the collective, and the process.

Victims as Persons

The general usage of the term *victim* refers to individuals who have suffered criminal wrongdoing. The human dimension of the victim's suffering is often extraordinary. Of course, the costs of being subjected to crime are quite different depending on the crime itself. The excruciating results of a rape are different from those of other assaults; those who suffer from business fraud suffer differently from those whose cars are stolen, or who are kidnapped. To know the real harm suffered by victims is not an easy task.

Yet the harms victims suffer must be comprehended, if there is to be an understanding of the link between the harms of crime and penal harms. Burglary provides an example. According to recent studies of victims (*BJS Bulletin* 1991), four and one-half million households experienced a burglary in 1990. It is estimated that almost half of all urban households will experience multiple break-ins (BJS, 1988). Each break-in produces two types of direct injury. There is the loss of property, of course, which amounts to up to $50 billion annually, or $1,143 per break-in. For many, the property loss is trivial—insurance covers much of the replacement cost. For others, the few who lose priceless items or the many who have no insurance, the loss is often permanent—only about one-third of burglarized items are recovered (FBI 1990).

The property loss often pales in comparison to the intangible loss of security that the burglarized so often feel. In the USA, home security has become a six-billion dollar industry (*The Bellringer* 1989), and by the mid–1980s was the nation's fifth largest employer (*N.Y. Times*, cited in Elias 1986: 113) The growth in private security, estimated to be at least 15% annually (Elias 1986: 119) is fed very much by the fears of victims and their acquaintances. A remarkable 40% of respondents to a survey of 10 major U.S. cities indicated they had installed a home security system (Cunningham and Taylor 1984).

But even this is a crudely impersonal measure of the sense of insecurity a burglary will normally produce; mere dollars cannot adequately capture the scale of the injury. To the direct losses must be added the indirect impact of crimes of burglary: maintenance of a black market for stolen goods, victim's loss of work time, marginal opportunity costs of large industries of insurance and security, and so forth. And all those who have been burglarized feel an emotional loss, a personal violation and a loss of self-control.

There is a third type of injury that sometimes results from burglary—the injury which occurs when an offender breaks into a dwelling that turns out to be occupied. Although this injury occurs in a minority of such crimes, the burglary can culminate in a more violent event, such as an assaultive act against the homeowner.

To realize, then, the human impact of just this one type of crime, the various sorts of injury must be multiplied across the millions of households experiencing a burglary each year. When the human costs of crimes such as burglary are fully recognized, the importance of victim experiences for penal harm policy seems obvious. The experience of victimization is so widespread, so common, that ordinary citizens feel alarmed about their prospects for suffering at the hands of offenders.

Some studies suggest that such fear is well-founded. The probability of living in a household that experiences a burglary during any given year is estimated to be 6.1% (UCR 1990); it is estimated that 72% of households will experience a burglary in the next 20 years (BJS 1988). The probability of being the victim of a violent crime in a given year is 730 per 100,000 citizens—approaching 1% (UCR 1990). Eight percent will report one or more sexual assaults after the age of 12 (BJS 1988), though the extensive underreporting of this crime leads some researchers to estimate the proportion of victims as much higher—with studies suggesting rates of rape ranging from 14.5% (Kilpatrick, et al., 1987), to 27.5% (Koss and Wisniewski 1987), or even an astounding 44% (Russell 1984). Without question, becoming the victim of a felony crime is an experience widely shared in our society.

The link between an individual's victimization and penal harms is direct: offenders are harmed penally in order to return in some measure the harm they have done to a victim. This is in large part a result of sympathy (or outrage) felt by those who know, either first-hand or through friends, the injuries suffered by victims. The idea that victims of criminal wrongdoing wish to strike back at their violators is so deeply ingrained in our culture that it has been called "instinctive" (Mackie 1982) and has been named "the punishment response" (Newman 1978).

The Victim as Collective

There is a sense in which the use of the term *victim* connotes not just the specific target of a specific crime, but the whole of the larger society. Some aspects of this viewpoint are discussed in chapter 5, but here we recognize the ways in which the notion that the victim of crimes is society becomes meaningful.

For one thing, the experience of criminal events is almost as skewed as the behavior of criminals. One-third of all multiple victimizations for violent crime are committed against less than one-fiftieth of the population (Klaus 1981). This concentration of victimization is not experienced by a random sample of the population. Victims of serious crime are predominantly economically disadvantaged urban dwellers, especially minorities and children (Flowers 1986; BJS 1990), although criminal victimization is also most widely experienced by young males (BJS 1990). Blacks, for example, are two to five times more likely than whites to become victims of the various predatory street crimes, depending on the crime (Elias 1986). Young persons (under the age of 25) are 17 times more likely to be assaulted than the elderly (Whitaker 1990).

The collective image of the victim is often distorted to support particular social agendas, as when the crimes of a black man, Willie Horton, against a suburban white couple are emphasized for political gain (Johnson 1991). That does not mean the usage is purely manipulative. Where a person lives, the color of a person's skin, and the person's wealth and occupation are important correlates of victimization. The term victim should bring to mind a particular social group as a collective: the poor, the ethnic minority, the very young, the very old.

Often, however, when people use the term to refer to a collectivity, they mean it in a much more general sense, as though they are suggesting that all of society suffers as victims of crime. The indirect tally to support this idea is quite remarkable—the costs of the criminal justice system are estimated to be $65 billion annually (BJS July, 1992), and the costs of private social protection are half again those costs per year (Lipman 1988; BJS 1988). But again, to use the financial impact as a way to gauge what might be called the "victim as society" is to illustrate the point, not really to grasp it.

In many respects, the United States is obsessed with crime, to borrow a phrase from Adler (1983). Newspapers and the nightly news are filled with stories of crime; they are considered good ways to sell papers and sustain viewers. Concern about crime consistently ranks high on public opinion polls about social problems, and "fear of crime" is itself a phrase with a stylized meaning in the U.S. lexicon. It is not stretching things too much to view the U.S. self-concept as deeply affected by images about crime.

It is as though all of us are victims. When, in the theater halls of the nation, an excited audience's approval greets the so-called "protector's" (often gory) evisceration of the villain, it becomes apparent that we all carry around within us a sense of our own victimization, perhaps a sense that when one of us suffers, we all suffer. This is a type of societal identification that is perhaps more true in America than elsewhere.

Identification with the victim plays into the punishment agenda. The ordinary citizen takes on the role of the injured victim, and thereby comes to accept and even glorify penal harms not as expressions of legal judgements, but as manifestations of what feels like a personal investment in carrying them out. Penal harms cease to be actions taken in behalf of others who have suffered, and instead become extensions of every citizen's felt sense of violation by criminals. This is more than a case of acting as the victim's agent; it is the citizenry, as a collective, taking on personal emotions of the victims. It is a powerful type of identification, one which dominates thinking about victims and corrections.

The result of the identification is that non-victims, in sympathy with actual victims, assume the mantle of the injured. They feel for the perpetrator the same vitriol they themselves would experience if they were the victims of the crime. In this sense, every crime makes all members of society into victims—in experiencing the crimes against others, we identify and transfer into ourselves the emotions we believe are being experienced by the victim.

The Victim as Process

Another way in which the term *victim* is used is as something like a code word for what we call "the loss of social control," which is both a process and a symbol of a process. This is the most abstract usage, and yet in some ways it is the most important, for when expressed in this way, the word stands for a social philosophy. When the popular media describe a victimizing experience, many people hear a subtle message that goes something like this:

This is another indication about how unsafe it is to live in this society. A person cannot go through normal daily experiences (any more) without the fear that harm will be inflicted by this or that threatening stranger. It is so bad that simply to walk the streets is to take your life in your hands. It has gotten entirely out of control. Drastic measures are needed to reestablish the rule of law.

This is a powerful message about what people think is happening to U.S. society, and it is a message that reinforces the usage (described above) of the term *victim* as a collective social judgement. But the message also conveys a picture of a society at a loss for control, and by so doing justifies the expanded use of penal harms to regain the streets.

For if the *victim* stands for a process, then the way to not be a victim must also be a process (or more accurately, a reversal of a process). The symbolism is as powerful as it is subtle, and its result dramatically public and tangible. When victimization is represented as a social process, people develop a sense that "things are headed in the wrong direction" and that this is an irresistible drift. The word *victim* evokes the vision of a world that has become abnormal, and suggests that abnormal reactions are called for to confront the malaise. This feeling serves to sustain the advancing levels of penal harm described in Chapter 2: every bite of news about crime confirms the idea that the social fabric is fraying; it is taken as more or less axiomatic that solutions, in the face of the onslaught, must be terrible.

Why go through this summary of the various meanings of the term *victim*? Because it must be emphasized that the victim is a complex concept: a person, a group of persons, and not least, a symbol. Even though public portrayals of victims evoke in all of us strong feelings of sympathy and outrage, we cannot conclude that, somehow, the whole thing is a magnification of the media.

Yet as some critical analysts have wanted to argue, the symbolic imagery of victims is used often in service to political interests (Elias 1986). These analysts build their argument by focusing on latent functions of the victim's movement, to show that "victimology" serves unpalatable political interests.

The Dark Underside of Victim Imagery

Although anybody can become a victim in the United States, the reality of victimization is that it is far and away a lower-class experience. Crime—that is, the predatory street crime that generates most penal harm—is committed by the poor against the poor far out of proportion to their numbers in the general population (Davis 1987, in Maguire: 198).

Yet one would not come to this conclusion by observing the makeup of some of the high-profile organizations of the victim's movement. A good illustration is provided by Mothers Against Drunk Driving (MADD), one of the earliest and certainly one of the most successful victim groups. The organization was started by a middle-class victim who lost a child to a drunk driver, and its advocacy is concerned about a type of crime that arguably is not a lower-class event (Weed 1987). This organization has been extremely successful in achieving legislative change, nearly always involving tougher sanctions, with regard to drunk driving. Much of this work is based on contrasting the victims who are children to drunk drivers, who display utter disregard for the safety of those around them. Despite considerable evidence that many drinking drivers are alcoholics, the efforts of MADD to define the problem as one of law-breakers unwilling to exert self-control—people who can be punished into compliance with the law—have been quite successful.

In contests over the social definition of social problems—debates over "what should be done" about them—definitions are everything. The victim's movement has had two agendas. The first agenda has been to increase services to victims; the second, to increase legal rights of victims, especially through participation in the criminal justice system. In the United States, the latter agenda has more success than the former.[33] The main result has been to define the problem of victimization in terms of the criminal's decisions, not the victim's experiences—sympathy with victims is not used to give victims anything; rather, it is used to urge actions against criminals.

The National Organization for Victim's Assistance (NOVA) has argued for the insertion of the victim's interests at various stages throughout the criminal justice process. The bulk of what they ask for involves the capacity to exert greater influence on the penalty experienced by the offender (Bard and Sangrey 1986).

As a result of this type of advocacy, the victim's movement has redefined the victim's circumstance. The victim's suffering is used as a lever to create a version of legal standing in the penalty the offender should receive. The state becomes the agent acting in the victim's interest against the offender. What had heretofore been seen by legal theorists as a contest between the state and the accused becomes, after the rise of the victim's rights movement, a struggle between the state and the victim over who gets to determine the offender's fate.

The big winner in all this is, ironically, the state, which goes from having two claimants for its dominion to only one. Without the victim's movement, the state is faced with the claims of two different citizens, claims that can be thought of as essentially unrelated. The offender claims the right to be treated according to the law, to be treated as a person whose interests in just punishment are an obligation of the state. The victim, on the other hand, stands as a citizen who has experienced the trauma of an unfair loss—property, injury, financial and emotional strain. In a way, the very existence of the unfair loss stands as an accusation of the state's ineffective promotion of general welfare. The state, in an obligation to be fair, seems required to remediate that loss somehow, to support the victim, who is a citizen in need of compensation for the extraordinary physical, financial, and emotional losses resulting from crime.[34]

But the advocacy of the victim's movement coalesces these otherwise divergent interests by linking them in this way: the need to support the victim is transformed into the need for harsh treatment of the offender. Now the state can regain a more ascendant symbolic posture by rejecting the accusation that it fails to protect its citizens; the state asserts itself as the victim's champion. Instead of being required to give both the offender and the victim their due, the state can answer these claims by giving neither their due.

Many crime victims are so poor that they cannot afford to address their injuries and losses; most report that concrete services are more helpful than counseling (Skogan, Davis, and Lurigio 1990), though in U.S. victims services, the latter are more commonly found than the former (Davis and Henley 1990). The public image of the crime victim is more likely to be one who has suffered at the hand of a recidivist rapist, or the child victim of a brutalizing adult. These images support the state's claim that it must, in the interest of not only the particular victim, but of all victims, respond with the harshest possible treatment of the offender.

What seems never open for discussion is the almost irremedial failure of victim compensation programs to effectively repay the financial costs of crime (Skogan, Davis and Lurigio, 1990). Also never discussed are the absence of effective crime prevention programs in communities caught in the grips of victimization, the cynically narrow definition of victim interests to exclude wider forms of corporate and official harm, and the many other possible ways the existence of harms against citizens might threaten the state's claim as servant of the people's interests. In short, the victims do not get what they need; they only get what the state can afford or is willing to discuss:

> Research suggests that victims may function to bolster state legitimacy, to gain political mileage, and to enhance social control. By championing the victim's cause, the government may deflect criticism about ineffective law enforcement, and portray itself as the

friend of victims, instead of as possibly their greatest threat. (Elias 1986: 231)

Despite the ascendancy of the victim's movement in recent years, most of what has happened as a result of this movement has happened *to* offenders rather than *for* victims. When President Ronald Reagan established a special Federal Office for Victims of Crime within the Department of Justice in 1983, the victim's movement became firmly placed as an aspect of the punishment-and-control Federal agenda—a place many victims may have felt very comfortable to occupy. Instead of criticizing government inaction, many of these organizations began to receive Federal funds. When Attorney General Barr (1992) announced 24 recommendations to combat violent crime, six were under the heading "respecting the victim." Three had as their aim the improvement of victim cooperation with the prosecution of the offender, and another one was designed to increase pressure on the judge at sentencing and the parole board. Obviously, all of these are designed to do something *to* offenders. The only two which improved the lot of victims were a call for restitution (to be paid, of course, by the offender) and mandatory HIV testing in sex crimes.

Some Doubts

There is certainly something to be said for a little healthy cynicism-with regard to the victim's movement. But we should not take this cynicism too far, for three reasons.

First, a radically cynical point of view does not lead to a conclusion. Perhaps most victimizations do not involve traditional street crime. Yet the link between the victim of traditional street crime and the increasing use of penal harms remains intact, and continues to exert an influence on the practice of penal harms. The issue of victims must be analyzed on its own terms if there is to be an understanding of a new way to approach this problem.

Second, cynicism fails to explain *why* there is so much support for the victim's point of view. To argue merely that there is sympathy for victims seems an oddly anticlimactic analysis. On the other hand, to find a conspiratorial manipulation of the public strains credulity. A common problem for radical analyses (Garland, 1990) is that they tend to underestimate the considerable explanatory power of integrative (or consensus) models of social relations. In the case of victims, perhaps their fellow citizens share with them their sense of loss, and seek recompense for themselves as well as for the victim. Perhaps the influence of the victim's movement stems from the commonly shared experience of being a victim at someone else's hands—or at least the shared fear that victimization may happen. To the degree this is true, then the response of the general citizenry to support the outrage felt by victims is understandable without a radical explanation.

Third, and perhaps most important, a radically cynical perspective tends to belittle the tremendous emotional importance that penal harshness seems to have for so many victims. The victim's outrage about the offender's harm-doing is so profound, so uniformly felt, that is seems unreasonable to see it as a creation of alien state interests. The state may take advantage of these feelings to promote its agenda, but that does not explain the feelings themselves. To ignore them is to once again paternalize those who suffer as victims, a problem to which the radical criminological perspective has been far too susceptible (Taylor and Young 1973).

THE NATURE OF THE VICTIM'S EXPERIENCE

To understand the relationship between the newly-expressed interest in the victim and the acceleration of penal harms, we return to the three distinct usages of the term offered at the outset of the chapter. Two of those usages are wrong, in fact, despite their popularity. To continue to understand the term according to these meanings is confusing. The purpose of the next few sections of this chapter is to clarify why these usages are wrong and troublesome, and to offer a more accurate definition of the term *victim*.

Throughout this discussion, and for the remainder of this chapter, I rely heavily on an excellent analysis of victims and punishment developed in a recent book by two philosophers, Jeffrie Murphy and Jean Hampton (1988). Theirs is the most insightful treatment to date of the philosophical issues surrounding the victim, and the articulate way in which they present their insights finds its way repeatedly into the discussion below. I hope to borrow upon and extend their treatment.

Let us begin with a definition: A victim is a person who suffers harm as a result of the wrongdoing of another; the nature of the harm is an attack upon the victim's self-worth. The first part of this definition is not remarkable, but the reader may feel that the second is. The 'self-worth' portion of the definition is merely an attempt to be more specific about the first part of the definition: the way a criminal act makes the victim suffer is that it damages self-worth.

It should be noted that this is a much more narrow use of the term than is common in the United States. The definition recognizes that the larger society in which the victim lives cannot truly be thought of as a party to that harm, nor as a colleague in the wrongdoing of another. The larger society can sympathize with a victim, but it cannot share the victim's loss. It is, in fact, the loss that separates the victim from society.

It should also be obvious that, according to this definition, the term cannot rightly be used to denote a process of social change, real or imagined. A person who is confronted with the status of victim faces prospects of a process that is personal, not social. The victim is challenged to regain a level of self-worth commensurate with full citizenship, and this is an intensely personal process. It is not the process of a declining society, nor is it an experience of a collective. (The impression of the declining society may ring true precisely because it is such a potent metaphor for the declining self-worth of the victim.)

There are two realms, the symbolic and the practical, in which the victimization occurs.

The Symbolism of Victimization

A person who has been made to suffer wrongly, and this is especially true of victims of crime, feels an injury to basic self-worth that is experienced as a diminishment of well-being. Jeffrie Murphy has described this aspect of victimization as:

> *messages*—symbolic communications. They are ways a wrongdoer has of saying to us, 'I count but you do not,' 'I can use you for my purposes,' or 'I am here up high and you are there down below.' Intentional wrongdoing *insults* us and attempts . . . to *degrade* us—and thus involves a kind of injury that is not merely tangible and sensible. It is a moral injury. . . ." (Murphy and Hampton 1988: 25, emphasis in the original)

The explanation of the importance of this feeling is deeply imbedded in the democratic ideal, especially the version of moral philosophy espoused by Kant, which views the individual morally as an end and never as a means. The idea that all people are of equal worth, that all well-being counts equally, is a core foundational idea in the United States, as embodied in the assertion of the Declaration of Independence that "all men are created equal." The wrongdoer criminally violates these cherished values by saying, "I am above the law; I use you for my own pleasures." The victim experiences this attack as a deeply disturbing statement about the victim's self-worth and an extremely damaging attack upon his or her well-being. The most troubling aspect of this attack may be the unstated assertion of the wrongdoer that the victim is a person who has no right to well-being. The injury resulting from the act stands as evidence of the accuracy of the wrongdoer's accusation.

It is understandable, then, that in the face of this wholesale attack upon the victim's self-worth and belief in a right to pursue well-being, a profound resentment might emerge (Smith 1982). The feeling of anger and resentment is a defensive reaction against the symbolic meaning of the crime—that the victim does not count. It is a "feeling of hatred—call it revenge, resentment, or what you will—which the contemplation of such conduct excites in healthily constituted minds" (Stephen 1967: 152).

It is difficult, then, to separate what Murphy calls "the moral injury" from the more tangible effects of victimization. The temptation is to focus attention on what is thought to be the "real" injury of the crime—property loss and physical suffering. But this desire to focus on the tangible is likely to understate seriously the moral suffering that results from crime. The rape victim's fear of returning to the streets, after all, may be as much (or more) a product of the guilt and humiliation she feels at having been degraded as it is physical trepidation (Mawby and Gill 1987; Parks 1990). But it is also the case that "shame and anger have a deep affinity." (Karer, 1992: 52).

The Realities of Victimization

The actual injuries that result from criminal acts have already been described, but it is worth returning to this problem. Much of the discussion of the costs of crime to victims is expressed in statements such as "victims lose X days of work per year." This type of analysis, one which presents *average* losses of victims, portrays all citizens as victims of crime, and supports the so-called "collective" usage of the term that we have already rejected.

In fact, what a victim really loses as a result of a crime varies across victims and across crimes (see, for example, Cook, Smith, and Harrell 1987). An insured person whose automobile is stolen may be able to arrange for its replacement within hours, at very little or no actual financial loss. With a proper trade-off, the victim may even get a better car out of the deal. Another victim may lose the means for traveling to work and may be financially unable to replace the car. A woman who is raped by an intimate acquaintance will surely suffer physically and mentally, but may, with help from others and contrition from the assailant, be able to recapture a renewed self-confidence and even reestablish a relationship with the attacker and move beyond the crime. By comparison, who can claim to understand the loss experienced by the victim of a violent sexual assault such as befell the Central Park Jogger, who was gang-raped, disfigured, and left for dead?

The point is that what we call "real" damage to victims is highly individual in nature, and cannot be thought of accurately or usefully in any other way. There are patterns, of course, to the way victims tend to respond to the wrongs they experience (Viano 1990), but these patterns play out in idiosyncratic ways. Besides, it is crudely paternalistic *not* to see the victim in any other light than as a unique person with unique needs—and the desire to express those needs in a particular way.

Yet the penal process struggles to differentiate victims. There may be a kind of individualization of the victim's situation, as when at the sentencing hearing, the prosecutor recites the harms experienced at the hand of the perpetrator; or in preparation for sentencing, the probation officer records these facts in the "victim impact statement" (Erez and Tontodonato 1990). These are actions designed not to deal with the victim's loss, but rather to extend to the offender the appropriate degree of penal harm.

What the victim needs, what these experiences require in the way of support or assistance, the system may be able to do very little about. If the loss is financial, the government is seldom in a position to offer full recompense; if the victim needs emotional support and psychological treatment, how can the state do otherwise than pay the costs? Faced with an inability to help the victim recover self-worth, the state chooses an alternative course: to attack the offender.

The Punitive Response to Victimization

The punishment of the law violator is aimed at ameliorating both the symbolic and the practical harms the victim experiences.

Symbolic Functions

The crime symbolizes the vulnerability of the victim's well-being to unscrupulous wrongdoers. Punishment, since it is an attack upon the offender's well-being, seems an appropriate response. It carries symbolic weight, because it calls attention to the wrongness of the act; as some retributivists say, it "expresses" the social disapproval of the conduct by declaring a defiant "No!" to the act (Feinberg 1970; von Hirsch 1985). In C.S. Lewis's famous, graphic metaphor, the offender's experience of punishment "plants the flag of truth within the rebel soul" (1944). The act of punishment

> seeks to communicate to the criminal a proper understanding of his crime: by imposing some material injury which can be seen as injurious even through the eyes of egotistical self-interest, we hope to represent, and to force on his attention, the harm he has done both to others and to himself. . . . [It also] aims to bring the

criminal, though an understanding of his crime and his punishment,
to repent his crime (Duff 1986: 1986).

That is why some argue punishment is required. To fail to punish
an offender for a crime is to participate in that crime by failing to
proclaim its wrongness. Moreover, the penal sanction is properly
thought of not merely as a threat, but as a *promise* to uphold certain
values of the society (Van den Haag 1975). When the state fails to
carry out its promise in the face of a crime, it mocks its own
moral legitimacy.

For this same reason, it is required that the offender experience
the punishment as painful and feel damage to self-worth. This is
true whether the punishment is viewed as a way of "balancing the
advantages" that the law seeks to regulate (Morris 1968), as a means
to advancing the moral education of the offender and society (Morris
1985; Hampton, 1984), or merely as an expression of society's moral
repulsion of the act (Stephen 1967; Feinberg 1970; von Hirsch 1985).
That the punishment is indeed harmful to the offender is the cornerstone of its value as a message.

The punishment must also be fashioned in certain ways. Because
the penalty is a statement about the act's reprehensibleness, it must
contain the information about the relative censure the act deserves.
This is the requirement of *proportionality,* that the punishment imposed reflect the seriousness of the crime. The degree of the victim's
diminishment is dependent upon the act's harm to the victim's well-
being.[35] It is not feasible in modern society to implement the *lex
talionis* of the biblical commandment, "an eye for an eye," so the
social order must settle for the next best thing: a range of punishments
scaled to reflect our moral disgust at the conduct.

The scaling of penal harms individualizes the institutionalized
concern about the victim's suffering. It is a poignant method of siding
with the victim against the offender, of saying that the victim does
indeed count and that his or her self-worth matters. To the degree that
the crime has served to communicate a particular kind of moral
imbalance in the social order of human worth, the punishment is a
symbol for its lack of victory.

Practical Functions

It is less obvious how the punishment deals directly with the nonsym-
bolic loss suffered by the victim. Until recently, Western law has
generally not recognized any particular right of the victim to be
compensated for the losses suffered from the crime—one reason was
that the offense was actually seen as a violation of "the King's peace,"
and thus a problem to be dealt with by government. But modern

concerns about victims have led to a recognition of their very real suffering at the hand of offenders, and this in turn has translated into provisions for their recompense.

The most common form of repaying victims is restitution (Thowaldson 1990; Staples 1986). It is now a commonplace idea that the court, at the time of sentencing, will consider the direct financial cost of the crime to the victim and order the offender to repay those costs in the form of restitution. Because it is a relatively new idea, good statistics are not available on the successfulness of restitution schemes. Some studies suggest that restitution is not always paid by the offender (Thowaldson and Krasmick 1980) and several studies describe the difficulty the poor offender often has in making restitution (Mullaney 1988).

Sometimes there is a conflict between the symbolic function of the law as it imposes harms on the perpetrator, and the practical function of securing recompense. In order to be able to pay restitution, most offenders need to remain in the community rather than be incarcerated, and this may strike the victim (or the prosecutor, who claims to take on the values of the victim) as an inadequate level of penal harm, given the offense's seriousness. Indeed, the crimes that result in the greatest losses for victims are, by virtue of their seriousness, the least likely to call for a non-prison punishment. If those who most need restitution are denied it by the sentence of the court, then the only explanation to be given is that victim restitution is but a secondary aim of the law.

In view of the shortcomings of restitution, many systems have determined to develop "victim compensation" laws to provide money for victims to repay their losses. These laws are often notoriously inadequate—they impose upon the victim a bureaucratic maze of claims and thereby encourage padding of reported losses; they seldom pay the full costs of the victimization; and they normally only apply to a minority of victims (Elias 1983).

In the end, it is far too restrictive to view the victim's loss in purely financial terms. Some analysts assert that the emotional impact of experiencing diminished self-worth is often a far more profound loss to victims than the financial injury could ever be (see, for example, Maguire and Corbett 1987); and the injury itself, physical and emotional, stands as a constant reminder of the victim's vulnerability to such diminishment.

Problems with the Punitive Response

The preoccupation of the law with the tangible suffering of the victim is part of its deficiency in reestablishing the victim's sense of self-worth. Because the victim feels not only a personal loss, but also a personal diminishment, the focus of the law on the tangible loss to the exclusion of the symbolic suffering heightens, for the victim, a sense of the split between the self and the community.

THE VICTIM'S DILEMMA

After the crime, the law often encounters a victim steeped with bitterness and resentment about the crime. It is natural to expect the victim to feel outrage of two types: specific fury directed at the offender, and general rage (that is the predecessor of grief) at the loss the crime has caused.

These feelings often lead to a kind of hatred that is, in part, a moral repulsion at the loss the victim has experienced. It is also a defensive reaction, by which the victim seeks to proclaim unmistakably: "I am not of less worth than others!" Contained within this proclamation is a subtle, but important, irony. It is the feeling that gives rise to the victim's urgency in broadcasting a message of moral self-worth and moral equality with others—in his or her secret heart, the victim also worries: "Perhaps you believe I am of less worth than others; perhaps I am tempted to believe the same."

This kind of analysis is difficult for many of us to accept, for we are so used to romanticizing the innocence of the victim that we often do not take seriously the submerged doubts most victims feel. All true victims are legally innocent, of course, and most victims are factually innocent. Yet we all learn how it feels to be victims as children, when adults or superior peers use us in small and not so small ways for their own ends. We learn, then, that we *can* be made less than others against our will. The bewildered resentment that accompanies repetition of that experience is understandable: "Why me?"

This cognitive and emotional transaction is a kind of reaction formation that can be explained by a variety of normal psychological processes: perhaps the victim envies the attacker's mastery, identifies with the attacker's success, suspects a personal role in the suffering, or projects self doubts upon others (Jain 1990; Gerber 1990). A detailed defense of the psychological structures of the self-doubt need not be made here, however, for it is enough simply to call attention to the obvious point that a person who feels no doubt about self-worth feels no need to proclaim it, certainly not so dramatically.

Of course the victim is not inferior; to hint otherwise would be an outrage. The existence of the offense, however, is a public claim against the victim's equality. Unanswered by denial, it is natural the victim would feel affront and rage. As an extreme illustration, we think it natural that we seek to punish Nazis nearly a half-century after their atrocities. To do otherwise would be to silently affirm the Nazi claims. There is a way, of course, that this desire links the victim to the offender even more closely.

Readers who doubt this analysis are called upon to look over any of several excellent reviews of the victim's experience of painful association with the wrongdoer (see, for example, Miethe 1987). It is difficult, of course, for a person who has never been the victim of a serious, predatory crime to admit that it could so easily shake confidence in self-worth. Likewise, it is difficult for a victim to admit these same misgivings. So we are inclined to shy away from them. The victim focuses directly on the rage, as though it were the only important emotion. The bystanders experience sympathetic indignation about the crime, seeing as they do the magnitude of the victim's loss, and imagining how painful that loss would feel. Not being the actual victim, the bystander (fellow citizen) is incapable of identifying with the self-doubt the crime has engendered in the victim, and can only focus on the practical costs (financial and emotional) of the loss. Caught up in the resentment of powerlessness (Nietzsche 1967), the victim—and we, the observers—can imagine no action more meaningful than the full expression of the outrage: revenge upon the person of the wrongdoer.

But this circumstance is also a dilemma, one that is easily expressed but difficult to explain. The dilemma is that the more the victim focuses on the instincts of revenge, the less likely it is the emotions underlying the diminished self-worth (brought on by the crime) can be overcome. The mechanisms of hatred, no matter how justified the moral outrage underlying it, cannot produce well-being. Hampton, herself a victim of serious wrongdoing, recognized this when she found herself "becoming increasingly critical of the kinds of anger we victims generally feel toward those who wrong us" (1988, 10).

There are two ways in which the call for retribution fails to resolve the victim's suffering. The first has to do with the practical losses the victim has suffered: the imposition of pain obviously cannot undo the harm already experienced by the victim. People who advocate extreme penalties while invoking the victim's name obviously cannot mean that the penal harm will accomplish that kind of balancing. To make such a claim would be inane. What is meant is that the imposition of the penalty deals with the symbolic loss of the victim.

As attractive as this line of argument may seem, it has severe limitations. The aim of the victim is to reclaim a status of moral worth equal to everyone's, to support self-esteem by claiming to "count." The act of punishment, however, delivers a different message. It does not say to the world "the victim counts," but rather to the offender, "now you do not count."

> "The wrongdoer inflicts one pain; the victim (or the society which represents him) reciprocates with a second. Aren't both parties merely engaged in a kind of competitive struggle for standing, in which harm is taken either to effect or prove a diminishment of the other's position relative to one's own, a diminishment in which one glories?" (Hampton, in Murphy and Hampton 1988: 119)

Rather than raising the victim, the punishment merely succeeds in damaging the offender in return. After the crime, in addition to the losses caused by the crime, what really hurts the victim's psyche is the sense of having been made less than whole at the hands of another. To make that other also less than whole, in turn, cannot lead to anything more than a hollow victory, no matter how promising the strategy feels to the victim at the time of suffering. For

> as he looks down upon the wretched and pathetic figure of the wrongdoer, the avenger invariably finds that he is getting no pleasure from her victory. He has shown that the wrongdoer is nothing, so that now he is the lord of nothing." (Hampton, in Murphy and Hampton 1988: 73–4)

We hope that the imposition of the penalty upon the offender would right the wrong by declaring the law to be standing in behalf of the victim, thus elevating the victim back up to the level of full and equal moral worth. We forget two things, however. First, we forget that the act of the law is directed at the offender's status, not the victim's. Second, and more grievously, we exhibit sympathy for the victim, but not empathy, for we forget the importance of the victim's own doubts about self-worth. In the face of these grave doubts, to do something only to the offender is to say, "You should never have been diminished," but it does not say, "You are not diminished."

This is an important point, one to which we will return. The advocates of retributive models are fond of saying that, like Kant, they base their legal thinking upon the deontological assumption that all humans share the same moral worth, and are thus to be treated with the dignity that is due them. Indeed, Hampton points out that Kant himself has argued the folly of a person who would take on the right to judge the moral worth of another (Kant 1964). But the vision of the law as expressive about conduct devolves easily into expressions about the basic worth of the person who is the target of the punitive act. This is the tragedy of victimization that injures so deeply. To answer the repulsive, harming tone of the crime with an expression in kind is not likely to establish a case for equal moral worth; rather, it supports the idea that moral worth is a product of judgments. Thus, to follow this strategy is to engage in actions of great moral riskiness—to wear the mantle of the final arbiter of moral desert:

> To commit to a strategy of retributive hatred is to take on strong assumptions of moral epistemology and moral qualifications— assumptions that may prove insupportable. If they do, then one's hatreds, however motivated initially by a righteous desire to defend one's moral worth, will have in fact accomplished nothing but the diminishment of that worth. (Hampton, in Murphy and Hampton 1988: 103)

Just before the execution of Ted Bundy, the slick murderer of dozens of young women in several states, the television news interviewed several parents of victims, asking them if the execution of Bundy would finally allow them peace. The family members uniformly answered, "Yes." But who really believes them? If the television news were to go back to these homes, years later, and ask if they now felt peace, who really expects them to answer in the affirmative? The execution of Bundy may have given them some measure of closure, but the losses he imposed upon them can no more be overcome by his execution than by his abject contrition, had he been so inclined. Bundy's acts permanently damaged these families, and his execution cannot undo the damage.

THE STATE AS STAND-IN FOR THE VICTIM

The situation confronting the victim often has been described in the personal terms of victim and offender, which is not the way that the justice system works. The victim and the offender are not left alone to sort out this dilemma. As a third party, the state claims the right of sole arbiter in cases of crime.

The state's role is hardly neutral. On the surface, of course, is the appearance of an "adversary" process in which the accused has an advocate, the state is an accuser and there is an "impartial" judge. These terms are given in quotes because it is a surprise to no one that the system does not work in quite this way, except in unusual cases. Judges, especially those elected, seem often to be the staunchest and sometimes most publicly visible advocates of tough penalties for offenders. Prosecutors, whose official responsibility is to "do justice" (ABA 1966), often seek instead to outshine even the legislature in advancing the availability and imposition of draconion penalties for the convicted. Defense attorneys, except for the most successful—those whose typical clients are wealthy—are themselves often extremely disheartened by the endless flow of hopeless miscreants with whom they deal. They are overworked to boot, and therefore unable to spend much time with their clients, even should they wish to do so (for compelling descriptions of urban trial courts, see Rosett and Cressey 1976; Feeley 1979).

The seemingly paralyzed bureaucracy of the courts, confronted with the victim's movement as a political entity, has reacted by siding with what is perceived to be the victim's interest in ways that make the claim of impartial adversariness even more dubious than it was before. Prosecutors establish victim's services offices and provide specialized training for Assistants to teach them ways to deal sensitively with victims of crime. Courts often provide protections to victims by managing routine procedures in ways especially designed to take victims into account. In virtually every stage of the justice process, from complaint to parole consideration, there is a claim of a new awareness of the victim, a claim that translates into victim impact statements, rights of appearance and testimony, and so forth (Erez 1990). In almost every instance, the thrust of this new awareness is to make the case easier for the state to prosecute fully and punish severely.

It is hard to argue against most of these advances in victims' interests. The victim, having already suffered at the hands of the criminal, should not be made to suffer again at the hands of the system designed to enforce the victim's rights. It is nothing less than fundamentally fair to respect the plight of the victim. In terms of procedural law, at least, this plight has had considerable impact. In most current systems, virtually no decision is made without the law requiring at least some consideration for how the victim might feel about it.

Many of us might think of the court's reduced impartiality as a small detriment, in comparison to the huge advantage of providing aid and assistance to victims of crime. The promise of the pro–victim revolution of the 1980s was precisely that: to elevate the needs of the victim to a centerpiece status in order to be certain victim's needs are served. However, in two ways, this revolution has been incapable of materially changing the plight of the victim.

First, these procedures often operate under a stereotyped caricature of the victim who suffers and craves the offender's suffering in return. Often, the victim is portrayed as weak, vulnerable, and irreparably damaged. The creation of this stereotype stands as an open rejection of the victim's heartfelt need to be treated as an individual, and it ironically serves both to symbolize and to support the subterranean fear many victims feel, that they have suffered irreparably and will never be worth what they once were (Mezey 1987). Parading the victim as a political or media symbol objectifies the victim's life and represents the victim as a caricature of a person rather than a real person.

Almost always, the powerful appeal of the image of the victim— the symbolic meaning of the term—is invoked as an act of politics. Those who draw upon the symbol do so as an entryway into a claim that much tougher policies—"my policies" and "vote-for-me" policies—are called for in these times of evil. The real suffering of the real victim is transformed into imagery about a society in which the undeserving take unfair advantage of the weak, and this is an image that supports potently the need for a strong leader to protect the weak among us.

The political use of victim symbolism is at best unfortunate and at worst, downright reprehensible. This cynical political gain is a type of the invasion of privacy, and constitutes another kind of victimization. Just as we deplore the media who sell papers by exposing the private grief of victims, so should we disdain political leaders who turn victims into political capital.

Such political symbolism advances the interests of those who invoke it, but the crass use of victims' lives to manage public opinion cannot help but backfire. The citizenry are whipped into a froth about this or that horrible crime—we are reminded nightly when we watch news of the victim's suffering. Attempting to identify with the victim as we see him or her, we dress ourselves in what we think is the victim's self-righteous rage. Like voyeurs, we anticipate the parade of victims marching before our eyes. Mixed in our self-righteous sympathy for their suffering is a kind of repulsion—we cannot empathize with their plight, for empathy requires touching their lives in a real way, not just seeing them from afar. Whatever impersonal fury we are able to arouse within ourselves in their behalf is tinged with our own needs. Out of our fear of our own vulnerability to crime, we often succumb to a need to see victims as *different* from us in some fundamental way, perhaps worthy of their diminishment in some small way (Ryan 1971). As if on cue, the justice system officials help these victims appear before us on camera, enraged by their hatred and desire for revenge. This, too, serves our need to see ourselves as different, as above these victims, "whose faces are twisted with rage as they clamor for harsh punishments of their assailants . . . so that however much we may sympathize with them, we still find them repulsive" (Hampton, in Murphy and Hampton 1988: 145).

The first failure of the public display of the victim as sufferer, then, is this: instead of being presented with victims who are persons deserving of our compassion and our tangible acts of caring assistance, we come to see the victim as a class of persons unlike us, who are perhaps mildly repulsive to us and whose own unsavoriness absolves us from responsibility for the injury. Instead, we are left simply to join the symbolic protectors in a call for action against the perpetrator.

The second failure of the system stems from this exploitative use of victims' lives by officials of the government. Perhaps the actors in the system are unable to do otherwise, given their alienation from the victim's life. They are bureaucrats, and they are "processors of people" (Lipsky 1980). In this role, they must protect themselves from an identification with the victim, because such an identification would produce intolerable self-absorption. Faced daily with the endless line of lives damaged by crime, they become not inured to it, but intolerant of it, in a particular way. They want to find a way to strike back against crime and make it go away.

It is easy to build a surface identification with the victim's loss. The life-changing heartbreak of a parent of a murdered child is impossible to ignore; the terrified countenance of the rape victim and the mugging victim are easily apparent both to workers in the system and viewers in the television room.

What is much harder to see is the symbolic suffering over moral worth that the victim experiences. The bystander has not experienced and can barely imagine this suffering. Though the bystander hears the victim's anguished cry for retribution, he or she does not hear the unstated plea within the cry: "I feel damaged utterly." Instead, the bystander, apparently secure in his or her own self-worth and protective of any challenge against it, hears only the words as they come forth on the surface: "Find and hurt my assailant." In a valiant desire to support the victim, the system of justice, through its actors, follows the demand as those actors they are able to hear it.

It is a kind of a cliché. The long-suffering victim finally gets to hear "justice" pronounced as a measure of pain upon the wrongdoer, a public declaration that the person who was once wronged is now avenged. The victim's response can only be a kind of emptiness.

The care and feeding of the victim's animosity toward offenders is not merely a failure to serve their most fundamental needs of reaffirmation, but is also a failure on the part of public officials to recognize the kind of society that all of us, victims and non-victims, seek:

> One legitimate concern of social life is what *kind of people* will grow up and flourish. Will their personalities be rich and full and

integrated . . . or will they be stunted and limited and alienated? . . .
We are all . . . products of whatever system of socialization is in our
culture. If this socialization process activates certain irrational or
destructive or self-demeaning emotions, we will become prisoners
to those emotions—no matter how free we may think ourselves in
acting upon them. . . . (Murphy in Murphy and Hampton 1988,
emphasis in the original: 8–9)

As our political and justice system leaders encourage the spectacle
of the victim, they do little to materially aid the victim's recovery
from loss. But these leaders do a great deal to continue the cycle of
hostilities in our society, and they encourage the very kind of egoistic
views of life that provide the groundwork for harming each other.

WHAT THE VICTIM NEEDS[36]

The powerful and counterproductive seduction of hate with which
victims must deal was brought home to me during my televised
debate with Ernest Van den Haag regarding the death penalty. Set in
an audience-participation format, the studio was more than half-full
of the Parents of Murdered Children, a New York State self-help
group. When it came time for questions, they stood up one by one to
challenge my opposition to the death penalty, first telling their story
of the tragic loss of a child. Out of the corner of my eye, I could see
my own daughter, who had come to see the show as it was being
filmed. I could not help but wonder how I would feel, how I would
react if my own daughter were murdered.

As each person rose to speak, his or her unrelieved anguish was
apparent, and the same pattern repeated: first, the speaker would tell
the story of his or her personal victimization, then struggle with tears,
recalling vividly the sorrow of loss; then each would exhibit a kind of
furious anger at a generalized "criminal"—they all wanted to know
from me why anyone who would commit such a heinous act could
fairly escape death. The speakers would then sit down, cloaked in a
triumphant self-righteousness that barely contained their despair. One
by one, they stood and repeated this pattern, and I began to regret the
television program—to me, these people seemed to be asking for help,
but no matter what I said, there remained the same furious despair.

Then an older woman stood up. Again she started into her
story—as brutal a depiction as each of those before her. But her
question was not for me; it was for Van den Haag. She asked him
why he advocated death, when he could as easily use his intelligence
and persuasiveness to fight to get handguns and drugs off the streets
and actually save lives. As she talked, I noticed that her emotional

presence was different from the others of her group; there was a kind of quiet confidence about her, almost a kind of peace. Certainly her loss had been no less painful than any of her peers, but she was no longer its captive—it no longer held her. When she sat down, she was not in the throes of tears, as the others had been, but attentive and alert to the exchange she had begun with her questions.

Later, when I met her, I discovered she was the President and founder of the organization; she had started the POMC in response—in testimony—to her daughter's rape-murder. She told me not a day went by without a memory of her daughter and a pang felt over her loss. But she also said she was not bitter. To anyone who cared to notice, she was different from her fellow members, not in her fate, but because she had survived her victimization and turned it into an opportunity to give her life meaning. The others seemed, by contrast, to be tragically mired in their despondency over their loss. My heart went out to all of them, but this woman commanded my profound admiration.[37]

What this woman had achieved was a remarkable release from the impact of the symbolic message sent out by her assailant's victimizing action. Told that she did not matter by the action of the person who killed her daughter, she was able to transform her loss into acts that had meaning, not merely as additives to the punitive outrage around her, but in ways that reestablished her connection to the world in which she lived. Unlike others who felt what must be an unbelievably torturous pain at losing a child, she had been able to come out of the abyss and find a way to advocate for life, not against it.

I was reminded of meeting her when I recently read a story about one of the "Birmingham Six"—men who had been falsely accused of a terroristic bombing in England, then framed by the police and incarcerated for over 16 years until an appellate court ordered their release. Referring to one of them on the day after their release, the writer remarked:

> He displays an astonishing lack of bitterness. You ask, didn't he ever scream 'Why me?', but you know his answer before he gives it: 'Why not me? Children die in wars, there are others, lots of others, suffering now the same fate as us. What makes me special? If I started to think that in the cells, I'd tell myself I was getting three meals a day and somewhere to sleep, there are people out there who don't even get that.' (Merrit and Stanton 1991, 22)

There is an important kernal of truth in these two experiences, something neither victims nor their advocates want to admit. But it is true, nonetheless. For those who would shed their status as victims, strip themselves of the self-doubt about their worth that afflicts them, the punitive bitterness is a stage that must be overcome. It can only be overcome one way: the victims must establish a reconnection to life, a renewed commitment to the shared worth of all people, an ability to identify not just egoistically with the pain of one's own crime, but with the universality of human suffering and the universality of human hope. This is the true basis for the equality of human worth.

What this amounts to is a version of what people think of as "forgiveness." The meaning of forgiveness lies in the victim's decision to let go of self-protective hatred, and to accept the inescapable human condition of life: all people are capable of dignity, and life is a constant struggle to reaffirm all moral worth, even in the face of extreme immorality, and even when the immorality is experienced personally. The victim is worthwhile because all people are worthwhile, regardless of their circumstance. As Hampton has put it:

> "The first stage in the forgiveness process . . . involves regaining one's confidence in one's worth despite the immoral action challenging it. This is accomplished by overcoming, in the sense of 'giving up' or 'repudiating' emotions such as spite or malice and 'transcending' resentment." (Hampton, in Murphy and Hampton 1988: 83)

Too often, the victim's services advocates refuse to acknowledge the victim's deep, perhaps preconscious need for reconnection to society. Service providers are often indefatigable in reinforcing the initial feelings of rage that so many victims experience. This is done to validate the victim's sense of loss and provide an opportunity for the victim to fully express feelings about the loss. There is a danger in stopping at this point, for to summon the open expression of these feelings of rage without helping the victim to move beyond them is a type of pandering. It pretends an empowerment, but delivers only sustained attention to the loss. It is hazardous, for it misleads the victim into thinking that the solution to loss is rage. But rage is merely a stage that must be passed through on the way to recovery, and fixation on rage can retard the victim's recovery process. Moreover, it can lead to

> "dangerous excesses. Excesses that would harm others through our oversevere treatment of them and harm us through our own corruption. . . . Such a caution is particularly appropriate when directed toward one who is . . . a victim of wrongdoing. For such persons . . . have a natural tendency to make hasty judgements of responsibility, magnify the wrong done to them, and seek retribu-

tion all out of just proportion to what is actually appropriate." (Murphy, in Murphy and Hampton 1988: 100)

Instead of encouraging the victim to conquer the temptation toward self-destructive rage, the system caters to the rage, and thus fails the very victim it claims to represent.

The focus of traditional victim advocacy is not wrong, of course, but it is incomplete. Rather than focus on the victim's understandable rage, the system needs to develop a process that victims can be helped to navigate. Borrowing from Kubler-Ross (1972), we might say that there are four notable stages through which most victims need to pass.

Rage

The first stage of any loss is rage. The existence of the rage stems partly from the expectation (some would say, the myth) to which most of us are attached, that our lives are supposed to proceed without unfair interruption. Becoming a victim exposes the falseness of that myth. Self-absorbed fury is an appropriate response to the lesson that one is not special or golden, but is subject to all the random attacks with which the rest of the earth is afflicted. The justice system can support the victim's rage by encouraging its expression and allowing it to be expressed freely, without criticism—this is something commonly done in contemporary victim's services approaches.

Confirmation

Since the experience of victimization is an attack on self-worth, the victim will naturally seek to have the worth reconfirmed. This is an important symbolic task of the criminal law, and it is accomplished by the ceremonies of justice (Braithwaite, 1989). The official agencies of the state penally harm the offender in order to proclaim that the act was a wrongful violation of accepted rules of society and of the person who was victimized. The formal confirmation of the victim's true worth is achieved through the legal conviction of the offender for a crime that he or she committed. Again, this is a stage that is frequently performed within the system, although the practice of informal plea bargaining may detract from it.

Mourning

The victim must accept the reality of the loss (this is different from accepting its legitimacy). Depending on the nature of the loss and the strengths of the victim, this may be an extremely difficult stage to work through. Any loss is humbling, just as any unfair violation seems a debilitating thing to accept. But the loss, once experienced, is fact. To support a fantasy that somehow the loss has not occurred or otherwise can be erased is to sustain a fanciful belief in personal invulnerability—a belief that cannot be honestly retained in the face of the factual loss (Kubler-Ross 1972).

It is a common error of the system to pretend that this stage is unnecessary, that the conviction and punishment solves the victim's problem. The conviction merely confronts the victim with the undeniability of the loss by removing the offender as an object of the victim's emotions. The victim can no longer believe that the pain is embodied within the life circumstances of the criminal, for the criminal stands confirmed as wrong and is consigned to penal harm. But still the loss remains. This, in fact, is the time of the victim's most tender need. Having pinned hopes on a conviction and a punishment, the victim now emerges from the dark halls of the court with a painful realization that the case is over but the crime is not.

It is a sign of the system's astonishing tunnel vision that most insiders consider their work to be finished when the sentence is imposed. They ask the victim to agree to a myth: as soon as the offender has been successfully blamed and purposefully harmed, the cycle is complete. That the system's agents assert the myth is understandable, for they are well versed in the methods of blaming and harming offenders. But when it comes to joining in the victim's mourning of loss, not only is there an inability, there is also the lack of desire, for to mourn another's loss is to feel also their pain—and to admit one's own fundamental vulnerability to unfair events. It is to recognize that our moral equality is encased not just in the rubic of fairness, but also in the universal existence of unfairness and wrong.

Ultimately, most victims realize that the loss has not been overcome. In fact, the victim's real work of recovery begins at this point. The sad tragedy is that so few official resources are provided to reinforce this work.

Reconciliation

The final stage of the victim's emergence from loss involves an experience of reconnection to the human community. The victim rejects bitterness, and—changed by the humbling experience, no doubt—reengages with the world as a person of worth. The paradox is this: in order truly to believe in self-worth, the victim has to accept a belief in the self-worth of everyone, even the attacker. This does not mean forgetting the attack, but it does involve rising above its implications for the human condition. This reconciliation neither defies life's limitations nor signals a resignation to its inherent unfairness. The victim overcomes victimization by declaring allegiance to the human race, and by recommitting to membership in it as a person who behaves in a fair and even-handed manner toward others, who believes that "to strike a blow for morality and thus for the idea that all human beings have great moral value, the victim must make sure that she fights in a way that recognizes the wrongdoer's very real value" (Hampton, in Murphy and Hampton 1988: 137).

Thus, the strategy of the system that pits the victim against the offender is ultimately not in the best interests of anyone (except perhaps the persons who seek political advantage by being viewed as the victim's champion). In reality, the victim is a member of a society that includes lawbreakers and law enforcers, victims and innocent bystanders. To be able to rise above the status of 'loser' (and overcome the permanent disadvantage in that arrangement), the victim needs to find a way to understand the experience of the crime not as confirmation (or cause) of a lesser status of worth, but as irrelevant to worth.

Eventually, however this road is traversed, there is a point at which the victim confronts guilt, or culpability for all the things done and not done. It sounds outrageous to say it, but it is at this moment, the moment when the victim gives up 'special' ownership of a role as victim, that the healing process can begin. There is a way in which this process involves a deeply personal acceptance of the ubiquity of moral inadequacy, one's own need for tolerance, and one's own moral frailty. Such acceptance leads inexorably toward tolerance:

> Each of us, if honest, will admit two things about ourselves: (1) We will, within the course of our lives, harm others—even others about whom we care deeply; and (2) because we care so deeply about these others and our relationships with them, we will want to be forgiven by them for our wrongdoings. In this sense we do all want and need forgiveness and would not want to live in a world where the disposition to forgive was not present and regarded as a virtue. Given that this is the sort of world that we all need and want, is it not then incumbent upon each of us to cultivate the disposition to forgive—not the flabby sentimentality of forgiving any wrong, no matter how deep or unrepented, but at least the willingness to be open to the possibility of forgiveness with hope and some trust? Only a person so arrogant as to believe he will never wrong others or need to be forgiven by them would consistently will membership in a world without forgiveness. (Murphy, in Hampton and Murphy 1988: 32)

In a way, what the victim learns is a profound truth about the human race: one is constantly in the process of creating the world in which one has to live. In that respect, what one does to another, one does to oneself as well. This is the real reason why all democratic theories of government emphasize the humane treatment of all citizens, for they realize that no society can condone diminishment of anyone, no matter how repulsive the person's behavior, without becoming a society tolerant of self-diminishing and exploitative relationships. Society is, after all, a "moral community," in which the offender is treated "not just as an object whose behavior we want to control, but as a subject whom we must address, whose understanding we must try to engage" (Duff 1986).

This is not an easy lesson; it actually is a lifetime challenge. The victim is thrust into a situation in which the salience of the issues cannot be avoided. For the community at large—the bystanders to crime—it is a slightly different matter of the same problem, to which we will turn in Chapter 5.

As a final point, before leaving this discussion of the victims, we must return to the topic of penal harm. It is in the case of the victim that we find our first fundamental evidence of a need for penal harm as a tool to achieve the objective of victim support. Penal harm stands as the public repudiation of the criminal act. But the penal harm also stands exposed as a two-edged sword. When it receives inappropriate prominence as solution to the victim's dilemma, it not only becomes, at best, irrelevant to the dilemma, but at worst, exacerbates the victim's struggle to overcome the loss of worth inherent in the crime.

5

Community Protection

> And I remember that my darling mother, my
> beautiful mother, my innocent mother would
> say, "Now be very careful. Don't go near
> First Avenue. That's a bad neighborhood.
> There are tough kids there." And I had no
> idea what she meant. She had no idea. We
> thought that certain kids were tough—maybe
> they just liked to be. And they lived in certain
> neighborhoods—maybe because their friends
> were there. Nice people had gathered in our
> neighborhoods, had formed a community, and
> it was a good neighborhood. On First Avenue
> and other avenues, there were bad
> neighborhoods, where tough people gathered
> together, and those were the neighborhoods
> we had to avoid. We still avoid them—all of
> my friends. Bad neighborhoods. The people
> who live in places like that would hurt you,
> beat you, cut you, kill you. All the ones
> who would hurt you collect in those
> neighborhoods, like water in drains. And it's
> terrible. It's awful.
> —Wallace Shawn, *The Fever*

The central claim in behalf of expanded punishment is that it is a bitter but necessary medicine that protects the community from crime. I have already touched upon this claim in chapters 2 and 3, addressing first, whether the punishment experiment has reduced crime, and second, whether the punishment-and-control paradigm is based on a solid scientific foundation. In this chapter, I provide a broader critique of the community protection rationale.

My argument can be summed up as follows: the contemporary meaning of the term *community protection* promotes a separationist view of public order, in which distinct communities are isolated and insulated from each other; an integrationist view of public order would promote better harmony in communities and, properly construed, could also improve the safety of citizens in those communities. In the final section of the chapter, I illustrate how an integrationist approach might work with two types of offenders.

WHAT DOES *COMMUNITY PROTECTION* MEAN?

The subtle irony of community protection rhetoric is that its imagery is not that of community, but of its opposite: a vision of community subgroups divided against each other. The ideology of community protection is deeply imbedded in what has become known as "we-they" thinking. This thinking has been described as a foundational myth of U.S. culture (Edelman 1971; Combes 1981), and it holds that the populace must be perceived as composed of people 'like' us—good people, honest and dependable—and people 'different' from us— dishonest, even dangerous. The politics of community protection refers to these groups as separate and in need of separation from each other.

The commonsense idea of crime, according to the community protection formulation of it, is that so-called "ordinary" citizens have come under siege of "unordinary" criminals who have turned our streets into war zones and made it unsafe to live in America. Ask the average American citizen about crime, and be ready for a monologue of complaints about alarming increases in victimization, ineffectual courts, and puny punishments. The common wisdom about criminal justice is so at odds with the facts (Walker 1989) that it leads us to wonder what purposes are served when such inaccurate ideas are so widely held.[38]

The social myth that there are groups of bad people trying to hurt us helps to sustain a truism about criminal justice: what happens to victims is unforgivably unfair and should not be tolerated. The paradigm becomes a social justice folk wisdom, in which it is assumed that the victims of crime are undeserving of their fate because they come from the innocent classes of law abiders; whereas the criminal, (predatory) class, taking advantage as they do of the vulnerability of the everyday citizen, deserves whatever punitive evil an overburdened system can arrange to inflict.

The Ordinary Citizen and the Ordinary Offender

Central to the we-they model is the idea of a divided society, composed of the many who are innocent and the few (but certainly too many) who are predatory. How accurate is this idea?

Criminological research has firmly established that the decision to engage in criminal behavior is common among citizens. Studies have found, for example:

- As many as 20% of Americans misrepresent their taxes in any given year (Yankelovitch, and White, 1984)
- 1,371,236 adults were arrested in 1990 for driving under the influence (UCR 1991)
- About 13 million persons used "illicit" drugs in 1990 (NIDA 1990)
- Up to one in six children—one in five female children—experiences sexual abuse (Finkelhor 1979; Russell 1983); some studies put the estimates even higher (Hyde 1984), and the crime is vastly underreported in official records and self-report studies (Robinson 1990)
- About one in four female college students experiences a sexual assault (Koss 1990), over one-third by nonromantic dates or acquaintances (Koss, Gidycz, and Wisniewski 1987)
- In England, it is estimated that 44% of males will be convicted of an offense at some time in their lives (Farrington 1981)
- In a U.S. cross-sectional sample of adult men and women, 99% admitted to at least one criminal offense (Wallerstien and Wyle 1947)
- About one-half of a sample of San Francisco youths reported committing a delinquency in the previous year (Hirschi 1969)

Thus, large numbers of offenses are committed by ordinary citizens. This is the only conclusion to be drawn from the numbers of offenses reported by victims, and the frequency with which ordinary citizens admit their offenses in confidential surveys.[39] What does it mean that so many among us commit offenses?

Some of these statistics are not very surprising. That males have very high rates of illegal and aggressive behavior is well-known (Campbell 1993); that women more frequently suffer unwanted sexual advances of varying levels of seriousness than was previously thought has received much recent publicity (Center for Women's Policy Studies 1991). The high rates of noncompliance with tax codes probably surprise nobody.

But though the ubiquity of offending behavior is no surprise, that does not mean we should take it lightly. The sorts of crimes listed above, committed by so many among us, carry serious costs:

- It is estimated that the total loss of federal revenues due to misrepresentation of tax liability is $113 Billion, a major portion of the revenue deficit (GPO 1990)
- Illicit drug use results in $21–24 Billion in various kinds of business and medical losses, while drunk drivers kill 20,000–25,000 persons annually, and maim another 700,000, permanently injuring 125,000 (Highway Traffic Safety Administration 1986)
- One of the most consistently documented patterns of generational criminality is that adult child sexual abusers were themselves victims of sexual assault by other adults when they were children (Russell 1984; Hunter 1991)
- Fear of being sexually victimized leads women to restrict their social and economic mobility (Gordon and Reiger, 1989)

It is wrong, then—or at least, simplistic—to view criminal acts as events in which an anonymous wrongdoer who is considered to be "not like us" chooses freely to engage in a predatory act against an innocent who is "just like us." Many of these offenses are committed by persons whom we would ordinarily feel quite comfortable to know and even to care about; by friends and family members and persons of otherwise normal circumstances. These offenders are people who are more like us, perhaps, than we would like to admit.[40]

Because so few are caught, the offenders we do apprehend serve a vital function for us all. The myth of the criminal-as-other helps us deny our own culpability for the rules we like to break—or want to break. We engage in symbolic behavior that says, "It was he who offended." The audience is ourselves, and the ritual is our modern version of the ancient ritual of scapegoating.

This is inherent in the concept of deterrence, which is based on the idea that we are willing and able to offend.[41] We shore up our resistance to evil by punishing those who have been caught. We ask the system to punish those who are apprehended with such ferocity that others, who would behave in similar ways, are threatened to forbear by fear of the harshness. And who are these others? They are all of us.

> At the symbolic level, social control must fulfil the functions of creating scapegoats, clarifying moral boundaries and reinforcing social solidarity. The primeval form of scapegoating directs aggression towards individuals not responsible for the group's frustration. . . . These functions remain when societies move towards putting

blame not on the community . . . but on certain individuals who are *properly* caused to suffer. (Cohen 1985: 233, emphasis in the original)

Thus, what we create with the we-they model of community protection is a false vision of a society. It is false because there is only a very blurred distinction between who *we* are and who *they* are. The life stories of lawbreakers are not so odd; they are all modern American stories about *our society*, how it works and what it is like to live here. It is a story not about *them* but about *us*.

Community Protection and Penal Harm

Despite its flaws, the idea of a community of good people under siege by a community of bad ones remains a cherished vision of contemporary thinkers about crime and its control. In 1975, Wilson set the tone for this idea when he said: "When I speak of concern for 'community,' I refer to a desire for observance of standards of right and seemly conduct in the public places in which one lives and moves, those standards to be consistent with—and supportive of—the values and lifestyles of the particular individual." (24)

It is notable that the focus of this definition is upon "standards of right and seemly conduct" rather than, say, standards of well being. The apparent idea is that a recognizable standard exists for a citizen's conduct, that there is no controversy about it, and that its observance is a core element of desirable community. This is a vision of community that is synonymous with order. For some, it is an article of faith that, as Attorney General William French Smith put it, "a free society presupposes an orderly community" (1981: 1). Inherent is the idea that order is the desire of the many, and disorder the product of the few.

Community protection, from this point of view, proposes a vision of social harmony about the kinds of lives people want to lead. Advocates of social democracy have struggled against the temptation to use the power of the criminal law to enforce lifestyles. As the law concerns itself with fringe considerations, such as pornography, sexual deviance, drug use, abortion, and marital lifestyles, it begins to deal with acts that are not obviously dangerous. The use of the law to declare that certain forms of living are approved while others are not fosters a belief that there is an American lifestyle to which people should conform.

Recent political pressure in behalf of laws favoring sexual abstinence, drug abstinence, and heterosexuality portray a packaged version of right living for American youth. The natural extension of this idea is that the community, unanimous in its values concerning the ways it seeks to live, requires protection from the purveyors of wrong modes of life. Because in the United States there is actually a pluralism of lifestyles and ambivalence about many moral values, standards of conduct occupy a potential battleground of ideas and values. We should be wary of simple promises that the legal enforcement of certain lifestyle choices will promote order, and thus safety.

The uneasiness stems from the way the idea of community protection stands for separating some members of society from others. If what is meant by the term *community* is certain approved standards of conduct that equate closely to lifestyle choices, and if what is meant by the term *protection* is the removal of those who have chosen the lifestyle, then as a free society we have much to fear from this *community protection*.

This is no debate about street crime, of course. Let us stipulate from the outset that such conduct is harmful, reprehensible, and not a lifestyle choice that a person ought to be free to make. Here, the community protection model holds out an appealing promise: that the result of acts of community separation will be safer communities.[42]

One of the side effects of this type of thinking has been the aggravation of race conflict and the rise of race politics under the mantle of community protection. The problem partly has to do with symbols. By creating an image of so-called "bad guys," the rhetoric of community protection is used to support a portrayal of certain groups as dangerous.[43]

The blatantly racist use of Willie Horton by the Bush 1988 Presidential Campaign to intermix the fear of crime with the resentment of black people provides a profound example, all the more remarkable because studies show the public media joined the Bush campaigners in portraying blacks as criminals and whites as their victims (Johnson 1990). This is simply one example in a pattern that repeats itself over and over again in the nightly news and the daily paper.[44] The image that those whom we should fear are strangers to us—black strangers—is nearly emblazoned on our public consciousness. The community protection model feeds the notion that the people who harm us are not of us, and this makes it a bit easier to accept the divisive implications that follow.

Yet while law-violating is a widely distributed behavior, the effects of fighting crime are not. They are focused primarily upon the young, especially minorities hailing from inner cities. It is estimated that one in four black youths aged 21–29 is in prison or under community supervision (Austin and Killman 1990)—more than are in college (Mauer 1990). With statistics such as these, the separating actions that undergird the contemporary idea of community protection take on overtones of covert racism.[45]

Rethinking Community and Community Protection

An alternative definition of the term *community protection* would begin with the recognition that crime is an aspect of the communities in which we live, and cannot be effectively confronted by pretending otherwise. Strategies that attempt to improve the safety of communities must approach the problem of crime as a problem of community and deal with crime within communities, rather than try to separate the crime problem from the community in which it occurs.

This is not a new idea. Even though the predominant focus of crime prevention has generally been to do things with and to offenders who have been removed from their own communities, there has long been a contrary voice that calls for another type of thinking. The strongest statement of this strategy was made by the much discredited President's Commission on Crime and the Administration of Justice (1967). They argued in favor of a correctional strategy of "reintegration," which called for "change in social institutions as well as behavioral change of offenders, since both are necessary" (Weber 1969: 128).

Theirs is not the only vision of this type. Duffee (1980), for example, has argued that both crime and criminal justice can only be understood within the community context, and "if we are to make effective changes in some type or level of social order, we must begin outside the criminal justice system with redesign of basic living and working arrangements" (Duffee 1980; 137). Similar arguments have been posed by Cloward and Ohlin (1960), Sutherland and Cressey (1978), Miller (1969), Cohen (1955), and many others.

Recently, Elliot Currie (1985) has shown how social problems in the cities such as unemployment, inadequate schools, family break-down and inequality have been the wellsprings of crime in America. He is critical of the recent community crime-prevention emphasis on removing offenders and thereby "taking back the streets," and he shows how these programs fail to address the nature of urban communities and the problems faced by people who live there. According to Currie, the so-called "get tough" view of the cities "is hollow and often hypocritical. The emphasis of the reconstruction of community responsibility . . . must be . . . grounded in a more adequate sense of what a community really is and what is required to nourish and sustain it" (263).

These arguments were abandoned by many policy analysts whose work was led by Wilson's (1975) articulate critique. He urges that a distinction be made between causal analysis and policy analysis, and sensibly suggests that policy analysis is concerned only with those factors that can be changed to influence society. He then asserts that "ultimate causes cannot be the objective of policy efforts precisely because, being ultimate, they cannot be changed," adding later that "social problems . . . are almost invariably 'caused' by factors that cannot be changed easily or at all" (50).

Exactly why the institutional forces such as racism, income inequality, unemployment, school dropouts, family disintegration, and family violence cannot be addressed by policy is never adequately answered by Wilson. He seems to be suggesting that police clearance rates can be more easily altered than, for example, practices of hiring and pay in the workplace, taxes, or school retention rates. Still, Wilson is unequivocal in his condemnation of the reintegrative idea, when he says that the "experts" advising crime policy "were speaking out of ideology, not scholarship [without] built-in checks against the premature conversion of opinion into policy" (62).

In chapter 3, I argued that by the time Wilson wrote his argument, the tide had already shifted dramatically against the treatment idea, and offender-change views were under sustained attack by a new breed of social scientists. Whether these ascendant speakers for tough crime policy were any less prone to couching their ideologies in the comforting fabric of science is debatable. What is not debatable is that their arguments helped fuel the abandonment of reintegrative community action.[46]

But what was abandoned, really? The policy of reintegration as practiced was essentially offender-based. It sought to treat offenders as the unit of analysis in dealing with crime, but to approach them not as persons to be frightened or coerced into compliance with the law, but as people to be enabled to comply. The vision of offenders was of people who, if they could, would choose to be law-abiding rather than criminal citizens. It is this somewhat romantic vision of the offender that has been abandoned. In the face of mounting evidence about the nature of criminal careers, it is difficult to continue to see offenders as mere victims of failures of opportunity. Perhaps this is a view of crime rightfully left behind.

Yet even the criminal career model gives reason to hope that community change might be an important element of community protection. The desistence rate, after all, is a variable in the model, and at least a portion of its variance is a product of forces acting upon it. Among those forces are jobs, marriages, and maturation. The reintegration and criminal career models come together at the point where community forces such as inequality, opportunity, and family have been weakened as sources of desistence from crime.

Traditional reintegration theory is not the only theory that uses the community as a relevant target in the crime control problem, however. There are at least two alternatives.

The first alternative is a crime prevention model that seeks to prevent crime by understanding how it occurs, rather than who does it. There are numerous specializations within this line of inquiry, but there are three examples that are well-regarded. The first person to explore this type of inquiry was Newman (1972), whose concept of "defensible space" proposed that crime can be made easier or more difficult by the design of physical structures within which people work and live. A different crime prevention analysis is derived from the "routine activities" approach (Felson, 1987), which argues that crime results from the intersection of a set of predispositional elements that occur in regular patterns. A variant of the "routine activities" model (Cornish and Clarke 1986) represents offenders as persons who decide to commit crimes and then desist, due to more or less normal, rational reasons based on their understanding of the decisions they face.

While these three versions of the crime prevention school have been subjected to sometimes strident criticism (Gottfredson and Gold-kamp 1990) they are, for our purposes, remarkable for what they do not do. They do not rest their analyses on the idea that crimes are abnormal events springing from sinister minds, something done by 'them' to 'us.' Instead, they proceed with the understanding that most crime is a relatively common social behavior that is best understood in its social and spatial context, including fairly ordinary psychological motivations on the part of the offender as well as an important situational community component.

The various schools of the situational prevention model have proven to be much more promising in preventing crime than the older version, which focussed on enabling offenders to desist (see, for example, Clarke 1993). By contrast, the situational school treats the community as an entity contributing to criminality, albeit often unwittingly, and seeks to alter the nature of the community as a means of reducing crime.[47]

Some critics of the prevention approach have argued that its logic blames the victim and so is offensive to those who suffer from crime (Ryan 1971).[48] But the crime prevention idea is not about locating and assigning blame; it is about analyzing a type of crime and finding ways to reduce it.

Separationist Logic

The animosity generated by the prevention movement may also stem in part from a more basic divergence of perspectives about the world.

It is normal to view the victim and the offender as essentially separate people whose interests and experiences are entirely distinguishable. This is consistent with the separationist view of public protection. The criminal and the victim are viewed as essentially unrelated entities; the former is volitionally responsible for the damage caused by an act freely chosen, while the latter is tragically and wrongfully diminished by the results of that act.

The mechanisms of the law take a separationist view. The criminal and the victim are separated one from the other. Just because a homeowner did not lock his house, just because a person flashed a wad of money when paying a cashier, just because the auto buyer did not ask for an anti-theft device on the car—none of these actions on the part of victims excuses the offender. From the point of view of law, the courtroom houses a contest between the state and the accused, which assumes that the circumstances of the accused and the victim are in opposition. The disputative nature of the law is so central to its theory and operation that no other construction of the Western criminal law seems possible. Even the literature on mitigation (von Hirsch 1975; Feinberg 1984) provides frameworks for making distinctions between the motivation and understanding of the offender on the one hand, and the vulnerabilities and contributions of the victim as a separate actor in the criminal event. In its conceptual foundations, then, the law promotes a view of 'we-they' contests, wherein communities composed of innocents are afflicted by the blameworthy guilty, who must be forcibly separated from the rest of us and specially censured.

Deeply ingrained as this idea is, we know its inaccuracies. Most often, the victim of violence is a person well-known to its perpetrator (BJS 1991: table 49); most child abusers learned their sexually adaptive modes directly from others who abused them (Finkelhor 1984); burglaries producing stolen goods that translate into dollars to buy drugs are made possible only by vast networks of economic franchises for reselling the stolen goods to ordinary people (Johnson 1985). Further, the law acts to set a false floor on the cost of street drugs, which in turn makes street drug networks extremely profitable enterprises for persons who are unable (or unwilling) to become involved in other businesses (Moore 1990). Wherever we care to look, those who commit crimes are deeply dependent upon the circumstances, fates, and action of those whom they victimize. The interdependence of offender and community is seldom exculpatory, but it is generally contributory.[49]

Integrationist Logic

What if we were to view crime from an integrationist perspective,[50] and thus try to understand the ways in which criminals and their communities are interdependent? We would approach crime control by focusing on individuals as they live in their communities, recognize that communities are formed of more or less integrated social networks from which offenders originate, and understand crime as a product of various forms of interdependence within those communities (Hope and Foster 1993).

Recognition of the importance of intra-community patterns for understanding crime is by no means new to criminology. A host of studies and theories rely on community dynamics to explain crime and to speculate about its control (see Krohn 1988; Kornhauser 1978, cited in Hope). These studies concern themselves with a wide array of different types of crime. The dynamics of drug markets are now understood through ethnographic studies of the very localized interpersonal practices that constitute the markets (Williams 1989). Housing projects with high crime rates are being studied as local social networks (Hope 1991).

These community-oriented studies promise to yield significant insights about the nature of crime and ways to reduce the harms crime generates. An ethnographic study of 60 repetitive property criminals found they are "impulsive and disorganized when committing crimes . . . [and] over time, offenders tend toward specialization" (Tunnell 1992: 161). Studies such as these provide an understanding of the nature of criminal behavior that is grounded in observation and comprehension, and help to explain why offender control policies have not had much impact on street crime. As an alternative strategy for responding to crime, community-based crime prevention uses the grounded understanding of crime to mobilize community groups and networks to challenge the crime in its midst. Bright (1992) has described a range of successful community crime reduction programs that address housing, education, physical environments, employment; these programs take advantage of a grounded knowledge about crime.

The critical importance of understanding relevant communities is not limited to the crimes of the street. Braithwaite (1984), for example, considers the norms and practices of financial institutions in understanding white collar crime, and his analysis treats these institutions as though they were small communities. Nor is the analysis limited to economic crime. Various types of interpersonal violence are best understood by focusing upon the role of community values and traditions, from spouse assault (Burgess 1985) to barroom brawls (Gibbs 1990), from assaults against children (Kempe and Helfer 1980) to acquaintance rape (Parrot and Bechhofer 1991).

The powerful importance of the community as the context for

crime has even lead some writers to posit formal theories of the relationship between community practices and crime. Braithwaite (1989) has argued that the prevalence of crime can be attributed to the way in which the community responds to it—when "reintegrative shaming" approaches are taken, crime is suppressed. Adler, (1983) argued that a social force defined as "synomie" suppresses criminality in societies. These theories have not been without their critics, of course—most people find unilateral explanations of crime simplistic and inconclusive. Nevertheless, the popularity of these ambitious theories demonstrates the strong empirical and conceptual attraction to community integration as a means to understanding crime.

A grand theory is really unnecessary to make the rather limited point of the argument here. It is a sensible idea that crime is a relatively common behavior within the community; those who would understand crime find themselves forced to take into account both the lawbreaker and his community context. Because crime varies across communities, there must be ways in which variations in communities influence rates of crime.

But what of Wilson's complaint that contexts cannot be changed by intentional policy? By now this argument must begin to sound like an anachronism. Do we really think that new industry cannot change a community's unemployment rate? That an after-school program cannot reduce the number of unsupervised children? That gang-based programs cannot reduce youth violence? That block watch programs cannot reduce burglaries? That all of these policy interventions, and more, targeted at a high-crime neighborhood, would have no impact on criminality there? Studies suggest otherwise (See, for example, Clarke 1993).

CRIME AND COMMUNITY INTEGRATION

The traditional argument about crime and community is a familiar one: the existence of crime "impedes and, in the extreme case, even prevents the formation and maintenance of community" (Wilson 1975: 21). In a later explanation of his theory, Wilson (with Kelling 1982) argued that while crime promotes the disintegration of neighborhoods, the resulting disorder actually leads to further crime. Wilson's idea of crime and neighborhoods has been used to support the separatist idea that crime, seen as abnormal, is best fought by removing criminals from the streets.

It is hard to understand what realistic theory of community this point of view may be based upon; no community has ever been crime free, and even the highest crime neighborhoods in our most troubled inner cities are communities with their own special characteristics. Crime is a part of all vibrant communities, even tightly integrated ones, and especially modern, heterogeneous ones. That is certainly not to say that crime is desirable, merely to say that it is an inevitable part of the human—and particularly the social—condition. What is needed is a model for thinking about crime that takes into account its permanent, in many cases functional presence, without ignoring how crime injures the citizens within a community—a model that represents communities trying to minimize crime and its costs.

This approach to the problem of crime in communities holds several implications for the way offenders are dealt with after they are convicted of crime. The most obvious implication is that offenders are not enemies to be conquered, but fellow citizens whose well-being is important to the community, despite the damaging nature of their behaviors.[51] Thus, the integrationist model possesses moral, political, and practical benefits, which recommend it to us.

Moral Benefits

The strongest moral statement in behalf of the separationist idea is that punishment treats the offender with the dignity due to a responsible moral agent (Lewis 1944). When a citizen offends against the law, it is argued, the state treats the citizen with an act of punishment that affirms his or her status as a responsible moral agent equal to any other member of the society. By separating the offender from society, the offender's moral membership in that society is confirmed.

But the offender, in this instance, might be excused if he or she does not derive a sense of moral enhancement or moral confirmation from the punishment. The act of punishment—the deliberate and measured imposition of harm—cannot help but contain another message for the offender, one that undercuts the morally affirming message separationists would have the law contain. The message does not say that "you fully count as a moral citizen;" rather, it serves as a condemnation: "Because of what you have done, your interests do not count any more." Yet the thin line between the phrases is made fuzzy by modern versions of bureaucratic harm. Instead of hearing the law's positive message, which is that everyone counts as an agent of moral worth, the punished offender hears a personal accusation: "You are bad—you are spoiled and deficient." The result is a contradiction in the separationist's desires, for the punished offender certainly feels he or she has been made less than a whole person and counts less than others. The penal law may not intend the message, but it cannot do otherwise.

This switch in moral status occurs because the offender's circumstance no longer figures into the scheme of things—at the very least, the harm the offender already has caused is seen as more important than the harm the penal system is about to cause, which is a measure of suffering unlike the harm produced by the crime, which is past and therefore cannot be diminished. Penal harm says unequivocally that "this suffering is good," and tells the offender that of all the harm people experience, his or her suffering is not to be avoided.

How does it enhance the integration of a community to select some of its members for official harm by the community?[52] There is reason for a community, in symbolic form, to exert itself and insist that certain types of acts, because of the nature of their harmfulness, will not be allowed to occur without censure. In this way a community affirms its own moral interest in minimizing the harms its members experience. But at the same time, would not that community also seek to minimize the harms experienced at its own hands, even against offenders within its midst? To do otherwise would make sense only if the offender has lost the status of membership within the same community—only if he or she ceased to count as an agent of moral worth. But if the objective is to use the law as an affirmation of everyone's moral worth, then is it not important to minimize the pains experienced by those who themselves have gratuitously caused pain?

The argument here is not that harm for offenders is impermissible for a community that would define itself as moral and would reinforce itself as integrated. The very act of apprehending, accusing, and convicting a citizen—and declaring that person an "offender"—is inherently coercive and harmful. The argument is much narrower: that all harm experienced within a community, even that which has as its aim the reaffirmation of the community's values, counts in the moral order. In expressing those values, the community must count the harm it imposes against its wrongdoers not simply as a victory for community, but also as a loss for itself as a society of equal members. Thus, it is in the community's interest to minimize harm, including penal harm, in whatever ways are possible.

The community lives with a contradiction. Too little suffering imposed upon those in its midst who offend against its rules will mock the rules by failing to deplore the harm caused by those who break the rules. It will also mock the suffering of the victim who, after all, is a member of the community as well. Yet the purposeful use of penal harm as a social instrument to deplore the wrongdoer's conduct belittles the larger aims of freedom, autonomy, and well-being sought by the community.

There is no way out of this dilemma. Separationists solve it by moral sleight of hand. They convince themselves that it is no vice to add harms into the community membership through punishment, because the recipient of the harm no longer counts as a member. Because communities are forever faced with crime—precisely because the idea of community without crime is a fantasy—the separationist model is a recipe for accelerations in harm.

The integrationist view offers an exit from this moral dilemma, for it would not discount the harms anyone experiences. Should one community member harm another, the response would be a measured action. It would seek to reconfirm the wrongdoer's bonds to the community in a way that endorses the norm that people not commit offenses against each other, yet also endorses the claim of the offender to be treated as a person whose well-being matters. The situation would be seen as an opportunity to reaffirm, even strengthen the community members' interdependence and mutual commitment. The offending act would be seen, in part, as the law-breaker's false denial of interdependence with others in the community, and thus would become a symbol that must be corrected.

Political Benefits

If anything dominates the surface of conversation about penal harms, it is the degree to which such harms function as political currency. Since Barry Goldwater in 1960, political leaders have made crime and its control a part of their election campaigns and political sloganeering. The politics of crime are such that politicians must stand steadfastly and firmly against it and eagerly and unremittingly favor tough measures to fight it. Toughness inevitably refers to an expanded willingness and capacity for penal harming.

The differential exposure of minorities to penal harms makes the traditional separationist politics about crime—"law'n'order politics" (Finckenauer 1978)—take on an aura of race politics. Indeed, numerous political observers have remarked upon the abiding connection between the fear of crime, as a political agenda, and the fear of black men (Moeller 1989). When the White House announced plans to increase the prison Federal capacity by 75% in order to carry forward the "War on Drugs" (The White House 1991), the less enthusiastic observers realized, with a cold shudder, that the increased imprisoning capacity would be used mainly for young black males from the inner city.

It is not far fetched, then, to see the separationist definition of community protection as a rallying cry for an attack upon minority communities, particularly those living in the disadvantaged areas of our inner cities. Black and Hispanic communities in the United States are not protected by separationist policies of community protection;

rather, they are torn apart, especially by the removal of adult males, but more recently by the removal of teen-agers, who are targeted by enthusiasts of the boot camp model. As the growth of separationist penal harming continues, it foretells a vision of inner cities increasingly devastated by the loss of potential adult male role models and dominated by the sporadic removal of men and boys to prisons and jails.

An integrationist view of community protection would recognize the substantial damage done to communities, particularly minority communities, as a result of penal harm practices. The reliance on incarceration to censure criminal conduct guarantees a minimum floor of familial uproar in those neighborhoods hit the hardest by penal harms. Whatever destabilizing effect crime has on communities is certainly exacerbated by the destabilizing effect of living in neighborhoods where males are routinely removed for brief stays in prison and jail.

Aside from the damage experienced by the people who live in those communities, there is a kind of a national shame which attaches to the problem of race relations in the United States. That prisons are places for black people and poor whites is a disgrace for a nation that proudly declares itself the home of the free and the land of opportunity.

An integrationist view of community protection would count the damage done to these communities as part of the harm that a society seeks to minimize. It would consider the race differentials in imprisonment as a problem to be overcome through policy, not merely as a sad consequence of policy. As a result, an integrationist view would take the improvement of the quality of political life as an essential goal, in that it would seek to counteract the tempting appeal of racism in penal harms. In being against crime, a person would not necessarily be feeding a policy network that has the effect of being against the powerless.

Practical Benefits

It is important to stress that the integrationist view of community protection does not ignore the interests of victims. The model accepts responsibility for taking into account the well-being of all parties to crime and its control—the victim, the offender and the community—as it develops a correctional response. It is based in a recognition that the more allowance a community makes for harms against its own members, even penal harms, the more it loses its moral right to oppose harming in any form.

This is essentially a moral view of society that contrasts sharply with the traditional understanding of the moral operation of the criminal law. It is based on a set of affirmations that shape the response to offenders, among them:

- Crime is a normal and common aspect of modern social living, and in most respects it cannot be understood except in its social context.
- Offenders are not of less moral worth than non-offenders; otherwise, there would be very few people deserving of full moral status.
- Penal harms are necessary to publicly declare the community's opposition to the harms contained in criminal acts, but the imposition of those harms also damages the community in moral, political and practical ways.
- Because of the interdependencies of modern society, every citizen has an interest in the welfare of all members of the community, and all share a common interest in community safety, which is defined as "living together in safety," not "living apart in safety."
- The social context of crime, the interdependence of community members, the ambivalent value of penal harming, and the moral worth of offenders coalesce to establish a precondition to any act of penal harm: that it not exceed the minimum harm that is necessary to express the community's condemnation for the act.
- The interest of citizens in the safety of their communities calls upon correctional authorities to manage the penal harm they impose in a way consistent with sustaining and enhancing community safety.

Two Illustrations

The discussion below illustrates both the concept of integrationist penal sanctions and the fact of an evolving correctional practice, using two offenses: child sexual abuse and burglary. These two types of offenses are chosen purposefully. They represent a range of offenses—personal and property, compulsive and instrumental and interpersonal and stranger.[53]

Child molestation, a main version of child sexual abuse, is chosen as an example because it is a compulsive crime, often has a long active period in an offender's career, and is one of the most reprehensible of all offenses. Burglary/robbery by drug addicted offenders is the second example, chosen because these street crimes are often associated with impoverished inner cities, and constitute the kinds of crimes people most fear. People who commit these offenses often have lengthy criminal records.

For each type of crime, three stages of analysis are given. First, facts known about the nature of the crime and its prospects for control are summarized. Second, the array of interests of the key community members—victims, offenders and potential victims (community safety)—is laid out. Third, a description is provided of how penal systems might respond to offenders convicted of the crime, given what is known about it and about the interests arrayed around it. These illustrations are drawn to show how integrationist values can be made consistent with community protection interests in ways that are actually preferable to the more commonly proposed separationist models.

The reader should bear in mind that the purpose of this analysis is to demonstrate how the abstract idea of integrationist community protection can be given operational meaning. To do so requires we know something of the crime itself as well as pay attention to the interests and the well-being of those affected by the crime and criminal. The demonstration is meant to counter the easy assumption of the separationists that removing criminals from the community and harming them is the optimal strategy for ensuring community safety. My intention, however, is not to design a full-blown program for these offenders; rather, it is to illustrate the logic and analysis to be undertaken in the development of such a program.

CHILD MOLESTATION

Nature

Child molestation is a crime that occurs when an adult uses a child for sexual gratification. It is a crime that occurs frequently in regular society, and it is a crime committed by members of all social classes, both genders, and all ethnic groups (Finkelhor et al. 1986). A small minority of convicted child abusers have a specific mental illness diagnosed as causing their behavior, "but most people who molest appear perfectly normal in other ways" (Hunter 1991: 9). The onset of child sexual abuse seems correlated with marital disorganization and a personal sense of powerlessness (Groth and Burgess 1979), but in fact, a considerable case can be made for the existence of a deviant sexual preference for child partners, referred to as pedophilia.

The criminal career of a child abuser is often a long one, lasting throughout the offender's sexually active life. This is especially the case for pedophiles, who may have numerous victims over the years of their criminal activity (Lieblum and Rosen 1979). Although victims most commonly are members of the offender's immediate family, it is a frequent variation for isolated child abusers to befriend children and manipulate them into sexual contact. These offenders are the most frequently caught, it seems (Groth 1978), and they also have the most numerous victims (Lanning 1987).

The treatment prospects for child molesters are controversial. Some experts claim that "most sexual offenders can be successfully treated" (Seattle Sexual Assault Center, quoted in Hunter 1991: 10), but the consensus of opinion is that treatment is problematic for many types of offenders (Abel 1984; Rice, Quinsey, and Harris 1991). In most cases, the best solution to be hoped for is control of the appetite and propensity to seek children as sex partners (Groth 1978). Control is reinforced by behavior therapy (often including aversive deconditioning) and constant monitoring. There is a substantial body of opinion that a prison sentence is a critical component of treatment for many child molesters, especially pedophiles, because it has a confrontational effect on the denial that so commonly surrounds their offending (Hunter 1991). Some researchers believe the need for a prison sentence is overstated (Kempe and Kempe 1978).

Interests

The victim of the child molester most frequently is seen as having a great interest in being separated from the perpetrator. This may be so, but in the common situation in which the abuser is a parent, this requirement results in family disintegration, which may not always be in the victim's long-term interest. Indeed, dissolution of the family is nearly always at least somewhat damaging to the child's well-being. While it is certainly the case that removal of the perpetrator from the child's environment is normally a necessary first step in dealing with the child's need, it is quite often the case that successful treatment of the victim may ultimately result in reestablishment of the family with the perpetrator present (DePanfilis 1986).

Regardless of the victim's need in relation to the offender, there is a well-established need for the victim to receive treatment for the traumatic syndrome that so often follows abuse. Failure to provide effective treatment can result in depression, damaged self-esteem, alcoholism, and eventually, incidents of child molestation perpetrated by the victim (Courtois 1988).

Very often, it is necessary to see the child as only one of the victims involved in the crime. Adult members of the family may feel traumatized by the disclosure of the criminality—and they may feel guilt at their own direct or indirect role in the abuse (spouses of abusers often play enabling roles in the drama of abuse). Non-victimized children in the family may likewise feel emotional trauma, for they may wonder why they were not loved as their sibling was loved. All members of the family may require some level of supportive therapy, if the lasting emotional effects of the abuse are to be overcome (Mayer 1983).

Because child molestation is often a compulsion, an appetite on the part of the offender, it is important to recognize the interests of potential victims. For every victimization prevented, a host of harm is also prevented across the generations. Child sexual abuse is perhaps an extreme example of the way in which the occurrence, aftermath, and prevention of crime can best be seen as a web of interpersonal interdependencies.

The offender's interests are more complex. Even though advocates of man–child sexuality argue forcefully that it is an acceptable sexual lifestyle, it is inconceivable that sexual contact with children at a very early age can be consensual. It is equally apparent that such contact will result in emotional damage to the child. Therefore, it is not possible to think of continued sexual contact with children as being in the self-interest of the offender (as defined in Chapter 1), in the sense that self-interest reflects a prudent understanding of personal and interpersonal well-being. The actual interest of the active offender is to come to see the drive for sexual contact with children as an appetite that should not be satisfied, and to learn effective techniques for resisting the appetite. Within that larger interest, the offender has a natural desire for a more or less ordinary life within the community.

Approach

Locking up a child sex offender is never a complete solution to the problem, for three reasons. First, the offender will eventually be released, and the desires for sexual contact with children, if they were not situational (for example, caused by family stress), will continue for a lifetime, and may even become more pronounced in later years. Second, child sex offenders usually experience brutality during their incarceration, and the brutality often promotes bitterness and reinforces the denial that is essential to continued offending. Third, when the offender is removed from the family, the family suffers a loss of financial and human support as long as the offender is incarcerated.

On the other hand, some period of incarceration may be essential to treatment. In the case of incest (and for certain pedophiles) the incarceration is a public statement of wrong that the offender finds literally undeniable, and therefore forces him to jettison the techniques of denial that explain away the molestation as "harmless," "teaching," "loving," and so forth. The law's objection stands as a stark rejection of those claims.

But soon—maybe after a few months and certainly within a year or two (Hunter 1991)—the beneficial effects of incarceration are eroded and the negatives, listed above, begin to become important. A plan must be prepared to help the offender reside in the community.

If the plan is to take the community's safety seriously, it will require attention to a number of facts about child molesters:

- There is a high rate of repeat offending
- Repeat offending can occur after years of abstinence and at any age
- Offenders often signal readiness to reoffend by changing patterns of living
- Therapy is central to sustained abstinence, both as a support of abstinence and a check on compliance (Pithers et el. 1987)

These facts suggest that the corrections system may need to be prepared to provide therapy on a continuing basis, in some cases perhaps for life. Certainly corrections must be prepared to remain in some form of contact with many offenders for years, decades—even for a lifetime.

According to specialists experienced in working with child sex offenders (Schwartz 1988), the contact will have certain elements. First, it will be designed to ensure that the offender continues in some type of therapy. The first stages of the therapy may have involved aversive conditioning or some other packaged strategy used for molesters, but the later stages will almost certainly be insight/support-related counseling. The counseling will be designed to continue the offender's learning about the dynamics of his offending behavior, and it will offer an independent way to assess the offender's continued abstinence from sexual contact with children. This means that the therapy will need to be delivered by specialists who are not directly linked to the corrections process, but who have a close working relationship with correctional authorities. This is not, obviously, the traditional physician-patient relationship.

The corrections agency will have monitoring responsibility. It will assess the various types of 'signals' (Pithers et al. 1987: 125) to be concerned about in each particular offender's circumstance, and will lay out a plan to monitor those signals. The corrections agency will maintain regular, unsystematic contact with neighbors, family members, employers, and therapists, in order to be certain that stability remains in the offender's life (Vermont Department of Corrections 1988). There will be a search for behavior irregularities: has the offender started drinking (more)? Is he missing work? Has he started missing therapy appointments, or is he evasive or otherwise different in therapy? Have there been contacts with neighborhood children, or, if the offender is back in the family, do family children exhibit any symptoms of new intrusion into their sexuality?

These questions reflect only a part of what might be done—the specifics depend on the case itself. The thrust of the intervention is supportive—to help the offender abstain and to keep the offender in the community. Should a problem arise, the response will be rapid. A rapid response is needed in order to reinforce the external pressures for abstinence, to avoid the situation that a signal foreshadows, and to support the offender's adjustment.

Skeptics about corrections are likely to be concerned that an integrationist strategy of relapse prevention will be extremely intrusive with offenders. Little will be gained if the integrationist approach merely makes life worse for offenders by turning their control over to treaters instead of jailers, as has been true in the past of "medical model" strategies in the past (Kittrie 1971). The need is for a strategy that considers the interests of the offender in terms of minimal intrusion (Rotman 1990).

The ultimate intrusiveness will be dependent upon the attitude of the representatives of the corrections system. If they see it as their role to be nasty to the offender, to give him pain so that he will suffer the consequences of his past actions, then the whole procedure is a charade. But if the corrections system takes a different view, namely that the offender is a valued member of the community who is worth supporting, but about whom there is a concern that he not injure children again—in short, if the correctional approach is to treat the offender as a morally worthy community member—then correctional practices could emanate from the correspondence of interests of victims, offenders, and their neighbors.

Robbing/Burglarizing Drug Addicts

Nature

The problem of drug addicts' crimes stands at the core of American drug policy. The separationist approach views drug-addicted offenders with alarm, for they are stereotypes of the kind of offender citizens should fear. The most recent expansion of prison beds has been predicated upon the need to deal with this type of offender. The separationist policy would be to lock up drug-addicted offenders up for as long as possible.[54]

The attractiveness of this idea has deep roots in research about crimes committed by drug-dependent offenders. Studies show that these offenders commit large numbers of crimes, often of a variety of types (Johnson and Wish 1987) and that their criminal behaviors correlate highly with their drug use—rates of criminality are high when they are getting high, low when they are off drugs (Ball, Shaffer, and Nurco 1983). But the incarceration of drug offenders appears to have little direct effect on either their drug use or their criminality after they are released (Platt 1986). In other words, the incarceration provides a kind of a 'breather' period, and enables the offender to return to the community with less of a debilitation, but with small hope of desisting from either drug use or crime (Wexler and Williams 1986).

It is important to make distinctions between various types of drug-using offenders, of course. Studies suggest that there is a type of offender for whom the drug use is a source of excitement, as is the criminal lifestyle (Chaiken and Chaiken, 1990). These offenders do not commit crimes because of drug use; rather, they use drugs and commit crimes for the same reason: they are offenders. Studies show that these offenders commit a large number of crimes and do not really specialize in doing so (Chaiken and Chaiken, 1982).

Treatment of drug offenders receives a better review. Coercive treatment programs that incorporate peer treatment elements with disciplinary components seem to work well, despite the initial resistance of the client (Wexler and Lipton 1985). But the effects of treatment are not miraculous: offenders often dabble in drugs (and as a result, in crime) over long periods of time after initial treatment programs end. Thus, it is more accurate to view treatment as a first stage of change—as an investment in change. The effects of treatment are additive, and the treatment processes are best understood as cyclical in nature (Ball, Rosen, Flueck, and Nurco 1982; DeLeon 1984).

The emphasis on treatment as the most effective way out of the drug-crime lifestyle should not obscure its limitations. Many, if not most, graduates of treatment programs experience so-called "slips" and return to using drugs. It is, after all, a dependency. Many offenders, when they slip back into drug use, return also to crime (Faupel 1992).

Interests

Drug-dependent offenders have an interest in freeing themselves from drug use. This, regardless of the drug-dependent offender's protestations, is a fact. (It may not be a fact for intermittent drug users who are able to constrain their drug use and therefore never disappear into the drug-dependent lifestyle—see Clear, Clear, and Braga 1993.) The negative effects of drug dependency, the testimonies of graduates of coercive drug treatment, the obvious deficits imposed by the law when drug using offenders are caught—all these factors contribute to an unassailable argument that the well-being of drug-addicted offenders would be better if they overcame the addiction. (Again, non-offenders who are addicted to drugs may have a different interest, but they are not the people who generate public fear, and so they are not being discussed here.)

The victims of the crimes of drug-addicted users have less of an interest in what happens to their predators. It is true that the victims of robberies and burglaries experience outrage and want to see their violators publicly defeated, but generally their well-being depends more on their being compensated for criminal losses than it does on the consequences that come to those who harmed them. Therefore, for the identified victim, there is a need for the offender to be able to replace the items stolen or their value. Since most victims of drug-dependent offenders never are linked to the specific offenders who robbed them, what actually matters is having a viable victims compensation plan to provide the restitution.

For the drug offender, there stands the problem of future victims. The most accurate prediction is that for any drug-dependent offender, there will be future victims. This prediction applies regardless of the penalty (short of death), for all drug-dependent offenders will be released eventually, most after a few months of incarceration. All will have to confront the cruel slavery of their dependency, many without any support to help them stay free of drugs. Thus, it is in the interest of future victims that actions be taken not simply to remove offenders from the community, but to carefully structure their living situation within the community.

Approach

The approach to treating drug offenders is very straightforward: deal with the drug addiction. There is some evidence that effective work with drug addiction can be done in institutional settings (Wexler and Williams 1986) but the bulk of the evidence is that this kind of treatment is most effectively done in special residential drug treatment centers that also work with people who are living in the community (Anglin and Hser 1992). If a drug-dependent offender is to 'make it,' his success will take place in the real context of the community, not in the artificial setting of the prison.[55]

The cornerstone of effective community management of drug dependent offenders is treatment (Byrne, Lurigio, and Baird 1989). Treatment challenges the drug offender to reconstruct his life; it provides a separate way to understand what is happening to him; it confronts his most cherished rationalizations; and, most of all, it provides a way to test whether he is still 'clean.' These benefits of drug treatment are all more salient in the community than in the institutional context.

The ever-present potential for relapse into drug use (and associated criminality) colors every aspect of dealing with the drug-dependent offender. Because he is likely to slip, authorities must be willing to sustain a continuing vigilance about drug use. This means that there must be a consistent and frequent program of drug testing, and that there must be a rapid response to indications of renewals of drug use. Such responses need not involve reimprisonment—they can range from increased frequency of drug testing to brief periods of incarcerations. These consequences act as reinforcements to drug-free living, and they are considerably more reasonable than programmatic threats such as "one dirty urine and you are back in prison."

In fact, the drug-dependent offender should be expected to be a high-failure client, and so the goal of total abstinence is unrealistic. What the program manager seeks is a much more restricted accomplishment: To reduce the duration of periods of drug use, to increase the length of drug-free time between periods of use, and to respond as rapidly (and consistently) as possible to slips. It is this kind of program that will, in the long run, maximize community safety and minimize harm to offenders and citizens alike.

6

Reducing Penal Harm

> *We are free to decide on the pain level we find*
> *acceptable. There are no guidelines except in*
> *values. . . . If there are any experts here,*
> *they are philosophers. They're also fond of*
> *saying that the problems are so complex that*
> *we cannot act. We must think. This may not*
> *be the worst alternative when the other option*
> *is pain delivery.*
> —Nils Christie,
> *Crime Control as Industry*

It is always perilous to proceed from a critique of a social problem to a plan of action. The most obvious reason this is true is that criticism and action have different intentions: the aim of criticism is understanding, while the aim of action is movement. My primary aim in this book has been to critique penal harms. Obviously, however, it is my hope that what is wrong with our penal system will get less wrong.

It is natural to think that an improved understanding will promote effective movement, but often these two aims get impossibly muddled: our desire to move on a problem contaminates our ability to understand it critically. This is certainly true for the problem of crime—we can get so caught up in the desire to eliminate crime that we fail to see, critically, the nature of crime and the role it plays in modern society. If we have learned anything in the last 20 years, we have learned, first, that understanding crime does not necessarily lead effectively to fighting it, and second, that an overly-developed desire to fight crime distorts our ability to understand it.

There is another reason to avoid mixing criticism and action. The pragmatic and utilitarian nature of most public policy debate in this country often accepts criticism as valid only if it can suggest a better idea. Thus, we are tempted to first evaluate the idea and its promise before we settle down to hear the criticism that serves to advance it. The theory of selective incapacitation was much more a product of the promises it made than of the analyses that supported it.

In the preceding chapters, I have tried to provide a critical description of recent trends in penal harm theory and practice in order to question the assumptions and results of the recent explosion in the size and scope of the penal system. My central argument has been that expansion of the penal system has been neither socially beneficial nor theoretically supportable, and I have framed my arguments by investigating the goals often attributed to the penal harm movement. It seems altogether reasonable to conclude my argument with a chapter outlining what we might call "the way out" of the current penal chaos.

The problem is that there is no way out. This is a point that John DiIulio (1991) made when he analyzed the now prominent clash between the constitution, political and programmatic realities, and public resources for the penal system. His work is that of a political scientist, describing the untenable fit between the various traditions that intersect to produce the U.S. prison system. For instance, he notes that the countervailing pressures from the electorate to be tough on crime and yet to reduce the taxes exist on a collision course.

Yet this kind of discussion misses the central point, namely that there is no way out of penal chaos, because the main thing Americans want from their penal system is crime control, and the system cannot deliver. It would strain credibility to argue that acts of penal harm have nothing to do with crime, but a generation of research and experience add up to a realization that the amount of crime has precious little to do with the amount—or nature—of penal harm.

The current penal chaos results from our stubborn insistence on sustaining an essential policy link between crime and punishment. This is not to say that our punishment policies should be designed with disregard for their crime control potential, but rather that we expect far too much crime control from our policies. This unrealistic expectation is a final reason to be hesitant in concluding the book with prescriptive advice for the system. For those who would use the arrangements of penal harm to make crime less common, my advice will probably seem to be unacceptably pessimistic, which will lead them to doubt my original analysis. Since one of my intentions is to bring the term *penal harm* into wider usage, it cannot help my cause to alienate anyone by my inability to offer "sound policy alternatives," a phrase that serves as a code for the idea that we might combat crime without extensive use of prison. Once I admit that I see no extraordinary way to combat crime through penal policy, regardless of the number of people put under penal control of one type or another, then any suggestions I have are bound to face serious doubts among those who have set the policy agenda to ensure that the penal system *shall* combat crime.

On the other hand, I must admit that the critical analysis in the preceding pages leads *somewhere*—if not, why have I bothered? The trepidation I feel is merely that the possible solution does not include a firm promise of less crime, though thankfully it does not contain a threat of more crime. My suggestions do, however, deal with the problem of penal harm; those who want to end crime by harming offenders need read no further.

This chapter describes some of the policy implications of the critical analysis provided in earlier chapters. It begins with a summary of the main points of my argument thus far, then moves on to suggest how we ought to approach policy-making regarding penal harm.

JUSTIFICATIONS OF PENAL HARM

The essence of a punishment is the harm it imposes upon the well-being of the law violator. We should be suspicious about the uses of punishment, because allowing government to intentionally damage the well-being of some of its citizens is inherently questionable.

The imposition of penal harms is justified by two general arguments: retributive and utilitarian. The retributive position is that law violators should be harmed because they deserve to be harmed, and it is good and proper that they be harmed. The utilitarian justification is that the penal harm is necessary in order to prevent the greater harms resulting from criminal acts. Neither of these justifications survives close scrutiny.

Retributive justifications are confronted with a series of contradictions that reduce their persuasiveness, especially in the context of modern society. Those who argue that penal harms are necessary to right a wrong are faced with the problem of showing how the state's decision to impose an otherwise avoidable act of harm can make up for the law violator's previous (and by definition irretrievable) act of criminal harm. The argument that the penal harm is necessary to teach the law violator a moral lesson also faces difficult questions: What if the lesson learned has nothing to do with morals and everything to do with the power of the state? Why is harm needed to teach moral lessons, when we know that most people learn best by reward, not punishment?

Utilitarian arguments are even more seriously flawed by a long history of research showing that even under ideal circumstances, the crime prevention benefits of most punishments are minimal or nonexistent.

THE EXPANSION OF THE PENAL HARMING APPARATUS

Because the justifications of penal harms are so shaky, it would seem that law violators would be harmed only with reservation and as a last resort. In the United States, this has not been the case. Since the mid-1970s, the United States has embarked upon a wholesale increase in the scope of its penal system, bringing the modern penal apparatus to a position of power unprecedented in history and second to no other place in the Western world. The United States has engineered a kind of social experiment in penal harm.

The expansion of the penal harming machinery can only be explained as a consciously chosen social policy. It cannot be explained as a response to an increase in crime, for changes in crime rates preceding this growth do not duplicate the penal harm expansion. Nor can it be explained as a crime prevention policy, for data confirm that few meaningful changes in crime rates have occurred since the policy of penal harm was undertaken.

Just as the philosophical justifications suggest restraint in the use of penal harm, so do the results of our social experiment in penal expansion: people are not more satisfied with the justice system; crime has not been reduced.

THE CRIMINOLOGICAL ROLE IN PENAL HARM

Science has always played a role in the evolution of modern penal policy. The claims of classical penology supported the initial invention of prisons to deal with crime. In later years, when the emphasis was on offender rehabilitation, scientists promised that the use of treatments for offenders would reduce crime. There was even a brief period of time when scientists suggested that communities could be changed in order to reduce crime.

The penal harm experiment was given intellectual legitimacy by science as well. Two research strands, prediction of criminal recidivism and incapacitation of active criminals, served to anchor policies that expanded punishment. Despite sometimes broad claims for the benefits of prediction and incapacitation, there are practical and conceptual problems with each scientific strategy.

The effectiveness of prediction is impeded by a human malady that is unlikely to be overcome: the uncertainty of human behavior. In addition, there are technical problems in prediction methods that seem to set outer limits on the potential of the technique. The theory of incapacitation is sorely tested by studies suggesting its research claims were overstated. Recent studies also suggest the incapacitation model of human criminal behavior is flawed, and that replacement, combined with the lack of desistence, eliminates the benefits of incarceration. This may explain the confounding result that despite a quadrupling of the prison population, crime remains about the same.

Though scientists seem to have failed in their quest to provide ways to reduce crime, their work has not been totally irrelevant with regard to penal policy. By responding to political interests in defining penal policy, they have provided policy makers with so-called "scientific" rationales to support policies that were politically expedient. They have also sustained a crime prevention focus on the individual offender, maintaining the tradition in this country that crime-fighting is synonymous with criminal-fighting.

The Victim

In contrast to the heady appeals of science, the issue of the victim speaks directly to the sympathetic heart. Punishing the offender, it is argued, is a way to tell the victim (and everyone watching) that the harm of the criminal act was wrong and condemnable.

The image of the damaged and enraged victim is familiar to us all, partly because being (or knowing) a victim is a common experience. The image is compelling also because we feel so helpless to assist a victim, and so fearful of becoming one ourselves. The journey from helpless fear to unrestrained rage is not a long one.

But in what way does a penal harm actually help a victim? It surely stands as a public statement that the victim deserved better, but after that, it does little. Penal harm cannot make the victim whole—indeed, the most heinous crimes may make this an impossible goal. In some ways, the focus on getting even with the offender diverts the victim from his or her personal path of recovery. It suggests that after the court has imposed a penalty, the victim's needs have been served by the state. Yet, for the victim, the long path of recovery really begins only after sentencing.

In this way, the emphasis on penal harm may actually be a disservice to the victim, in that it promises that if the state is only able to impose a penalty severe enough, the victim will be able to overcome the crime. The focus is placed on what happens to the law violator, not what happens with the victim. The victim's victory at sentencing is eventually exposed as a pyrrhic conquest, for the problem faced by the victim does not center on the offender. Punishment of the offender is an essential message to the victim about justice, but the degree of punishment has little to with the victim's task of recovery.

COMMUNITY PROTECTION

The phrase *community protection* engages in a conceptual sleight of hand: it acts as though there is a single, obvious community in need of protection, and by making that claim, creates a symbol of *two* communities—'them,' the bad guys, and 'us,' their victims.

This symbolism is false on two grounds. First, studies of crime show that there is not such a clear boundary between victims and offenders—they are often intertwined personally, and most people have been *both* victims and offenders. Second, the rhetoric of community protection has not only failed to reduce crime, but also exacerbated racial inequalities.

The larger question is whether or not separationist community protection is necessary. Using well-established research about serious felons as a basis for designing correctional programs, it is possible to demonstrate that segregation of convicted offenders is not necessary to protect the larger community—especially if one regards those offenders as members of the community. An integrationist model has both moral and practical benefits as an alternative theory of community protection.

FOUR FORCES IN THE PENAL HARM DILEMMA

Throughout this analysis of the growth of punishment in the United States from 1973–1993, four forces continually arise: race, politics, science, and drugs. A return to these issues will help us understand strategies that may reverse, or at least stall, the growth in the penal system.

Race

No moral problem haunts the United States' sense of identity more intractably than race relations. We are a society that has never successfully overcome its history of slaves and slave owners; this is true despite the heroic efforts of citizens of all races and ethnic backgrounds to make social justice a reality.

The penal system is a part of the problem, because penal harms are inequitably distributed among our racial and ethnic populations. The familiar fact is that one-fourth of black males aged 20–29 are currently under control of the penal system. Less familiar but equally troubling facts:

- The United States' incarceration rate for black males is 3,370 per 100,000, which is four times the rate for whites and five times the rate for black males in South Africa, the Western nation whose overall incarceration rate comes closest to that of the United States (Mauer 1992).
- Arrest rates for drug offenses committed by whites have remained steady at about 300 per 100,000 since 1973; the rate for blacks was twice as high in 1973, but soared to five times the white rate in 1989, and decreased slightly to four times the white rate in 1991 (Blumstien 1993).
- Between 1985 and 1987, detention of juveniles grew by 15%; almost all of this increase was due to the fact that the growth in detention of minorities was 30 times greater than the growth in detention of whites (Snyder 1990).
- The jail rate for blacks grew from 339 per 100,000 in 1984 to 619 per 100,000 in 1992; the white rates grew from 68 to 109 per 100,000 (BJS 1993).
- Three-quarters of New York state's prison population come from seven minority neighborhoods in New York City (Clines 1992).
- In some cities, more than half of all young black males are under correctional control (Miller 1992).

Criminologists debate the conclusions that can be drawn from these and similar statistics; some find evidence of racial disparity, while others do not.[56]

In some respects, the debate is moot. We have argued that the credibility of the criminal law lies in its ability to serve as the community's moral instrument; we have also argued that problems of race are this culture's main moral failing. It follows that the penal system cannot serve its moral function when it intensifies this country's central moral failing.

Politics

The U.S. political system has failed to provide its constituents with a penal policy that makes strategic sense and provides moral authority. Almost everyone, regardless of their politics, would agree with this statement.

Instead of building a rational, principled penal system, our political leaders have chosen to turn the correctional process into political capital. When it comes to crime and punishment, elected leaders do not lead; they pander. The determinate sentencing movement of the 1970s is a case in point. Griset's (1992) history of determinate sentencing reform in New York found that "liberal ideologues . . . hoped to introduce the rule of law into the sentencing system [but] as more people jumped on the determinate bandwagon . . . other, more conservative groups began to influence policymakers (176–177).

Politicians continue to call for mandatory minimum sentences, despite good evidence that these sentences fail to achieve any objective (see U.S. Sentencing Commission 1991) save that of promoting a reelection campaign. In the 1988 Presidential election, political concerns led the Federal Bureau of Prisons to cut furlough by 50% (Isikoff, 1992)—no Willie Hortons for candidate Bush! Yet, for many observers, the best criminological news in the 1992 Presidential campaign was that crime received so little attention.

There is no natural law that penal policy must work this way. Studies show that overall victimization rates in the United States are nearly identical to those in Canada, Australia, and the Netherlands (van Dijk, Mayhew, and Killias 1990: E1). Yet our incarceration rates are four times that of Canada, nearly six times that of Australia, and an astonishing ten times that of the Netherlands. England, despite a rising crime rate, a conservative government, and a longer and deeper recession than that seen in the United States, reduced its prison population in 1990 by 6% (Proband 1992), and plans a 35–50% decrease in that population by 1995 (Bean, 1992).

We come by our nonsensically large penal system as a product of our nonsensical political approach to crime. Elected officials can do little to affect the issue directly, and so there is a premium on instituting tough politics. Each new elected generation erects its tough policies on the failed foundations of the previous group. The direction of penal harms is ever upward in scale and scope.

The lack of sophistication with which the media report crime and punishment does play a role in the inadequate politics of the issue. For instance, under the headline, "For Petty Offenders, Toil Replaces Incarceration," (Sullivan 1992) the opening sentence read: "Petty offenders who once went unpunished because their crimes were so minor are now being put to work . . . under a new program." Thus, a story that actually was about a way in which the penal system became *tougher* was portrayed as a story about how the system is getting more lenient! New coverage of corrections is too often about dramatic program failures of recidivists and, too infrequently about the chaotic consequences of accelerating penal harms.

Science

As of July 1993, the National Rifle Association has run an advertisement on television claiming, among other things, that research shows the average rapist serves only a few days in prison for his crime. The advertisement concludes that we need to fight crime with tougher penalties and more prisons, not with gun control laws.

The study alluded to is Reynold's (1991) analysis of Texas data, which provides *per crime* estimates of prison sentences, not *per offender* estimates, as the NRA advertisement claims. There is much wrong with the study (see Baird 1993), but the NRA's mischaracterization of its results is an illustration of how, when it comes to crime and punishment, politics and science are often partners.

It is probably not possible for politics and science to work any other way. Criminology is, after all, a policy science, and any exhortations to separate research from its application are likely to be futile. Perhaps it is in recognition of this fact that both the American Society of Criminology and the Academy of Criminal Justice Sciences—two academic professional societies—have recently begun a debate about whether or not to take positions on certain policy matters affecting the field.[57] A more aggressive attempt to lessen the influence of politics on science is likely to be very controversial, not only because it would run contrary to academic freedom, but also because it would require reorganization of research funding structures.

Drugs

Scholars have written a great deal and will continue to write about drugs and drug policy. What makes drugs important for my purposes is that for the last 20 years, we have tried to punish our way out of a national drug problem (with vengeance during the last 7 years). Neither drug use nor punishment are the better for our efforts.

Drug arrests and punishment have been especially targeted at minority citizens (Blumstein 1993; Snyder 1990); and drug law enforcement has been accompanied by a distressing official attack on civil liberties (Johns 1992). More than any other type of crime, the so-called "war" on drugs has accelerated incarceration rates in the last seven years (Austin and Killman 1990). Between 1979 and 1988, prison commitments for drug offenders increased more than 2.5 times; prison commitments for marijuana cases more than tripled (Reuter 1991: 157, 158). The drug war has had particularly strong impact on recent incarceration trends, leading to ". . . an order of magnitude increase in sentences of more than one year [from 1980 to 1991] from 11,500 to 118,000" (Reuter 1991, 3).

It is no longer controversial to say that our drug policies do not achieve their aims and have considerable negative side effects. RAND's Drug Policy Research Center[58] has published a series of papers that empirically analyze U.S. drug policy to demonstrate unequivocally the inadequacies of our current policies: street prices of drugs remain the same; organized crime becomes a stronger part of domestic and foreign drug markets; violence is increased; and drug use patterns appear essentially unaffected (Reuter 1991; 1992; 1993; DiNardo 1993; Caulkins, Crawford, and Reuter 1993). Studies also show that pretrial drug testing does not improve defendant performance in pretrial programs (Jones 1991). Finally, studies of drug policy show ways in which these policies can be systematically linked to disparities in treatment by race (Helmer 1975).

As never before, drug policy is the engine that drives the punishment machine over and above the relationship between drugs and crime. The question is whether a political energy exists to reverse the machine's direction.

What Is Needed?

It is clear that a new conversation about our penal system is needed. The final pages of this book suggest directions we might take in pursuing that conversation. By no means am I proposing a fully-articulated view or theory of what we ought to be doing in place of what we are now doing. It will take more and wiser minds than mine to work out that problem—I hope to play a part in opening the dialogue.

The conversation must occur at two levels simultaneously. There must be a conceptual/philosophical level at which basic values about our society are engaged and critiqued. There must also be a practical level at which laws and programs are designed. What I say below is meant as a opening journey into these two levels of analysis.

The Social Meaning of Penal Harm

The first step in recasting the debate about penal policy is to stop focusing only on individual acts and their results and begin taking into account social actions and their results. In our thinking about crime and justice, we reflexively approach the problem as though it were one of individuals: judges sentencing lawbreakers, counselors treating clients, probation officers supervising offenders, and so forth. We can never dispense with this viewpoint, of course, since whatever a justice system does, it always comes down to individual workers and their actions *vis-à-vis* citizens under their control.

But a system of justice must not be seen merely as a collection of individual acts. The penal system also represents a social fact. It is a product of social forces, and stands as a mirror of the kind of society our collective actions produce. In this way, our penal system can be seen as the realization of our social values, at least with regard to the concept of criminal justice. We are used to observing individual events in the justice process and asking if they make sense to us, given our values. Thus, each of us reacts to a news story about a judge's sentence by asking, "Is this what I think is right?" We ought also to react to the collective results of those many individual decisions by asking, "Is this what we had in mind? Is this the society we were trying to create?"

We need to view the penal system as the socio-moral version of what we stand for as a society, and in doing so, we ought to look at the collective realization of the penal process. We should take this point of view, not to the exclusion of individual rights and duties, but in addition to the individual level of analysis.

Of course, there is nothing revolutionary about the idea that the penal system has to do with the morality of a society. Social scientists since Durkheim have made the point that crime and punishment are fundamentally issues of social morality. But we err when we treat the penal system as a socio-moral equivalent of what economists call the "invisible hand." Central to this economic point of view is the faith that the collective product of individually self-productive economic decisions will be a self-productive economic society. Whether the economic "invisible hand" exists is debatable. In the moral realm, we can say with certainty that its equivalent does not occur. The collective result of a large number of morally self-protective individual decisions is not necessarily a morally self-protective society.

This is true because there is a growing discordance between decisions that are individually self-protective and those that are so-cially self-protective. For individuals, *separation* always seems to promise the greatest safety: move away from the dilapidated urban core; send the burglars and drug dealers away; locate the criminally-likely child and incapacitate him. As we saw from chapter 5, the philosophy of separation proposes to move overt offenders to a place where they cannot commit crimes against supposedly law-abiding citizens.

Why does this simple formula not work?

The answer involves the interdependence that characterizes the modern age of information. For instance, the so-called "white flight" of the 1960s was largely the collective decision of many individuals to leave cities for safer, more desirable environments. One result has been the deterioration of cities. Another has been that the problems of cities have slowly worked their way out to the suburbs. It should be apparent by now that what happens in our cities deeply affects quality of life in the suburbs and beyond. For certain cases of (predatory) crime, it seems prudent to deny bail before trial. Yet failure to make bail is associated with a greater likelihood of a prison sentence, which in turn is associated with later failure under community supervision. The decision to deny bail may contribute to later criminal justice failures. It is in our interest to be concerned about what happens to the bail seeker, not just from his point of view, but also from ours.

These are but two divergent examples of the obvious modern fact that the world has gotten smaller and that societies—and the individuals within them—more dependent upon one another for the quality of their lives. Leslie Wilkins has made this point in his award winning book *Social Deviance* (1965). In earlier days, social interdependencies were centered in familial and community relations. Wilkins argues that it was easier for these highly integrated communities to absorb deviants into their midst. It was also easier for these communities to get rid of deviants.

These days, this is not the case. A crime committed yesterday in a city a thousand miles away is news in our own morning papers today; reading and knowing the details of this crime affects our sense of personal security. The deterioration of cities is a cancer that weakens every other aspect of our neighborhoods and economies. The people who live as far outside those cities as possible, but still struggle to go into them to earn a living wage—can they claim their lives are not deeply altered by the loss of the cities to decay?

The knee-jerk reaction is a further belief in the power of separatist thinking: build prisons and stick those we think responsible for the decay in them. But we can never really separate ourselves from the offenders in our midst. More than 90% of those who enter prisons eventually leave them, most in less than 2 years. To double their average stay would wreak unimaginable fiscal damage on government coffers, and would involve far more than a doubling of the prison population. It would mean that far more than one in four young black men would be in prison or jail. And they would still be only the tip of the offender iceberg.

Modern interdependence is inter-societal as much or more than it is a phenomenon of families or neighborhoods. In the United States, the average citizen moves 12 times in a lifetime; the modal child is raised in a non-nuclear family. This is not to discount the family or the neighborhood, but rather to argue the idea that the way these institutions insulated individuals from social malady no longer exists.

I am not seeking to argue that individual rights are outdated. To the contrary, the need for individual rights has never been greater, given the modern emergence of the powerful information-based state. My point is a much more simple and perhaps slightly subtle one: we no longer expect the justice system to really protect the integrity of our individual, familial, and neighborhood relations; we now place greater value on the way the justice system promotes the integrity of our larger social relations. We want the penal system to help support the social interdependence that pervades modern society.

This is not a wholesale shift in focus. When the modern penal system was invented, it was thought to relate to societal interests as well as individual reformation. Today, we still expect it to deal fairly and effectively with the individuals with whom it is concerned. Yet a shift in the balance of our expectations has occurred. The relationship of system actions to individuals is no longer more important than the relationship of those actions to broader societal well-being.

Most of the dissatisfactions we feel with the penal system have to do with its inadequacies with regard to our larger societal needs. In recasting the modern debate about penal harm, I rely on the way in which a penal system is a societal realization of the moral basis for interdependent social relations. I begin by returning to this basic starting point of my analysis: why and how do we harm each other's well-being through penal agency?

JUSTIFYING PENAL HARM

In the opening chapter, the anomaly of penal harm was discussed. Through government action, the individual citizen's well-being is harmed. How can this be justified?

Retributivists argue that the value of penal harm lies in what it symbolizes about interpersonal rights and duties, namely that certain acts are sufficiently reprehensible to be socially and publicly castigated. Certainly, to simply ignore criminal misconduct would stand as a symbol that these acts between people are tolerated. Yet a society in which the infliction of penal harm is commonplace is not an attractive one. When does the proliferation of penal intolerance begin to symbolize a deep fixation upon intolerance, especially when the intolerance is expressed as acts of harm against a person's well-being?

The problem is the contradiction between acts of self-protective penal harm that are employed in the pursuit of a desirable society, and the undesirability of a society in which the routine and excessive use of penal harm is one of its attributes. We find ourselves, like Br'er Rabbit, trying to punch our way out of the tar baby, only to be ever more caught in its sticky grasp. The more we punish each other in order to try to preserve order, the more we find ourselves living in a nation in which punishment is ordinary.

The Durkheimian view, that the way a social system deals with its rule violators defines its behavioral standards through the mechanism of the collective conscience, is perhaps accurate, but does not go far enough. To a certain extent, the institutions of penal harm also *define* the society. The use of brutal, physical punishments in some Middle-eastern societies define them as nations in which the instrumental use of brutality is characteristic. The comparatively conservative use of the prison in certain Western European nations defines them as cautious in the reliance upon prison as a device of social discipline.

How does our use of penal harm define us? We are a nation that spends more total dollars on imprisoning young black men than on providing them higher education; indeed, we deflect tax revenues away from our public education, transportation, and health budgets in order to afford the practice of penal harming. We are a nation in which minority group members, especially the poor from those groups, experience penal harm as virtually a right of passage to adulthood. We are a nation for whom the only growing portions of government expenditure are those that keep the aged alive and healthy and keep young men under correctional observation and control; and public debate occurs only around the issue of health and social security benefits for the aged.

This description of how our penal system defines us is only recently accurate. The growth in penal populations and their concentration of the poor and the black inner-city youth is a product of policy choices made in the 1970s and 1980s, when an emphasis was given to harsh treatment of individuals found to have broken the law.

It may be that the majority of individual acts of penal harm were justified by traditional retributive criteria, but it is beyond doubt that the aggregation of those decisions defines our society in ways that cannot make us proud to be U.S. citizens.

Could we change that self-definition? It would require setting limits on what we do in the name of justice, not just to individuals, but at the level of social priority. This is done quite frequently as a normal part of government budgeting—decisions are made as to "how much" a given government service will receive to do its work, and the level and amount of work it performs follows that decision. We could do the same for the penal system. For example, we could set a limit on the proportion of a budget devoted to punishment, and we could target the money in order to reflect values of social integration and interdependence. The money could establish educational scholarships, for example, or provide prenatal health care and infant day care.

Or the money could be spent on ways of confronting crime that involve more than merely building prisons and buying electronic monitors. We could say, for example, that for every dollar we spend on penal harms, we will dedicate two dollars to preventing crimes.

Not nearly enough is known about preventing crimes as we need to know, and so there is an extraordinary research agenda before us. In discussions of ways of preventing crime, we have placed an artificial restriction upon the topic by focussing only on the post-conviction controls of community supervision or prison. There is a whole panorama of other possibilities for preventing crime.

Crime prevention can be thought of as occurring in several domains of action. We may target the offender with interventions designed to reduce the motivation to offend. These are called "rehabilitation programs." We may target social forces that delay (or impede) onset of criminality and increase desistence. Programs that focus on improving schools, strengthening families, reducing violence in the home and so forth have been called "community crime prevention programs." Finally, we may target the conditions under which crimes occur, thereby reducing opportunities for successful offending. The research process underlying this approach has been called "situation crime prevention."

All three varieties of crime reduction have social advantages over penal harm, as a prevention strategy. They work via mechanisms that increase the target's well-being rather than attacking that of the lawbreaker. The side effects of effective programs are considerably less troublesome than the side effects of expanded programs of penal harm—for inner cities, children, minorities and even victims.

Critics say that we have limited firm knowledge about how to make these programs work to prevent crime. There are two responses. First, our knowledge is limited because we have invested very little in trying to find out—there is much that could be tried, much that is knowable, should we make a commitment to find out. Second, and perhaps more to the point, a utilitarian argument would insist that the only justification for an anti-crime action is that it works, and we have seen that the gains produced by a system of straight penal harms are minuscule. A crime prevention alternative that is not strategically very strong may still be marginally superior. And a crime prevention strategy will not have to overcome the onus carried by penal harm campaigns that are achieved through acts of damage to a utility (namely, the offender's well-being). Penal harm strategies touted as campaigns against crime have an extra dose of benefit they must produce to make up for the harm they certainly cause.

Thus, we can overcome some of the main objections to retributive and utilitarian strategies by recognizing the broader social utility we seek. This recognition leads to strategies of crime control that are far less onerous and less morally burdensome than traditional penal harm methods.

CARRYING OUT PENAL HARMS: CAUTIOUS SUGGESTIONS

I pause, once again, to remind the reader that what follows is intended as a stimulating list of options for conversation, not as a completed program. In the business of penal reform, any new method can backfire—this we certainly know from a long and tortuous history of failure. But if we are to make any improvements on the penal problems we have created for ourselves, we must address four broad areas.

Sentencing

Until some upper limits are set for the penalties imposed on offenders, there will be no solution to the problem of excessive penal harm in the United States. How can we set such limits?

The question is partly a philosophical one—on what moral or intellectual basis may we limit penalties? Inescapably, we must rely upon desert to set the upper limits of the penalty. This is true for a whole host of reasons: commensurate penalties meet the victim's need for confirmation of the wrong done; they define the state's interest in the penal harm; and they meet all the familiar and compelling arguments posed by recent retributionist perspectives. Desert limits involve both length of time and level of injury to self-worth.

On the other hand, desert should not be used to set a lower limit.[59] There will often be good reasons to do less—sometimes much less—than desert would allow. The relatively free reign of negative utilitarian aims could operate here: if a deserved penalty is not demonstrably likely to improve well-being through some crime-reduction benefit, then we ought to be free to not require the full penalty. We would do so in the interest of being the kind of country where justice and mercy are common; we would do so to avoid spreading harms more widely than is necessary.

Critics will ask, what of disparity in penal harms? The easiest way to reduce this problem is to set upper limits of desert at low levels. Then, the impact of treating one robber one way and the next robber another way will be minimized.[60] I am persuaded by the logic of von Hirsch (1993) that the moral benefits of low desert terms are considerable; I merely disagree that handing out deserved punishment is a moral necessity—especially when good and socially humane reasons can be found to do otherwise.

Limiting sentence lengths is also an enormous practical problem.

Finding political willpower to set these limits may seem as unlikely as finding the Cubs in the World Series. Yet there are promising signs. As antecedent to reasonable sentencing policy, we need rational, national debate on the topic; such debate is now underway.[61] The U.S. Attorney General speaks publicly in favor of less gruesome alternatives for drug offenders. The U.S. Sentencing Commission has advocated the elimination of mandatory minimum sentences. Some mandatory minimums have already been rolled back—in Colorado and Florida—and there is talk in the U.S. Congress of more such rollbacks. For the first time in many years, an environment friendly to discussion of more sensible sentences seems to be emerging.

Offender Management

We must make a commitment to minimizing the harm that results from the way we manage offenders while they are being punished. To do so will require us to confront issues of risk reduction, risk management, and coercion.

Any offender who wants to should be able to enroll in any risk reduction (in effect, treatment) program of his choice. Offenders who volunteer for risk reduction programs are more likely to succeed in them, and thereby reduce losses of well-being for both the offender and his or her potential victims. To deny an offender who wants one a risk-related treatment is worse than short-sighted; it is self-defeating.

A different issue is raised by offenders who do not want to enter risk-reduction programs. How does a fair and equitable system deal with the risk posed by these offenders?

In chapter 5, I illustrated a different view of community protection with two types of offenders who represent a large risk to the public well-being. I tried to show that we might engage in risk management with such offenders in ways that respected their lives, tried to maximize their freedom and autonomy, but did not ignore the fact that keeping them in the community is a risk. In this way, I believe a responsive penal system can attempt to minimize incursions into well-being and, at the same time, take seriously the obligation to impede destructive offenses against others' well-being. Thus, the penal system is obliged to control risk posed by those who are under its jurisdiction as long as they are under sentence.

The moral dilemma comes when a desert limit is surpassed by a risk control agenda. Let us use an unlikely case in which a sexual abuser of children is thought to deserve no more than two years' penal harm—yet we know he is likely to be risky for many years. Here, I think, is an excellent example of a case for which we must analyze all the interests. We would try to find the least intrusive, least coercive ways to manage the risk; these would most likely extend well beyond the two-year limit.[62] Any injury to well-being would, in our own minds, require a risk that met a stringent test of accuracy and reliability; only then would we would impose the limits in the least harmful way. To the degree possible, the offender would have a say in how those limits were imposed and monitored.

To be sure, there are contradictions in this model.[63] I would hope they would receive deep and continuing discussion among professionals in the penal harm system, as part of the effort to find marginal ways to reduce the incompatibility of ideas. In the end, we would try to manage risk humanely and justly; the offender's views would count, and science would, too.

Budgeting

Financial incentives for budgeting the costs of punishment tend to support system growth rather than cost control. This has partly to do with the structure of accountability in U.S. politics. Locally-elected judges find it financially wiser to send felons to prison systems funded by state revenues rather than to local jails funded by local taxes. Locally-elected sheriffs are encouraged to charge the state for the service of housing state felons, which facilitates overcrowding of state prisons. Local jobs and future political loyalties are created by floating big construction contracts for new prisons and jails (Christie 1993), even though the prisons may not be opened due to staffing costs, and jails may open only under court order as a result of overcrowding in prisons. In each case, elected officials are able to use correctional growth to build political strength in the electorate while passing costs on to other groups.

There are also organizational incentives that support penal growth. Probation and parole agencies can solve behavior problems and reduce their own workloads by revoking clients who violate their rules. Over half the prison admissions in some states are revocations of probation or parole. Collecting probation supervision fees is often a higher priority than managing risk, because the fees go directly into the probation budget (Baird 1986). Revocation and supervision priorities are organizational policies that shift goals away from fiscally prudent and programmatically effective practices (Robison & Takagi 1976).[64]

Eighteen states have recognized these incentive problems, and have sought to increase the use of less costly and often less harmful local correctional alternatives through Community Corrections Act legislation.[65] These acts' record for controlling costs and reducing penal harm has been mixed (Lerman 1975; Austin and Krisberg 1982), but there is enough good news to warrant the continued development and improvement of these approaches (Jones and Harris 1991). More radical and direct cost-control means could also be instituted on an experimental basis. For example, when judges impose a sentence that exceeds an established limit, for example that of a desert-based guideline, costs for the sentence might be supported by funds taken from court budgets; probation and parole could be charged for some of the costs of revocation.

In the end, systemic planning will be an essential component of any attempt to control the growth in the penal system. Fragmentation of authority and practice is widespread in corrections, so much so that piecemeal approaches to change usually backfire. The Edna-McConnell Clark Foundation's State Centered Program (1993) is based on the principle of inter-agency planning across institutional, judicial, and field service components of both adult and juvenile justice systems. The National Institute of Corrections, in its various projects to design and implement intermediate sanctions, has advocated establishing inter-agency coordinating boards to ensure the new programs meet the needs of the system. Significant budget implications of these strategies include sufficient staff support for planning personnel and sufficient information (across justice disciplines) with which to plan.

Research

Compared to other priorities, we spend little to learn about crime and how to deal with it. For every federal dollar spent on health research, we spend less than a half a penny on crime research. The National Institute for Dental Research receives a budget six times that of the National Institute of Justice; the National Eye Institute's budget is ten times bigger. It would take a seven-fold increase to make the federal crime research budget equal to its humanities research budget (see Petersilia 1991).

However, even a major increase in support for research and development on crime problems will benefit us little without a simultaneous depoliticization of the federal crime research bureaucracy. The federal government has molded the crime research agenda into a finely-honed tool of politics, and in doing so goes far beyond any practice justified by electoral mandate. Over the last 12 years, topics for research were increasingly selected based on how well they fit the 'get tough' philosophy of the Justice Department. Recommendations of external scholars and internal professional staff as to which research deserves support—though routinely solicited by the government—have been for the most part ignored.[66]

A long-term investment in improving our knowledge base would ask us to treat crime in the same way that we treat other public interest research priorities. We would put a research scientist, not a politician, in charge of the Research and Development program, and we would make better use of independent scholars to help us determine the research agenda and evaluate specific proposals for federal funding. There is also a need to encourage private foundations to develop a greater interest in funding programs and evaluations of responses to crime (foundations should have a natural interest in this area, since crime and punishment have impact on quality of life).[67]

Topics under study would broaden as well. The impact of short-term crime prevention practices would remain of interest to researchers. Long-term studies of communities and crime would be given a priority because they would help us see the impact of demographics on crime; such ethnographic studies would help us understand better the nature of crime. The impact on crime of policies not primarily housed in the justice system needs greater study; health, education, family supports, jobs, and income-maintenance programs all deserve our attention. We also need to study criminal careers to learn the factors that delay onset and increase desistence rates, because early results of these studies are promising (see West 1978; Loeber et al. 1991).

FINAL COMMENT: A REASON FOR OPTIMISM

In my introduction to this book, I said it was first drafted in 1990–91, when I was on a sabbatical made necessary by my profound dismay at the trends of the U.S. penal system. Some of these trends continue: the prison population grew in 1991–94 at about the same rate as it has for more than a decade—mostly as a result of drug offenders sentenced within the Federal system. The regular call of this or that politician for "tough measures" continues to be heard. Life in our cities deteriorates; budgets to confront problems that cause crime continue to be cut.

But those of us with our ears to the ground might also feel a reason for optimism. News coverage that reports the failure of tough policies is improving; editorial space is devoted to the issue and increasingly calls for an end to the more draconian sentencing policies of the past 20 years. Professional leadership in the field has reached a consensus and now speaks almost as a single voice against the wisdom of further expansions in our system of penal harms. Even some elected officials at the state and federal level are beginning to publicly wonder whether this expansion has been wise, and whether we ought to concentrate our limited crime-reducing resources elsewhere.

A debate is emerging, and I hope this book can be a part of that debate.

Notes

1. One problem of the penal harm strategy is that it scatters more widely than its intended target: spouses, partners, children and other family members—all innocent of the conduct leading to the harm—suffer not only shame and disappointment, but real losses in well-being as a result of an offender's conviction and punishment. Former inmate Bill Giddens observed:

> The mother of his children had become a crack addict, and . . . his 11-year old son and his 7-year-old daughter were separated and sent to live with what he believed were insensitive foster families. He became desperate to retrieve his children: "I felt they were doing time for what I had done." (Peter Kerr, "The Detoxing of Prisoner 88A0802." *The New York Times Magazine*, June 27, 1993: 27)

2. There is a hint of the tautological in this review of Feinberg: a penal harm cannnot be considered harmful because it would be illogical to criminalize this type of harm. Feinberg's purpose was not to decide whether punishments result in harm, but to provide a general theory of the types of harm that call for criminalization.

3. For example, one person spreads a rumor about another that results in damage to that person's reputation.

4. A case can be made that rehabilitation does not require penal harm, for it is based upon humanitarian aims with which the offender is sympathetic. This is often true, and therefore, in terms of penal harm, rehabilitation is the least objectionable of the utilitarian aims. But there are two problems with this argument. First, rehabilitative aims are often pursued through patently harmful techniques: negative reinforccments are frequently proposed as an effective treatment. Second, even the most indifferent treatment programs, when imposed coercively, harm autonomy—which is central to well being. But the point remains: rehabilitation is the only utilitarian aim that does not rely intentionally upon penal harm.

5. The case of a compulsion toward an illicit desire—which may be true for our hypothetical Tom—is a slightly different version of the same argument. This is illustrated in detail in Chapter 5, but the essential point is still the same: to interfere with a compulsion is not

the same as to punish for that compulsion. And it is hard to think of a serious compulsion that would need to be undisturbed in order to retain the person's prudential well-being.

6. The contemporary trend to add fines, penalty fees and supervision fees to community punishments illustrates the point. These penalties have no protective effect; they are merely harms against the offender's means for personal choices.

7. In the time since this report, several studies and authors have made the case that research on the effectiveness of rehabilitation deserves a more favorable review (Andrews 1990; Palmer 1992). I am inclined to agree with these arguments. Yet even the most supportive case for rehabilitation finds no more than small to moderate decreases in criminal behavior as a result of programs targeted for subgroups of offenders. An across-the-board crime reduction impact for all offenders is not claimed.

8. Writers have observed that it is here that classic utilitarian and retributive theories come together.

9. It may be that justice, thus defined, is an admirable end. But it is no less an end than public protection or 'the greatest good for 'the greatest number.' Why it is considered a preferable end might be a topic for debate, but clearly justice as an end, and the offender as an end are separable concepts.

10. The reader will note that in place of the term, *penal harm,* which has pervaded the discussion thus far, I will begin now to use the terms *punishment, corrections,* and *penal system.* The latter terms are more common usage and less cumbersome in the narrative of my argument, so for ease of presentation—and at kind suggestion of several readers of earlier drafts—I will use them. My emphasis and persistent use of the term in this opening chapter should, I hope, have made its point. What we are talking about is harms officially taken against law violators in our behalf, and conventional language about our actions should not mask that fact.

11. The experiment metaphor has been used by others, notably Currie (1989) and the National Research Council of the National Academy of Sciences (Reiss and Roth 1993), which has called the period from 1975–1989 "a case study for analyzing the effects of changes in the prison population on levels of violent crime" (292). I also want to recognize John Irwin's repeated use of the "punishment binge" metaphor in public speaking, and the later use of this conceptual frame in a recent book (Irwin and Austin 1993).

12. Having noted this wide disparity in tallies of crime, most writers proceed to argue that one is preferable to the other—and obviously they choose the one that most comports with the views they ultimately wish to express. Instead, I will use both measures, and see what conclusions flow from them.

13. The following estimates are used:

1) Probation data were unavailable for 1975–78, and 1980–82. Since the total growth rate of prisons and probation were nearly identical from 1973–1983, I used the annual growth rate of the prison system in each year to estimate the growth that may have occurred in the probation system.

2) Jail population data are unavailable for 1975–77 and 1979–1982. For the earlier period, I used the average annual growth rate from 1972–78 to estimate each year's changes—a technique that provides a consistent curve between the years with known data; for the later period I used the annual prison growth rate data, which jail rates mirror throughout the 20-year period.

3) Parole figures are unavailable for 1980–1982. To estimate growth in this period, I used the average annual rates from 1979–1983, which again provide a suitable curve to the data in known years.

Since changes from one year to the next in each of these periods are generally unimportant to my analysis, use of estimates should not be taken as a serious flaw in these data. They enable me to aggregate numbers across all correctional strategies, not just prison, and look at gross trends across time.

14. The only offenders whose sentences are expected to become shorter under the new code are those convicted of fraud.

15. It is worth mentioning, as an aside, that the pattern in England was quite different for that same time period; probabilities of incarceration and time served for property offenders actually declined.

16. It is interesting to note that the probability of arrest for a violent crime remained essentially constant throught the period 1975–1989 (Reiss and Roth, 1993: 292).

17. I will return to the idea of reintegration in chapter 5, and develop further the philosophical case to support it.

18. Today, there has been something of a rebirth of a belief in offender change. These new arguments are considered in chapter 5.

The point here is that in the 1970s a broad consensus against offender change arose among scholars, intellectuals and public figures.

19. Figures are not available for 1988–1990.

20. The attempt to make sure everyone got a copy left no mailing list untapped: I got 3 unsolicited copies in the mail.

21. In this section on criminologists, it should be recognized that among them there is a wide diversity of opinion about the offender control movement. Some participated actively, others wrote quite critically about these changes. I am referring, obviously, to the role played by participants in the offender/control agenda.

22. In a type of policy *non sequitur,* Texas Senator Phil Gramm used Reynold's study of predatory crime to advocate for mandatory penalties for Federal drug offenders ("Don't Let Judges Set Crooks Free." *NY Times,* July 8, 1993: A19).

23. An example of the deterioration in discussion of penal policy is provided by the change in *NIJ Reports,* an official publication that disseminates the latest in research on criminal justice to the field. In its May/June 1992 issue, it listed 13 free publications that might be of interest to corrections professionals. One was on preventing escapes. The other 12 had to do with cheaper or faster ways to build prisons and jails—almost as if no other correctional topic deserves mention. These are also the only listings for the July/August *NIJ Reports.*

24. It is actually a description of some of the forces that would reside in Factor X—chapter 2.

25. This is an 'all things being equal' estimate, which requires certain troublesome assumptions, such as (1) the increases in time served did not aggravate criminal careers after release, nor did it aggravate problems in the community that cause crime, and (2) the alternative to incarceration for these offenders would have been doing nothing.

26. My former teacher, Leslie Wilkins, is fond of saying about testing models, "Let's run them around the block and see if the wheels fall off." Perhaps these are models that have not survived that simple test.

27. These limitations all apply, assuming one accepts other assumptions underlying deterrence models, some of which are problematic. For a critique, see Tyler (1990).

28. Interestingly, research shows that most of the fluctuation in crime rates can be explained by changes in the age structure, especially

the size of the population in the criminally most active years (Steffens-meier and Harer 1991).

29. The Supreme Court has recently applied the Eighth Amendment to this practice, and set limits on the amount of property that can be seized.

30. When the 1992 figures came out showing a drop in most violent crimes except rape, the political forces were quick to claim the get tough approach was now working.

31. The selective use of studies was so baldfaced that one scholar said the report ". . . did not deserve to be dignified by a response" (Tonry, "General Barr's Last Stand." Overcrowded *Times*. 1993: 3).

32. The reader will see that I rely heavily on one particularly insightful treatment of these questions: the book by Hampton and Murphy (1988).

33. This is not true in England or Europe, as Maguire (1991) has pointed out. There, the victim movement has been more directed toward services than legal changes.

34. In fact, only New Zealand makes this public safety a right which leads to compensation when it is violated (Maguire, 1991).

35. And the culpability of the offender in causing the harm (von Hirsch 1976)

36. There is an extraordinary range among victims. Any general description of victims' needs will of necessity be broad and risk underestimating the importance of substantial differences among victims. For example, while every victim will experience some rage, not all will feel it or express it in the same way, nor will they dwell in it to the same degree. Victims are different in their personal predispositions and their resources to deal with crime. My model here is only a very general one.

37. One reviewer of this manuscript told me of other, similar experiences with victims who had turned their tragedies into positive change. He said it might strengthen this story to point out it is far from unique. This is undoubtedly so.

38. Radical criminologists have long maintained that the politicization of street crime emphasizes the criminal acts of the poor against each other and downplays the crimes of the wealthy against all of society (Reiman, *The Rich get Richer, the Poor get Prison*. 1984).

> By imprisoning certain types of people (especially lower class peo-
> ple, blacks and the young), capitalist forms of punishment create the
> belief that there is a 'class of criminals' who should be feared, not
> because of their actual behavior, but merely because they might
> exhibit criminal behavior. (Lynch and Groves 1986: 98)

Why is so much is made of an ordinary burglary that nets a
television set and is eventually recompensed by insurance or restitution, while so little is made of financial crimes that net billions
and create heart-breaking stories of destitution of elderly and other
vulnerable citizens? It is certainly convenient for elites that these
definitions of crime dominate public discourse.

Yet to attribute crime and its definitions to an entrenched elite is
to ignore, perhaps cruelly, the real experience of victims of predatory
crime; it degrades their loss and belittles their rage. This recognition
has led a number of influential radical criminologists to adopt a less
strident view they call "new realism," which emphasizes the lot of
the victim, and realizes that most victims of street crime are the very
underclass who most suffer under capitalism (Taylor and Young
1973).

39. I am tempted to ask the reader confidentially: "Have you
broken the law—used an illegal drug, misrepresented tax information,
taken sexual advantage of another, trespassed property, or worse—
knowingly, sometime in your life?" Of what relevance is the reader's
answer to the question? At a minimum, it casts doubts on the accuracy
of the common view that criminals are "them" and victims are "us."

40. In making this point, I am not insisting that we all have a
little Charles Manson within us. Instead I want to challenge the idea
that there are two clearly demarcated communities of the righteous
and the wicked. The existence of a small number of highly predatory
criminals should not obscure the fact that most crime is committed
by ordinary people, and that most ordinary people commit crimes at
one time or another.

41. We know this to be true because, in fact, the hidden secret is
that we have offended.

42. Without really saying it directly, the community protection
model has a kind of conspiratorial flavor when it portrays a vast
majority of good citizens immobilized by fear of a tiny minority of
cruel, remorseless victimizers. In 1990, with 770,000 people in prison,
another 400,000 in jails, and another three million under the scrutiny
of probation or parole agents, it seems no longer reasonable to think
of the criminal as rare in our society. If the community protection

model demands that we find the bad guys and separate them from the rest of us, we must wonder if the number of criminals is not in fact such a small minority after all. Statistics support a sober appraisal of the scope of the problem: it is estimated that less than 1 in 100 crimes results in an incarceration (Zeisel 1982: 17–18). If the model could really ever fully be realized, and all the citizens who show a willingness to treat others as victims could be found and removed, it is reasonable to ask whether the remainder would be a small minority, indeed.

43. And less than worthy of citizenship.

44. When, in 1989, the Boston police rampaged through Roxbury to find the black murderer of Carole Stuart, the image of the lone black who wantonly violates white people was so burned in the public consciousness that the fury of the mobs seemed an understandable reaction. The shock: the real criminal was her husband; the real motive, money. It shocked, because it contradicted deeply held prejudices about who attacks white women (Sharkey 1991). Likewise, when the Gulf War veteran, Anthony Riggs, was shot dead in Detroit, an alarmed public rose up in revolt against the drug-based random violence they were certain was the cause. When it turned out the real murderers were family members, people were stunned by the way the truth mocked their enraged, self-righteous indignation.

45. In addition to the damages of divisiveness, racism, and anti-democratic action, the community protection model of crime control results in a misdirection of resources toward instruments of separation such as the prison, to the exclusion of alternative strategies that could improve communities. Investments in communities might instead focus resources on schools, child development, mental health, employment, housing, and basic health. These are all community needs that are drastically underfunded and which continue to languish even as we increase spending on prisons and jails. These are all ills against which communities need protection. Yet in the 1980s, spending on all these community services dropped or remained stagnant, while spending on corrections increased by two-thirds (Austin, 1990). It is ironic that the rhetoric of community protection allows political leaders to ignore these needs of community.

46. Feeley and Simson (1992) have referred to the philosophy that took the place of reintegration as "a kind of waste management function" (470).

47. The situational model is not a panacea, of course, and it is not presented here as a potential new breakthrough in crime fighting.

Instead, it is used here as a way of showing how realistic concerns about crime need not focus merely upon the criminal. When the focus is broadened, new and important insights about crime often emerge.

48. While some enthusiasts for the prevention model may, in their excess, feel that the person who leaves his keys in his car or the homeowner who leaves her front door open when nobody is home deserves little sympathy, the scrutiny of victims seems less reasonable when the crime is a violent attack such as rape or another type of assault.

49. In the literal meaning of the term, not necessarily in its legal reasoning.

50. I borrow this term from Cohen (1985).

51. The reader is so reminded from chapter 1, where the case was made that an interest in the offender's well-being does not condone, excuse, or allow his criminally harming acts.

52. Incidently, a case can be made that removing offenders from the streets can add to community social disorganization by increasing family disintegration. Social disorganization may, in turn, promote more crime (Bursik and Grasmick 1993).

53. One reviewer of an earlier draft of the manuscript urged me to use two different illustrations, because they would provide a stronger challenge to the integrative model: so-called "power" rapists and for-profit burglars.

These two types of offenders would offer a different set of issues than those I have chosen. With the power rapist, the stakes for the community would be higher (though initial punishment followed by intensive treatment/monitoring for a very long period using relapse prevention strategies would be similar). The for-profit burglar would represent the same array of interests, but obviously the intervention issues would focus on control and substitution of legitimate means of acquisition. The literature for the alternatives would overlap with that presented here.

In the end, I have stayed with these examples because they are clearly offenses representing serious danger, and there is a role for penal harm in each. I think they illustrate my central point about integrative community protection.

54. The argument has been made that the drug suppression policy causes most of the problems of drug-related crime in the United States (Benson and Rasmussen 1991). These criticisms of

contemporary drug policy raise, without expressly saying so, the very appeal to integrationist arguments that define the alternative community protection view. My analysis of drug-dependent offenders will be based upon current legal policy—though strong arguments exist to change that policy.

55. Current thinking calls for treatment to begin in secure residential communities, followed by continuing treatment within the community.

56. Compare Wilbanks (1986) to literature review and analysis in Nelson (1991) for an illustration of the debate. However, the most convincing book in the area is Mann's (1993) analysis of race and justice, which defines the scope of the problem and shows how racial disparities in criminal justice actually work.

57. No doubt the decision also stems from considerable dismay shared by the membership regarding certain irrational policies.

58. RAND's Center is partly funded by federal research grants.

59. Here I borrow from my teacher and colleague, Don Gottfredson.

60. There is also the point that two different definitions of *equity* exist in our minds. One is to treat similar persons similarly; the other is to treat persons in ways that fit their lives. People may be treated differently and equitably, if we can show that the treatment fits them according to some moral criteria. The criterion might include the "social well-being" idea I have advocated in this chapter.

61. The Sentencing Project has begun a Call For A Rational Debate on Crime and Punishment.

62. And so we might be obligated to make the harms during those two years as inconsequential as we could, knowing we will be transgressing the desert limit on time.

63. Ralph Waldo Emerson wrote that "a foolish consistency is the hobgoblin of little minds."

64. Parole abolition schemes also throw off the distribution of incentives: "Eliminating or reducing the power of parole boards over the release of prisoners removed a significant means of controlling prison population from the level of government responsible for the cost of the prison system" (Zimring and Hawkins 1990: 212).

65. Alabama, Arizona, Colorado, Connecticut, Florida, Indiana, Iowa, Kansas, Michigan, Minnesota, Montana, New Mexico, Ohio, Oregon, Pennsylvania, Tennessee, Texas, Virginia.

66. Often, tentatively-approved studies languish on someone's desk without funding, until a Federal legislator or state-elected official calls to apply some political pressure. Under this regime, research is heavily focussed on short-term political payoff—the most recent example was the gutting of the crime research budget to fund the so-called "drug war."

67. Two recent cooperative efforts of government and foundations illustrate what can be done. The MacArthur Foundation and the National Institute of Justice are collaboratively sponsoring a lengthy and expensive cohort study; the Edna McConnell-Clark Foundation and the National Institute of Corrections co-funded the Prison Overcrowding Project.

References

Abel, Gene G. 1984. *The treatment of child molesters.* New York: SCV-TM.

Ackerman, Bruce. 1982. *Social justice in the liberal state.* New Haven: Yale University Press.

Adler, Freda. 1983. *Nations not obsessed with crime.* Littleton, Colo.: Fred B. Rothman.

Adler, Jacob. 1991. *The urgings of conscience.* Philadelphia: Temple University Press.

Allen, Francis A. 1964. *The decline of the rehabilitative ideal: penal policy and social purpose.* New Haven: Yale University Press.

American Bar Association. 1966. *Standards relating to prosecution.* Chicago, Ill.: American Bar Association.

American Friends Service Committee. 1971. *Struggle for justice. A report on crime and punishment in America.* New York: Hill and Wang.

Andrews, Don, Ivan Zinger, Robert D. Hoge, James Bonta, Paul Gendreau, and Francis T. Cullen. 1990. Does treatment work? A clinically relevant and psychologically informed meta-analysis, *Criminology* 28, 369–404.

Andrews, Don and James Bonta. 1993. *The psychology of criminal conduct.* Cincinnati: Anderson Publishing Company.

Andrews, Don, James Bonta, and Robert D. Hoge. 1990. "Classification for effective rehabilitation," *Criminal Justice and Behavior* 17:1, 19–52.

Anglin, Douglas, and Hser Yih-ing. 1990. *Treatment of drug abuse.* In Michael Tonry and James Q. Wilson, eds. *Drugs and crime,* vol. 13. Crime and Justice series. Chicago: University of Chicago Press: 393–460.

Archer, Dane, and Rosemary Gartner. 1984. *Violence and crime in a cross-national perspective.* New Haven: Yale University Press.

Ashworth, Andrew. 1983. *Sentencing and penal policy.* London: Weidenfeld and Nicholson.

Asimov, Isaac. 1950 *I, robot.* New York: Basic Books.

——. 1960. *Kingdom of the sun.* New York: Basic Books.

——. *Robots of dawn.* New York: Basic Books.

Austin, James, and David Killman. 1990. *America's growing correctional-industrial complex.* San Francisco: National Council on Crime and Delinquency.

——. 1993. *Reforming Florida's unjust, costly, and ineffective sentencing laws.* San Francisco: National Council on Crime and Delinquency.

——, and Barry Krisberg. 1982. The unmet promise of alternatives to incarceration. *Crime and Delinquency* 28, 374–409.

——, Mike Jones and Aaron David McVey. 1991. *The 1991 NCCD prison population forecast: the impact of the war on drugs.* NCCD Focus. San Francisco: National Council on Crime and Delinquency.

——, and Marci Brown. 1989. *Ranking the nation's most punitive states.* NCCD Focus, San Francisco: National Council on Crime and Delinquency.

Avi-Itzhak, Benjamin, and Revel Shinnar. 1973. Quantitative models in crime control. *Journal of Criminal Justice* 1, 185–217.

Bailey, Walter C. 1966. Correctional outcome: an evaluation of 100 reports. *Journal of Criminal Law, Criminology and Police Science* 57:2, 153–160.

Baird, S. Christopher. 1993. *The "prisons pay" studies: research or ideology?* NCCD Focus. San Francisco: National Council on Crime and Delinquency.

——. 1989. *Analysis of the diversionary impact of the Florida Community Control Program.* Madison: National Council on Crime and Delinquency.

——. 1986. *Fees for probation services.* Report by the National Council on Crime and Delinquency to the National Institute of Corrections. Madison: National Council on Crime and Delinquency.

——. 1984. *Classification of juveniles in corrections: a model systems approach.* Washington, D.C.: Arthur D. Little.

Ball, John C. 1980. The impact of heroin addiction upon criminality.

Problems of drug dependence 1979. Washington, D.C.: U.S. National Institute of Drug Abuse.

——, James Shaffer, and Dennis Nurco. 1983. The day-to-day criminality of heroin addicts in Baltimore: a study in the continuity of offense rates. *Drug and Alcohol Dependence* 12, 119–142.

——, L. Rosen, J. Flueck, and D. Nurco. 1982. Lifetime criminality of heroin addicts in the United States. *Journal of Drug Issues* 3, 225–239.

Ball, Richard A., Ronald C. Huff, and Robert J. Lilly. 1988. *House arrest and correctional policy: doing time at home.* Newbury Park, Calif.: Sage Publications.

Bard, Morton, and Dawn Sangrey. 1986. *The crime victim's book.* 2nd ed. New York: Brunner/Mazel Publishers.

Barnes, Harry Elmer, and Negley K. Teeters. 1959. *New horizons in criminology.* Englewood Cliffs, N.J.: Prentice-Hall.

Barr, William P. 1992. *Combatting violent crime.* Washington, D.C.: U.S. Department of Justice. (July 28)

——. 1992. *The case for more incarceration.* Washington, D.C.: U.S. Department of Justice. (October)

Baumer, Terry L. 1990. *The electronic monitoring of non-violent convicted felons: an experiment in home detention.* Final report. Indianapolis: School of Public Affairs and Environmental Affairs, Indiana University.

——. 1989. "Electronic monitoring: an interim report." Paper presented to the Academy of Criminal Justice Sciences, San Francisco. (March)

Bean, Philip T. 1991. British to reduce prison population by 35–50 percent. *Overcrowded Times.* 2:6 (November) 1–2.

Becker, Howard S. 1963. *Outsiders: studies in social deviance.* Glencoe, Ill.: Free Press.

Bellringer, The. 1987. Pennsylvania Burglar and Fire Alarm Association Newsletter Dowington, Penn. (April) 3.

Benn, S. I. 1958. An approach to the problems of punishment. *Philosophy* 33, 325–41.

——, and R. S. Peters. 1959. *Social principles and the democratic state.* London: Allen & Unwin.

Benson, Bruce L., and David Rasmussen. 1991. Relationship between illicit drug enforcement policy and property crimes. *Contemporary Policy Issues* 9, 106–115.

Bentham, Jeremy. 1982. *An introduction to the principles and morals of legislation.* London: Methuen.

Blumstein, Alfred, Jacqueline Cohen, Jeffrey A. Roth, and Christy Visher, eds. 1986. *Criminal careers and "career criminals."* Washington, D.C.: National Academy Press.

———. ed. 1978. *Deterrence and incapacitation: estimating the effects of criminal sanctions on crime rates.* Washington, D.C.: National Research Council.

———. 1993. Making rationality relevant—the American Society of Criminology presidential address. *Criminology* 31:1, 1–16.

———, Jacqueline Cohen, and Daniel Nagin. 1978. *Deterrence and incapacitation: estimating the effects of criminal sanctions on crime rates.* Washington, D.C.: National Research Council.

———, and Jacqueline Cohen. 1973. A theory of the stability of punishment. *Journal of Criminal Law & Criminology* 64, 198–207.

Boggess, Scott and John Bound. 1993. *Did Criminal activity increase during the 1980s? Comparisons across data sources.* Research report no. 93-280, University of Michigan Population Studies Center. July.

Boland, Barbara. 1990. *The prosecution of felony arrests.* Washington, D.C.: U.S. Department of Justice, Bureau of Justice Statistics.

Box, Steven. 1987. *Recession, crime and punishment.* London: Macmillan.

———, and Chris Hale. 1982. Economic crisis and the rising prisoner population. *Crime and Social Justice* 17, 20–35.

———, and Chris Hale. 1985. Unemployment, imprisonment, and prison overcrowding. *Contemporary Crisis* 9, 209–28.

Branham, Lynn S. 1992. *The use of incarceration in the United States.* Chicago: American Bar Association.

Braithwaite, John. 1979. *Inequality, crime and public policy.* London: Routledge and Kegan Paul.

———. 1989. *Crime, shame and reintegration.* New York: Cambridge University Press.

———. 1984. *Corporate crime in the pharmaceutical industry*. London: Routledge and Kegan Paul.

———, and V. Braithwaite. 1980. The effect of income inequality and social democracy on homicide. *British journal of criminology* 20: 45–53.

———, and Philip Pettit. 1990. *Not just deserts: a republican theory of criminal justice*. Oxford: Clarendon Press.

Bright, Jon. 1992. *Crime prevention in America: a British perspective*. Chicago: University of Illinois Press.

Brownmiller, Susan. 1975. *Against our will: men, women and rape*. New York: Simon and Schuster.

Brownstein, Henry H., and Paul J. Goldstein. 1990. Research and the Development of public policy: the case of drugs and violent crime. *Journal of Applied Sociology* 7, 77–79.

Bruck, Connie. 1991. "The world of business: no one like me," *The New Yorker* (March 11), 40–68.

Bukstel, Lee H., and Peter R. Kilman. 1980. Psychological effects of imprisonment on confined individuals. *Psychological Bulletin* 88 (3), 469–93.

Bureau of Justice Assistance. 1993. *Survey of state prison inmates, 1991*. Washington, D.C.: U.S. Department of Justice.

Bureau of Justice Statistics. 1990. *Criminal victimization: 1989*. Washington, D.C.: U.S. Department of Justice.

Burgess, Anne Wolbert. 1985. *Rape and sexual assault*. NY: Garland Publishing Company.

Burgess, Robert L, and Patricia Draper. 1989. The explanation of family violence: the role of biological behavioral and cultural selection. In Lloyd Ohlin and Michael Tonry, eds. *Family Violence*. Chicago: University of Chicago Press.

Burton, Velmer S., Francis T. Cullen, and Lawrence F. Travis III. 1986. The collateral consequences of felony convictions: a national study of state statutes. *Federal Probation* 51 (3), 52–60.

Bursik, Robert J., and Harold G. Grasmick. 1993. *Neighborhood crimes: the dimensions of effective community control*. New York: Lexington.

Byrne, James, Arthur Lurigio, and S. Christopher Baird. 1989. *The effectiveness of the new intensive supervision programs* (Research report No. 5). Washington, D.C.: National Institute of Corrections.

California Blue Ribbon Commission on Inmate Population Management. 1990. *Final report of the Blue Ribbon Commission on Inmate Management.* Sacramento: Governor's Office.

Campbell, Anne. 1993. *Men, women and aggression.* New York: Basic Books.

Casper, Johnathan D., David Brerton, and D. Neal. 1982. *Implementation of the California determinate sentencing law.* Washington, D.C.: U.S. Department of Justice.

Caulkins, Jonathon P., Gordon Crawford, and Peter Reuter. 1993. *Simulation of adaptive response.* Santa Monica: Rand Corporation.

Center for Women Policy Studies. 1991. *Violence against women.* Washington, D.C.: Center for Women Policy Studies.

Chaiken, Marcia R., and Bruce Johnson. 1988. *Characteristics of different types of drug-involved offenders.* Washington, D.C.: U.S. National Institute of Justice.

Chaiken, Jan M., and Marcia R. Chaiken. 1982. *Varieties of criminal behavior: summary and policy implications.* Santa Monica: Rand Corporation.

――――. 1990. Drugs and predatory crime. In Michael Tonry and James J. Wilson, eds., *Drugs and crime.* Chicago: University of Chicago Press.

Chiricos, Theodore G., and Miriam A DeLone. 1992. Labor surplus and punishment: a review and assessment of theory and evidence. *Social Problems* 39:4, 421–46.

Christie, Nils. 1981. *Limits to pain.* Oslo: Universitetflag.

――――. 1993. *Crime as industry.* Oslo: Universitetflag.

Clarke, Ronald V., ed., 1993. *Situational crime prevention: successful case studies.* New York: Harrow and Heston.

Clear, Todd R. 1988. Statistical prediction in corrections. *Research in corrections.* Washington, D.C.: National Institute of Corrections.

――――, Val B. Clear, and Anthony Braga, 1993. Intermediate sanctions for drug offenders. *The Prison Journal* 73:2 (June) 178–98.

――――. and George F. Cole. 1994. *American corrections.* 3rd ed. Pacific Grove, CA: Brooks/Cole.

————, and Patricia L. Hardyman. 1990. The new intensive supervision movement, *Crime and delinquency* 36 (1), 42–60.

————. John Hewitt, and Robert M. Regoli. 1978. Discretion and the determinate sentence: its distribution, control, and effect on time served. *Crime and Delinquency* 24, 428–45.

————, and Vincent O'Leary. 1983. *Controlling the offender in the community: reforming the community supervision function.* Lexington, Mass.: Lexington.

Clines, Frances X. 1992. Ex-Inmate's urge return to areas of crime to help. *New York Times* (December 23), 1ff.

Cloward, Richard A., and Lloyd E. Ohlin. 1960. *Delinquency and opportunity; a theory of delinquent gangs.* Glencoe, IL: Free Press.

Cohen, Albert K. 1955. *Delinquent boys: the culture of the gang.* Glencoe, Ill.: Free Press.

Cohen, Jacqueline, and Jose A. Canelo-Cacho. 1993. Patterns in incarceration and crime: 1965–1988. In Albert J. Reiss and Jeffrey Roth, eds. *Understanding and preventing violence:* dimensions and consequences. Volume IV: Report of the National Research Council of the National Academy of Sciences. Washington, D.C.: National Academy Press.

Cohen, Stanley. 1988. *Against criminology,* New Brunswick, N.J.: Transaction Books.

————. 1985. *Visions of social control.* Cambridge, Eng.: Polity Press.

————. 1979. The punitive city: notes on the dispersal of social control. *Contemporary Crisis,* 339–63.

Cohn, Ellen G., and David P. Farrington. 1990. Differences between British and American criminology: an analysis of citations. *British Journal of Criminology* 30: 467–82.

Cole, George F. 1988. The use of fines by trial court judges. *Judicature* 71 (6), 1–8.

Colorado Department of Corrections. 1989. *Annual statistical report, fiscal year, 1988–1989.* Colorado Springs, Colo.

Colorado Department of Corrections. 1980. *Annual statistical Report, fiscal year 1979–1980.* Colorado Springs, Colo.

Combes, James. 1981. A process approach. in Dan Nimmo, Keith

Sanders, eds. *Handbook of political communications*. Beverly Hills, CA: Sage.

Conley, John A. 1980. Prisons, production and profit: reconsidering the importance of prison industries. *Journal of Social History* 14:3, 251–73.

Cook, R., B. Smith, and A. Harrell. 1987. *Helping crime victims: levels of trauma and effectiveness of services*. Washington, D.C.: U.S. Department of Justice.

Cornish, Derek B., and Ronald V. Clarke. 1986. *The reasoning criminal: rational choice perspectives on offending*. New York: Springer-Verlag.

Courtois, Christine A. 1988. *Healing the incest wound: adult survivors in therapy*. New York: Norton.

Cullen, Francis, and Karen Gilbert. 1982. *Reaffirming rehabilitation*. Cincinnati: Anderson Publishing.

Cunningham, W. C., and T. H. Taylor. 1984. *The growing role of private security*. Washington, D.C.: U.S. Department of Justice.

Currie, Elliot. 1985. *Confronting crime: an American challenge*. New York: Pantheon.

Davis, Robert C. 1987. *Providing help to victims: a study of psychological and material outcomes*. New York: Victim's Services Agency.

Davis, R., and M. Henley. 1990. Victim services programs. In Arthur Lurigio, R. Davis, and Wesley Skogan, eds., *Crime victims: problems, programs and policies*. Beverly Hills: Sage.

DeLeon, G. 1984. Alcohol use among drug abusers: treatment outcomes in a therapeutic community. *Alcoholism Clinical and Experimental Research* 11, 430–36.

DePanfilis, Diane. 1986. *Literature review of sexual abuse*. Washington, D.C.: Clearinghouse on Child Abuse and Neglect Information.

DiIulio, John. 1991. *No way out: the future of American corrections*. New York Basic Books.

———. 1990. *Crime and punishment in Wisconsin: a survey of prisoners*. Milwaukee: Wisconsin Policy Research Institute. (December)

———, and Anne Morrison Piehl. 1991. Does prison pay? *The Brookings Journal*. (Fall)

DiNardo, John. 1993. Law enforcement and the price of cocaine use. *Mathematical and computer modelling* 17 (2) 56–64.

Duff, Anthony. 1990. Punishment, repentance and forgiveness, David Garland, ed. *Justice, guilt and forgiveness in the penal system*. Occasional Paper No. 18. New College, Edinburgh: Center for Theology and Public Issues.

Duff, R. A. 1986. *Trials and punishments*. Cambridge, Mass.: Cambridge University Press.

Duffee, David E. 1980. *Explaining criminal justice: community theory and criminal justice reform*. Cambridge, Mass.: Oelgeschliger, Gunn and Hain.

————, and Vincent O'Leary. 1971. Models of corrections: an entry in the Packer-Griffith debate. *Criminal Law Bulletin* 7:4, 329–52.

Durkheim, Emile. 1964. *The rules of the sociological method*. New York: Free Press.

Dworkin Ronald. 1981. What is equality, part I. *Philosophy and public affairs* 10 (2), 185–246.

————. 1979. *A matter of principle*. Cambridge, Mass.: Harvard University Press.

Edelman, Murray. 1971. *Politics as symbolic action: mass arousal and acquiescence*. New York: Academic Press.

Elias, Robert. 1983. *Victims of the system*. New Brunswick, N.J.: Transaction.

————. 1986. *The politics of victimization: victims, victimology and human rights*. New York: Oxford University Press.

Erez, Edna. 1990. Victim participation in sentencing: rhetoric and reality. *Journal of Criminal Justice* 18, 19–31.

————, and Pamela Tontonado. 1990. The effect of victim participation in sentencing on sentence outcome. *Criminology* 28, 451–74.

Erikson, Kai T. 1966. *Wayward Puritans: a study in the sociology of deviance*. New York: Wiley.

Erwin, Billie S. 1984. *Evaluation of Intensive probation supervision in Georgia*. Atlanta: Georgia Department of Offender Rehabilitation.

Fagan, Jeffrey. 1990. Intoxication and Aggression. In *Drugs and Crime*, edited by Michael Tonry and James Q. Wilson. Chicago: University of Chicago Press.

Fagel, David. 1979. *We are the living proof . . . the justice model for corrections,* 2nd ed. Cincinnati: Anderson Publishing Co.

Farrington, David P. 1985. Predicting self-reported and official delinquency. In *Prediction in Criminology,* edited by David P. Farrington and Roger Tarling. Albany: State University of New York Press.

———. 1986. *The Cambridge study on delinquency: long-term follow-up.* Cambridge: Cambridge University Press.

———. 1981. The Prevalence of convictions. *British Journal of Criminology* 21, 173–75.

———, and Patrick A. Langan. 1992. Changes in crime and punishment in England and Wales. *Justice Quarterly* 9:1, 5–46.

———, and Richard Tarling. 1985. *Prediction in criminology.* Albany: State University of New York Press.

———, and Donald J. West. 1984. The Cambridge study in delinquent development. In Saul Mednick and Alan Baert, eds., *Prospective longitudinal research.* New York: Oxford University Press.

Fattah, E. A., and U. F. Sacco. 1989. *Crime and victimization of the elderly.* New York: Springer-Verlag.

Faupel, Charles E. 1992. *Shooting dope: career patterns of hard core heroin users.* Gainesville: University of Florida.

Federal Bureau of Prisons. 1991. *National prisoner statistics bulletin No. 46. capital punishment 1930–1970.* Washington, D.C.: U.S. Department of Justice.

Federal Office for Victims of Crime—[within in Office of Justice Programs] created—1983.

Feeley, Malcolm M. 1979. *The process is the punishment: handling cases in a lower criminal court.* New York: Russell Sage Foundation.

Feeley, Malcolm, and Jonathon Simson. 1993. The new penology: notes on the emerging strategy of corrections and its implications. *Criminology* 30:4, 449–71.

Feinberg, Joel. 1988. *The moral limits of the criminal law: harmless wrongdoing.* New York: Oxford University Press.

———. 1986. *The moral limits of the criminal law: harm to self.* New York: Oxford University Press.

———. 1985. *The moral limits of criminal law: offense to others.* New York: Oxford University Press.

———. 1984. *The moral limits of the criminal law: harm to others.* New York: Oxford University Press.

———. 1984. *Harm to others.* New York: Oxford University Press.

———. 1970. *Doing and deserving; essays in the theory of responsibility.* Princeton: Princeton University Press.

Felson, Marcus. 1987. Routine activities and crime prevention in the developing metropolis. *Criminology* 25:4, 911–31.

Field, Simon. 1990. *Trends in crime and their interpretation.* London: Her Majesty's Stationery Office.

Finckenauer, James O. 1982. *Scared straight: and the panacea phenomenon.* Englewood Cliffs, N.J.: Prentice-Hall.

———. 1978. Crime as a national political issue: 1964–1976—from law and order to domestic tranquility. *Crime and Delinquency* 24:1, 13–28.

Finkelhor, David. 1979. *Sexually victimized children.* New York: Free Press.

———. 1984. *Child sexual abuse: new theory and research.* New York: Free Press.

———, Sharon Araji, and Larry Baron. 1986. *A sourcebook on child sexual abuse.* Beverly Hills: Sage.

Fischer, D. R. 1983. Better public protection with fewer inmates? *Corrections Today* 45, 16–20.

———. 1984. *Risk assessment: sentencing based on probabilities.* Des Moines: Statistical Analysis Center, Iowa Office for Planning and Programming.

Flew, Anthony G. N. 1954. The justification of punishment. *Philosophy* 29, 291–307.

Flowers, Ronald B. 1986. *Children and criminality. The child as a victim and perpetrator.* New York: Greenwood Press.

———. 1988. *Minorities and criminality.* New York: Greenwood Press.

Fogel, David. 1979. *We are the living proof. . . : the justice model for corrections.* Cincinnati: Anderson.

———. 1988. *On doing less harm: Western European alternatives to incarceration.* Chicago: Office of International Criminal Justice, University of Illinois, Chicago.

Ford, Paul Leicester. 1988. *The federalist: A commentary on the Constitution of the United States*. New York: Holt.

Foucault, Michael. 1977. *Discipline and punish: the birth of a prison*. New York: Pantheon.

Frankel, Marvin E. 1973. *Criminal sentences; law without order*. New York: Hill and Wang.

Furman v. Georgia 408 U.S. 238 (1972).

Garland, David. 1990. *Punishment in modern society: a study in social theory*. Chicago: University of Chicago Press.

Gendreau, Paul, and Bob Ross. 1979. Effective correctional treatment; biblio therapy for cynics. *Crime and Delinquency* 25, 463–89.

Gibbs, Jack P. 1975. *Crime, punishment and deterrence*. New York: Elsevier.

Gibbs, John J. 1990. Lager louts: violence in English pubs. Paper presented to the Cambridge University Centre for Criminology. London, November 23.

Glaser, Daniel. 1955. The efficacy of alternative approaches to parole prediction. *American Sociological Review* 20, 283–87.

Glueck, Sheldon, and Eleanor T. Glueck. 1930. *Five hundred criminal careers*. New York: Knopf.

———. 1934. *Five hundred delinquent women*. New York: Knopf.

Golub, Andrew. 1992. *Desistance of criminal careers*. Paper presented to the Rutgers University, School of Criminal Justice Colloquim series. Newark, New Jersey, February 17.

———. 1990. *The termination rate of adult criminal careers*. Pittsburgh: School of Urban and Public Affairs, Carnegie-Mellon University. (April 13)

Goodstein, Lynne, and John R. Hepburn. 1985. *Determinate sentencing and imprisonment: a failure of reform*. Cincinnati: Anderson.

Gordon, Diana R. 1990. *The justice juggernaut: fighting street crime, controlling citizens*. New Brunswick, N.J.: Rutgers University Press.

Gordon, M. T., and E. Reiger. 1989. *The female fear*. New York: Free Press.

Gorecki, Jan. 1979. *A theory of criminal justice*. New York: Columbia University Press.

Gottfredson, Don M. 1987. Prediction and classification in criminal justice decision making. In *Prediction and classification,* edited by Don M. Gottfredson and Michael Tonry. Chicago: University of Chicago Press.

————, and Michael Tonry. 1987. *Prediction and classification: criminal justice decision making.* Chicago: University of Chicago Press.

Gottfredson, Michael, and John M. Goldkamp. 1990. Some consumer guidelines for prison alternatives. In *Policy and theory in criminal justice,* edited by D. M. Gottfredson and R. V. Clarke. Avebury: Gower Publishing.

————. 1979. Treatment destruction techniques. Journal of Research in Crime and Delinquency 16, 39–54.

————, and Travis Hirschi. 1990. *A general theory of crime.* Stanford: Stanford University Press.

————, and Travis Hirschi. 1986. The true value of lambda would appear to be zero: an essay on career criminals, criminal careers, selective incapacitation, cohort studies, and related topics. *Criminology* 24, 213–34.

Gottfredson, Stephen D. 1987. Prediction: an overview of selected methodological issues. In *Prediction and classification,* edited by Don M. Gottfredson and Michael Tonry. Chicago: University of Chicago Press.

————, and Don M. Gottfredson. 1986. Accuracy of prediction models. In *Criminal careers and career criminals,* edited by Alfred Blumstein, Jacqueline Cohen, Jeffrey A. Roth, and Christy A. Visher. Washington, D.C.: National Academy Press.

————, and Don M. Gottfredson. 1992. *Incapacitation strategies and the criminal career.* LEIG Monograph Series, edition 8. Sacramento, CA.

Greenberg, David F. 1975. Problems in community corrections, *Issues in Criminology* 10, 1 (Spring).

————. 1991. Modeling criminal careers. *Criminology* 29:1, 17–46.

————, and Drew Humphries, 1980. The cooptation of fixed sentencing reform. *Crime and Delinquency* 26, 2 206–25.

Greenwood, Peter W. 1982. *Selective incapacitation.* Santa Monica: Rand Corporation.

Greenwood, Peter, and Susan Turner. 1987. *Selective incapacitation revisited: why the high rate offenders are hard to predict.* Santa Monica: Rand Corporation.

Gregg Power Company v. Georgia, 428 U.S. 153 (1976).

Griffin, James. 1986. *Well-being: its meaning, measurement, and moral importance.* Oxford, Eng.: Clarendon.

Griset, Pamela L., *Determinate sentencing: the promise and reality of retributive Justice.* Albany: State University of New York Press.

Griswold, Jack H., and Mike Misenheimer. 1970. Art Powers and Ed Tromanhausef. *An eye for an eye.* New York: Holt.

Gross, Hyman. 1979. *A theory of criminal justice.* New York: Oxford University Press.

Groth, A. N., and A. W. Burgess. 1979. Sexual trauma and the life histories of rapists and child molesters. *Victimology* 4, 10–17.

Groth, A. Nicholas. 1978. Patterns of sexual assault against children and adolescents. In *Sexual assaults of children and adolescents,* edited by A. W. Burgess. Lexington, Mass.: Lexington Books.

———. 1978. Guidelines for the assessment and management of the offender. In *Sexual assaults of children and adolescents,* edited by A. W. Burgess. Lexington, Mass.: Lexington Books.

Hale, Chris. 1989. Unemployment, imprisonment, and the stability of punishment hypothesis: some results using cointegration and error correction models. *Journal of Quantitative Criminology* 5:2, 169–86.

———, and Dina Sabbagh. 1991. Testing the relationship between unemployment and crime: a methodological comment and empirical analysis using time series data from England and Wales. *Journal of Research in Crime and Delinquency* 28, 400–17.

Hall, Jerome. 1960. *General principles of criminal law.* Indianapolis: Bobbs-Merrill.

Hammett, Theodore M. 1989. *AIDS in correctional facilities.* Washington, D.C.: U.S. National Institute of Justice.

Hampton, Jean. 1984. The moral education theory of punishment. *Philosophy and Public Affairs* (Summer), 245–73.

Harris, M. Kay. 1991. Moving into the new millenium: Toward a feminist vision of justice. In *Criminology as Peacemaking,* edited by H. Pepinsky and R. Quiey. Bloomington: Indiana University Press.

Hart, H. L. A. 1963. *Law, liberty and morality.* New York: Vintage.

———. 1961. *The concept of law.* Oxford: Oxford University Press.

Helmer, John. 1975. *Drugs and minority oppression.* New York: Seabury Press.

Hirschi, Travis, 1969. *The causes of delinquency.* Berkeley: University of California Press.

Hobbes, Thomas. 1937. *Leviathon,* London: J. M. Dent.

Honderich, Ted. 1984. *Punishment: the supposed justifications.* Harmondsworth, Eng.: Penguin.

Hope, Timothy, 1991. Construction of community safety and disorder. Paper presented to the American Society of Criminology, San Francisco. (November)

———, and Janet Foster, 1993. Conflicting forces: change: the dynamics of crime and community in a problem estate. Unpublished paper. Research and Planning Unit, British Home Office, London.

Hood, Roger. 1989. *The death penalty: a worldwide perspective.* Oxford, Eng.: Clarendon Press.

Hudson, Barbara. 1987. *Justice through punishment: a critique of the "justice" model of corrections.* New York: St. Martin's Press.

Hunter, Howard. 1991. *Man/child: An insight into child sexual abuse by a convicted molester, with a comprehensive resource guide.* London: McFarland.

Husak, Doug. 1987. *Philosophy of criminal law.* Totowa, N.J.: Rowman and Littlefield.

Hyde, Margaret. 1984. *Sexual abuse: let's talk about it.* Philadelphia: Westminister Press.

Ignatieff, Michael. 1978. *A just measure of pain: the penitentiary in the industrial revolution, 1750–1850.* New York: Pantheon.

Inciardi, James A. 1991. *The drug legalization debate.* Newbury Park, Calif.: Sage.

IRS Income tax compliance research. 1990. *New tax gap and remittance gap estimates.* Publication 1415 (4-90), Washington, D.C.

Irwin, John and James Austin. 1993. *Its about time: America's prison population crisis.* Belmont, CA: Wadsworth.

Isikoff, Michael. 1992. Debate rises on prison Furlough Counts. *Washington Post* (March 15), 28.

Jackson, George. 1972. *Blood in my eye.* New York: Random House.

Jain, Ranjana S. 1990. The victim-offender relationship in family violence. In *The victimology handbook,* edited by Emilio Viano. New York: Garland Publishing.

Johns, Christina Jacqueline. 1992. *Power, ideology and the war on drugs.* Westport, Conn.: Praeger.

Johnson, Bruce D. 1985. *Taking care of business: the economics of crime by heroin abusers.* Lexington, Mass.: Lexington Books.

―――, and Eric D. Wish. 1987. *Criminal events among seriously criminal drug abusers.* Final report to the National Institute of justice. New York: Narcotic and Drug Research, Inc.

Johnson, Joyce. 1990. *What Lisa knew: the truths and lies of the Steinberg case.* New York: G. P. Putman's Sons.

Johnson, Rose. 1991. *Myths of justice: the presentation of criminal justice issues in the 1988 presidential campaign.* Unpublished Ph.D. dissertation. Newark: Rutgers University.

Johnston, Lloyd D. 1988. *Illicit drug use, smoking and drinking by America's high school students, college students, and young adults.* By Lloyd D. Johnston and others. Rockville, Md.: National Institute of Drug Abuse.

Jones, Peter. 1991. Measuring the impact of drug testing at the pretrial release stage. Paper presented to the American Society of Criminology, San Francisco. (November)

Jones, Peter, and M. Kay Harris. 1991. *Evaluation of community corrections in Kansas.* Report to the Edna McConnell-Clark Foundation. Philadelphia: Temple University.

Kant, Emmanuel. 1965. *The metaphysical elements of justice.* Indianapolis: Bobbs-Merrill.

―――. 1964. *The metaphysical principles of virtue.* Trans. James Ellington "Library of Liberal Arts," no. 85. New York: Liberal Arts Press.

―――. 1887. *The philosophy of law: an exposition of the fundamental principles of jurisprudence as the science of right.* Edinburgh: T&T Clark.

Kaplan, Helen Singer. 1979. *Disorders of sexual desire: and other new concepts and techniques in sex therapy.* New York: Simon and Schuster.

Karer, Robert. 1992. Shame. *The Atlantic Monthly* (February), 40–70.

Katz, Jack. 1988. *Seductions of crime.* New York: Basic Books.

Kelman, Herbert C. 1961. Processes of opinion change. *Opinion Quarterly* 25:2, 57–78.

Kempe, Ruth S., and Ray E. Helfer, eds. 1980. *The battered child.* Chicago: University of Chicago Press.

———, and Henry C. Kempe. 1978. *Child abuse.* Cambridge: Harvard University Press.

Kennedy, Peter. 1992. *A guide to econometrics.* Cambridge: MIT Press.

Kilpatrick, Dean G., Lois J. Veronen, Benjamin E. Saunders, Connie L. Best, Angelynne Amick-McMullen, and Janet Pudahovich. 1987. *The psychological impact of crime: a study of a random sample of victims.* Charleston: Crime Victims Research and Treatment Center.

Kittrie, Nicholas N. 1971. *The right to be different: deviance and enforced therapy.* Baltimore: Johns Hopkins University Press.

Klaus, Patsy A. and Michael R. Rand. 1985. *The crime of rape.* Washington, D.C.: Bureau of Justice Statistics.

Klein, Malcolm, 1979. Deinstitutionalization and diversion of juvenile offenders: a litany of impediments. In Norval Morris and Michael Tonry, eds., *Crime and justice: an annual review of research,* vol 1.

Kornhauser, Ruth Posner. 1978. *Social causes of delinquency: an appraisal of analytic models.* Chicago: University of Chicago Press.

Koss, M. P. 1990. Rape incidence. Testimony to the Senate Judiciary Committee. (August 29).

Koss, M., Gidycz, C., and Wisniewski, N. 1987. The scope of rape: incidence and prevalence of sexual aggression and victimization in a national sample of higher education students. *Journal of Consulting & Clinical Psychology* 55, 162–70.

Kramer, John H., and Robin L. Lubitz. 1985. Pennsylvania's sentencing reform: the impact of commission-established guidelines. *Crime and Delinquency* 31, 481–500.

Krohn. Marvin D. 1988. *Rochester youth development study project.* Albany: Hindelang research Center.

Kubler-Ross, Elisabeth. 1972. *On death and dying.* New York: Macmillan.

Langan, Patrick. 1991. America's soaring prison population. *Science.* 251 (March) 1565–77.

Lanning, Keith V. 1987. *Child molesters: a behavior analysis. For law-enforcement officers investigating cases of child sexual exploitation.* 2nd ed. Washington, D.C.: National Center for Missing and Exploited Children.

Latessa, Edward J., and Vito Gennaro F. 1988. The effects of intensive supervision on shock probationers. *Journal of Criminal Justice* 16, 319–30.

Laub, John. 1983. *Criminology in the making: an oral history.* Boston: Northeastern University Press.

————. and Robert Sampson. 1993. Turning points in the life course: why change matters to the study of crime. *Criminology* 31, 301–25.

Lauen, Roger, J. 1990. *Community-managed corrections and other solutions to America's prison crisis.* Laurel Md.: American Correctional Association.

Law Enforcement Assistance Administration. 1970. *Program plan, 1971.* Washington, D.C.: U.S. Government Printing Office.

Lemert, Edwin M. 1967. *Social deviance, social problems and social control.* Englewood Cliffs, N.J.: Prentice-Hall.

Lerman, Paul. 1975. *Community treatment and social control.* Chicago: University of Chicago Press.

Lewis, C. S. 1944. *The problem of pain.* New York: Macmillan.

————. 1954. On punishment: a reply. *Resjudicatae* (August), 519–523.

Lipman, Ira A. 1988. The private security industry: issues and trends. *Annals of the American Academy of Political and Social Science.*

Lipsky, Michael. 1980. *Street level bureaucrats: dilemmas of the individual in public services.* New York: Russell Sage.

Lockwood, Dan. 1980. *Prison sexual violence.* New York: Elsevier.

Loeber, Rolf, Magda Stouthamper-Loeber, Welmact van Kamman, and David P. Farrington. 1991. Initiation, escalation and desistance in juvenile offending and their correlates. *Journal of Criminal Law and Criminology* 82:1, 36–82.

Lynch, Michael J., and Byron W. Groves. 1986. *A primer in radical criminology,* New York: Harrow and Heston.

Mabbot, J. D., 1939. Punishment. *Mind* 48: 150.

Mackenzie, Doris. 1990. Boot camp prisons: componens, evaluations and empirical issues. *Federal Probation* 54, 44–52.

Mackie, J. L. 1982. Morality and retributive emotions. *Criminal Justice Ethics,* 3–9.

Maguire, Mike. 1992. The needs and rights of victims of crime. In Michael Tonry, ed., *Crime and justice: A review of research,* vol 14. Chicago: University of Chicago Press.

———. and C. Corbett. 1987. *The effects of crime and the work of victims support schemes.* Aldershot, Eng.: Gower.

Maltz, Michael D. 1977. Criminal statistics. *Crime and Delinquency* 23, 32–40.

Mann, Cora Mae. 1993. *Unequal justice: a question of color.* Blooming-ton: Indiana University Press.

Martinson, Robert. 1976. California research at the crossroads. *Crime and Delinquency* 22, 2, 178–91.

———. 1976. What works?—questions and answers about prison reform. In *Rehabilitation, recidivism, and research,* by Robert Martinson et al. Hackensack, N.J.: National Council on Crime and Delin-quency.

Mathiesen, Thomas. 1990. *Prison on trial.* Newbury Park, Calif.: Sage.

Mathews, Roger. 1992. Reflections on realism. In Roger Matthews and Jock Young, eds., *Rethinking criminology: the realist debate.* New-bury Park, Calif.: Sage.

Mauer, Marc. 1992. *Americans behind bars: one year later.* Washington, D.C.: The Sentencing Project. (February).

———. 1990. *Young black men and the criminal justice system: a growing national problem.* Washington, D.C.: The Sentencing Project.

Mawby, R., and M. Gill. 1987. *Crime victims: needs services and the voluntary sector.* London: Tavistok.

Mayer, Adele. 1983. *Incest: a treatment manual for therapy with victims, spouses and offenders.* Holmes Beach, Fla.: Learning Publications.

McCleary, Richard. 1980. *Applied time series analysis for the social sciences.* Beverly Hills, Calif.: Sage.

McCleskey v. Kemp 481 U.S. 279 (1987).

McDonald, Douglas. 1989. The cost of corrections: in search of the bottom line. *Research in Corrections* 2:1.

―――. and Keith E. Carlson. 1992. Federal sentencing in transition. *Bureau of Justice Statistics Special Report.* Washington, D.C.: U.S. Department of Justice. (June)

McDonald, William. 1976. Towards a bicentennial revolution in criminal justice: the return of the victim. *American Criminal Law Review* 13, 649–74.

McGuinan, Patrick B., and Jon S. Pascale, eds. 1986. *Crime and punishment in modern America.* Washington, D.C.: Free Congress Research and Education Foundation.

Meierhoefer, Barbara. 1992. *The general effects of mandatory minimum prison terms.* Washington, D.C.: Federal Judicial Center.

Melossi, D., and Pavarini, M. 1981. *The prison and the factory: origins of the penitentiary system.* London: Kegan Paul.

Menninger, Karl. 1968. *The crime of punishment.* New York: Viking.

Merrit, J. and Stanton, D. 1991. The release of the Birmingham Six. *The independent.* January 18.

Merton, Robert K. 1957. *Social theory and social structure.* Glencoe, Ill. Free Press.

Methvin, Eugene H. 1992. Doubling America's prison population will break America's crime wave. *Corrections Today.* (February) 13–15.

Mezey, G. 1987. Hospital-based rape crisis programs: what can American experiences teach us? *Bulletin of the Royal College of Psychiatrists* 11:2, 49–51.

Miethe Terrance D., 1987. Stereotypical conceptions and criminal processing: the case of the victim-offender relationship. *Justice Quarterly* 4, 571–93.

Mill, John Stuart. 1926. On Liberty. In *On liberty and other essays,* E. Neff, editor. New York: Columbia University Press.

―――. 1951. *Utilitarianism, liberty and representative government.* New York: Dutton.

Miller, Jerome. 1992. 56 percent of young black males in Baltimore under justice system control. *Overcrowded Times* 3:6 (December), 1, 10.

Miller, Walter B. 1969. *White gangs.* Boston: Transaction (rpt.).

Mitford, Jessica. 1973. *Kind and usual punishment, the prison business.* New York: Knopf.

Moeller, Gertrude L. 1989. Fear of criminal victimization: the effect of neighborhood racial composition. *Sociological Inquiry* 59:2, 208–21.

Monahan, John. 1981. *Predicting violent behavior: an assessment of clinical techniques.* Beverly Hills, Calif.: Sage.

Moore, Mark H. 1990. Supply reduction and drug law enforcement. In *Drugs and crime,* edited by Michael Tonry and James Q. Wilson. Chicago: University of Chicago Press.

Morris, Herbert. 1968. Person and punishment. *The Monist,* 52.

———. 1985. The paternalistic theory of punishment. In *Punishment and Rehabilitation,* edited by Jeffrie Murphy. Belmont, Calif.: Wadsworth.

Morris, Norval, and Michael Tonry. 1991. *Intermediate sanctions: between prison and probation.* Oxford: Oxford University Press.

———. and Michael Tonry. 1990. *Between prison and probation: intermediate punishment in a rational sentencing system.* New York: Oxford University Press.

Moynihan, Daniel P. 1969. *Maximum feasible misunderstanding: community action in the war on poverty.* New York: Free Press.

Mullaney, Fahy G. 1988. *Economic sanctions in community corrections.* Washington, D.C.: U.S. National Institute of Corrections.

Murphy, Jeffrie G., and Jean Hampton. 1988. *Forgiveness and mercy.* New York: Cambridge University Press.

Nadelman, Ethan. 1988. The case of legalization. *The public interest* 92, 3–32.

Nagin, Daniel, and David P. Farrington, 1991. The stability of criminal potential from childhood to adulthood. Unpublished paper.

Nathanson, Stephen. 1987. *An eye for an eye? the morality of punishment by death.* Totowa, N.J.: Rowman and Littlefield.

National Drug Control Strategy. February 1991. Washington, D.C.: U.S. Government Printing Office.

National Institute on Drug Abuse. 1990. *National household survey on drug abuse.* Washington, D.C.: NIDA.

National Institute of Law Enforcement and Criminal Justice, *Program Plans, 1978, 1982, 1985, 1986, 1987.* Washington, D.C.: U.S. Department of Justice.

Nelson, James F. 1991. *The incarceration of minority defendants: an identification of disparity in New York State.* Albany: Office of Justice Systems Analysis. (July).

Nettler, Gwynn. 1984. *Explaining Crime,* 3d. ed. New York, Mc-Graw Hill.

Newman, Graeme. 1983. *Just and painful. A case for the corporal punishment of criminals.* London: Macmillan.

———. 1978. *The punishment response.* Philadelphia: J. B. Lippincott.

Newman, Oscar. 1972. *Defensible space.* New York: Macmillan.

Nietzsche, Friedrich W. 1967. *On the genealogy of morals.* Trans. by Walter Kaufman and R. J. Hollingdale. New York: Vintage.

Nimmo, Dan, and James Combes. 1980. *Subliminal politics: myths and mythmakers in America.* Englewood Cliffs, N.J. Prentice-Hall.

O'Leary, Vincent, and Todd R. Clear. 1984. *Directions for community corrections in the 1990's.* Washington, D.C.: National Institute of Corrections.

———. and David Duffee. 1971. Correctional policy—a classification of goals designed for change. *Crime and Delinquency* 17, 373–86.

———. and David Duffee. 1970. *Correctional policy inventory.* Hackensack, NJ: National Council on Crime and Delinquency.

Packer, Herbert. 1968. *The limits of the criminal sanction.* Stanford, Calif.: Stanford University Press.

Palmer, Ted. B. 1992. *The re-emergence of correctional intervention.* Newbury Park, CA: Sage.

———. 1975. Martinson revisited. *Journal of Research in Crime and Delinquency.* 12, 133–52.

Parent, Dale. 1990. *Boot camps: assessment of the literature.* Cambridge, Mass. Abt Assoc.

———. 1989. *Shock incarceration: an overview of existing programs.* Washington, D.C.: National Institute of Justice.

Parenti, Michael. 1983. *Democracy for the few,* 4th ed. New York: St. Martin's Press.

Parks, M. Jean. 1990. Rape victims' perceptions of long-term effects; three or more years post-rape. In *The victimology handbook,* edited by Emilio C. Viano. New York: Garland Publishing.

Parrot, Audrea, and Laurie Bechhofer. 1991. *Acquaintance rape: the hidden crime.* New York: Wiley.

Pashukanis, E. B. 1978. *Law and Marxism: a general theory.* London: Routledge and Keegan Paul.

Patterson, James. 1991. *The day America told the truth.* Englewood Cliffs, N.J.: Prentice Hall.

Pearson, Frank S. 1987. *Research on New Jersey's intensive supervision program: a final report.* New Brunswick, N.J.: Institute for Criminological Research, Rutgers—The State University of New Jersey.

Pennsylvania Commission on Crime and Delinquency. 1990. *Containing Pennsylvania Offenders; final report.* Harrisburg, Pa.: Pennsylvania Commission on Crime and Delinquency Corrections overcrowding committee.

Pepinsky, Harold E., and Paul Jesilow. 1984. *Myths that cause crime.* Washington, D.C.: Seven Locks Press.

Petersilia, Joan. 1987. *Expanding options for criminal sentencing.* Santa Monica: Rand Corporation.

———. 1985. *Granting felons probation: public risks and alternatives.* Santa Monica: Rand Corporation.

———. 1989. Letter to Richard Abell, Assistant Attorney General, April 29.

———. 1991. Policy relevance and the future of criminology—1990 presidential address. *Criminology* 29:1, 1–15.

———. 1986. *Prison versus probation in California: implications for crime and offender recidivism.* Santa Monica: Rand Corporation.

———. 1985. *Probation and felony offenders.* Washington, D.C.: National Institute of Justice.

———. and Peter Greenwood. 1978. Mandatory prison sentences: their projected effects on crime and prison populations. *Journal of Criminal Law and Criminology* 69, 604–15.

———. and Susan Turner. 1985. *Felony probation: public risks and alternataives.* Santa Monica: Rand Corporation.

———. and Susan Turner. 1994. Intensive Probation and Parole. in

Michael Tonry and Norval Morris, eds. *Crime and justice: a review of research*. Vol 17. Chicago: University of Chicago Press. 281–335.

———. and Susan Turner. 1990. *Intensive supervision for high-risk probationers. Findings from three California Experiments*. National Institute of Justice and The Bureau of Justice Assistance/Rand Corporation.

Pithers, William D. 1987. *Relapse prevention of sexual aggression*. South Burlington: Vermont Department of Corrections.

———. M. M. Buell, K. Kasher, K. F. Cummings, and L. S. Beal. 1987. Precursors to sexual aggression. Paper presented to the Association for Behavioral Treatment of Sexual Abusers, Newport, Okla.

Platt, J. 1986. *Heroin addiction: theory, research and treatment* Malabar, Fla.: Krieger.

President's Commission on Law Enforcement and Administration of Justice. 1967. *The challenge of crime in a free society; a report*. Washington, D.C.: U.S. Government Printing Office.

Proband, Stan. 1992. England's 1990 prison population falls 6 percent, *Overcrowded Times* 3:1 (February) 1–2.

Quinney, Richard. 1977. *The problem of crime: a critical introduction to criminology*. New York: Harper and Row.

———. 1970. *The social reality of crime*. Boston: Little Brown.

Raab, Selwyn. 1976. U.S. study finds recidivism rate of convicts lower than expected. *New York Times*. 1 November, 61.

Rawls, John. 1971. *A theory of justice*. Cambridge: Belknap Press of Harvard University.

Reiss, Albert J. 1988. Co-offending and criminal careers. In *Crime and justice: a review of research,* vol. 10, ed. by Michael Tonry and Norval Morris. Chicago, Ill. University of Chicago Press.

Reiss Albert J., and Jeffrey Roth. 1993. *Understanding and preventing violence,* vol. I. Report of the National Research Council of the National Academy of Sciences. Washington, D.C.: National Academy Press.

Report to the Nation on Crime and Justice. 1988. U.S. Department of Justice, Bureau of Justice Statistics. (March)

Reuter, Peter. 1991. *On the consequences of toughness*. Santa Monica: Rand Corporation.

————. 1992. *Limits and consequences of U.S. foreign drug control*. Santa Monica: Rand Corporation.

————. 1992. *Hawks ascendent*. Santa Monica: Rand Corporation.

————. Drug policy: recent lessons. Congressional testimony to the United States Senate Committee on the Judiciary. Washington, D.C. April 29.

————, and John DiNardo. 1993. *Law enforcement and the price of cocaine use*. Santa Monica: Rand Corporation.

Reynolds, Morgan. 1991. *Crime in Texas, NCPA policy report number 102*. Dallas: National Center for Policy Analysis. February.

Rice, Marnie E., Vernon Quinsey, and Grant F. Harris. 1991. Sexual reidivism among child molesters released from a maximum security psychiatric institution. *Journal of Consulting and Clinical Psychology* 15:3, 381–86.

Riggs, Anthony. 1991. Army Specialist. *New York Times*, 19 March, D22:6.

Robison, James, and Gerald Smith. 1971. The effectiveness of correctional programs. *Crime and Delinquency* 17, 67–80.

————, and Paul Takagi. 1976. The parole violator as organizational reject. In Robert M. Carter and Leslie T. Wilkins, eds., *Probation, Parole and Community Corrections*. New York: Wiley.

Robinson, Robin. 1990. *Violations of girlhood: a qualitative study of female delinquents and children in need of services in Massachusetts*. Unpublished Ph.D. dissertation. Brandeis University.

Rock, Paul. 1990. *Helping victims of crime: the home office and the rise of victim support in England and Wales*. Oxford: Clarendon Press.

Rosenbaum, Marsha. 1981. *Women on heroin*. New Brunswick, N.J.: Rutgers University Press.

Rossett, Arthur, and Donald R. Cressey. 1976. *Justice by consent: plea bargains in the American courthouse*. Philadelphia: J. B. Lippincott.

Rothman, David. 1971. *The discovery of the asylum: social order and disorder in the new republic*. Boston: Little Brown.

Rotman, Edgardo. 1990. *Beyond punishment: A new view of the rehabilitation of criminal offenders*. New York: Greenwood Press.

Rusche, George, and Oscar Kirchheimer. 1939. *Punishment and social structure*. New York: Columbia University Press.

Russell, Diana. 1984. *Sexual exploitation: rape, child sexual abuse, and sexual harassment*. Beverly Hills: Sage.

————. 1983. This incidence and prevalence of intrafamilial and extrafamilial sexual abuse of female children. *Child Abuse and Neglect* 7, 133–46.

Ryan, William. 1971. *Blaming the victim*. New York: Pantheon.

Sadurski, Wajceich. 1985. *Giving desert its due: social justice and legal theory*. Boston: D. Reidel.

Saks, Howard R., and Charles H. Logan. 1984. Does parole make a "lasting" difference? In George F. Cole, ed., *Criminal justice: law and politics*. Pacific Grove: Brooks/Cole.

Sampson, Robert, and John Laub. 1993. *Crime in the making: pathways and turning points through life*. Cambridge: Harvard University Press.

————, and J. O. Wooldredge. 1987. Linking the Micro and Macro Levels of Lifestyle: Routine Activity and Opportunity Models of Predatory Victimization. *Journal of Quantitative Criminology* 3, 371–93.

Schlossman, Steven L. 1977. *Love and the American delinquent: the theory and practice of "progressive" juvenile justice, 1825–1920*. Chicago: University of Chicago Press.

Schwartz, Barbara K. 1988. *A practitioner's guide to treating the incarcerated male sex offender*. Washington, D.C.: National Institute of Corrections.

Sechrest, Lee, Susan O. White, Elizabeth D. Brown, eds. 1979. *The rehabilitation of criminal offeneders: problems and prospects*. Washington, D.C.: National Academy of Sciences.

Sen, Amartya. 1982. *Utilitarianism and beyond*. New York: Cambridge University Press.

————. 1979. Utilitarianism and welfarism. *Journal of Philosophy* 76, 463–89.

Seven cities lead violence epidemic. 1991. *USA Today*. 30 April, 1.

Shafer-Landau, Russ. 1991. Can punishment educate? *Law and Philosophy* 10, 189–219.

Shane-DuBow, Sandra, Alice P. Brown, and Erik Olson. 1985. *Sentencing reform in the United States: history, content, and effect*. Washington, D.C.: National Institute of Justice.

Sharkey, Joe. 1991. *Deadly greed*. Englewood Cliffs, N.J.: Prentice-Hall.

Shaw, Clifford Robe, and Henry D. McKay. 1969. *Juvenile delinquency and urban areas*. Chicago: University of Chicago Press.

Sher, George. 1987. *Desert*. Princeton, N.J.: Princeton University Press.

Sherman, Michael, and Gordon Hawkins. 1981. *Imprisonment in America*. Chicago: University of Chicago Press.

Shinnar, Shlomo, and Revel Shinnar. 1975. The effects of the criminal justice system on the control of crime: a quantitative approach. *Law and Society Review* 9, 581–611.

Singer, Richard G. 1979. *Just deserts: sentencing based on equality and desert*. Cambridge, Mass.: Ballinger.

Skogan, Wessley, R. Davis, and Arthur Lurigio. 1990. *Victim's needs and victim services*. Final Report to the National Institute of Justice. Washington, D.C.: U.S. Department of Justice.

Smith, Adam. 1982. *The theory of moral sentiments*. Indianapolis: Liberty Press.

Smith, William French. 1981. *Task Force on violent crime: final report*. Washington, D.C.: U.S. Department of Justice. (August 17)

Snyder, Howard. 1990. *Growth in minority detentions attributed to drug law violations*. Washington, D.C.: U.S. Department of Justice. March.

Sparks, Richard F. 1980. A critique of marxist criminology. In *Crime and Justice: An Annual Review of Research*, edited by Norval Morris and Michael Tonry. Chicago: University of Chicago Press.

Spelman, William. 1994. *Criminal incapacitation*. New York: Plenum.

Stanley, David T. 1976. *Prisoners among us, the problem of parole*. Washington, D.C.: Brookings Institute.

Staples, William G. 1986. Restitution as a sanction in juvenile court. *Crime and Delinquency* 32, 179–85.

Steadman, Henry J. 1985. Prediction at the system level: measuring the presumed changes in the clientele of the criminal justice and mental health systems. In *Dangerousness: Probability and prediction, psychiatry and public policy*, edited by Christopher D. Webster, Mark

H. Ben-Aron, and Stephen J. Hucker. Cambridge: Cambridge University Press.

Steffensmeier, Darrell, and Miles D. Harer. 1991. Did crime rise or fall during the Reagan presidency? *Journal of Research in Crime and Delinquency* 28:3, 330–59.

Stephen, S. 1967. *Liberty equality, fraternity.* London: Cambridge University Press.

Struggle for Justice. 1971. A report on crime and punishment in America, prepared for the American Friends Service Committee. New York: Hill and Wang.

Sullivan, Ronald L. 1992. For Petty Offenders, Toil Replaces Incarceration. *New York Times,* 8 March, 40.

Sutherland, Edwin H., and Donald R. Cressey. 1978. *Criminology.* 10th ed. Philadelphia: J. B. Lippincott.

Sykes, Gresham. 1958. *Society of captives.* Princeton, N.J.: Princeton University Press.

Tahtinen, Unto. 1963. *The theories of punishment studied from the point of view of non-violence.* Turku: Turun Yliupistan.

Task Force Report: Corrections. 1967. *The President's commission on law enforcement and administration of Justice.* Washington, D.C.: U.S. Government Printing Office.

Taylor, Ian R., and Jock Young. 1973. *The new criminology: for a social theory of deviance.* London: Routedge and Kegan Paul.

Taylor, Sam. 1975. *Critical Criminology.* London: Routledge and Kegan Paul.

The tax gap and taxpayer noncompliance. 1990. Washington, D.C.: U.S. Government Printing Office.

Thompson, James D. 1967. *Organizations in Action: social science bases of administrative theory.* New York: McGraw Hill.

Thowaldson, Svei A. 1990. Restitution and victim participation in sentencing: a comparison of two models. In *Criminal Justice, Restitution, and Reconciliation,* edited by Burt Galaway and Joe Hudson. Monsey, N.Y.: Criminal Justice Press.

———, and Mark R. Krasmick. 1980. On recovering compensation funds from offenders. *Victimology* 5, 18–29.

Toborg, Mary A. 1989. *Assessment of pre-trial urine testing in the District of Columbia*. Washington, D.C.: National Institute of Justice.

Toch, Hans. 1989. *Coping: maladaptation in prisons*. New Brunswick, N.J.: Transaction.

Tonry, Michael. 1993. General Barr's last stand. *Overcrowded Times* 3:6, 2.

———. 1990. Stated and latent functions of ISP. *Crime and Delinquency* 36:1 (January), 124–91.

———, and Richard Will. 1988. *Intermediate sanctions: a review of the literature*. Unpublished manuscript.

———, and James Q. Wilson. 1990. *Drugs and crime*, vol. 13. Chicago: University of Chicago Press.

Trebach, Arnold S. 1987. *The great drug war*. New York: Macmillan.

Tunnell, Keith D. 1992. *Choosing crime: the criminal calculus of property offenders*. Chicago: Nelson-Hall.

Turk, Austin T. 1969. *Criminality and legal order*. Chicago: Rand Mc-Nally.

Tyler, Tom. 1990. *Why people obey the law*. New Haven: Yale University Press.

U.S. Bureau of the Census. 1990. *Statistical abstract of the United States: 1990*. Washington, D.C.: U.S. Department of Justice.

U.S. Bureau of Justice Statistics. 1991. *Crime and the nation's households, 1990*. Washington, D.C.

———. 1990. *Criminal victimization 1989*. Washington, D.C.

———. 1988. *Report to the nation on crime and justice*. *Washington, D.C.*

———. *1988. Profile of state prison inmates, 1986*. Washington, D.C.: (special report)

———. 1988. *Data report, 1987*. Washington, D.C.

———. 1987. *Elderly victims*. Washington, D.C.

———. 1992. *Justice expenditure and employment*. Washington, D.C.

U.S. Comptroller General. 1977. *Probation and parole activities need to be better managed*. Washington, D.C.: U.S. General Accounting Office. (October 17)

———. 1976. *State and county probation: systems in crisis.* Washington, D.C.: U.S. General Accounting Office. (May 27)

U.S. Department of Justice. 1991. *Criminal victimization in the U.S., 1989.* Washington, D.C.

———. Office of Justice Programs. 1990. *A survey of intermediate sanctions.* National Institute of Corrections.

———. 1991. *Crime in the United States: uniform crime reports.* Washington, D.C.

———. 1981. *Attorney generals' task force on violent crime, final report.* Washington, D.C.

———. 1973. *Crime in the United States: uniform crime reports.* Washington, D.C.

U.S. Sentencing Commission, 1991. *Mandatory minimum penalties in the federal criminal justice system.* Washington, D.C.: U.S. Sentencing Commission.

Van Den Haag, Ernest. 1975. *Punishing criminals: concerning a very old and painful question.* New York: Basic Books.

van Dijk, Jan, Pat Mayhew, and Martin Killias. 1990. *Experiences of crime across the world.* Boston: Kluwer.

Van Dine, Stephen, John P. Conrad, and Simon Dinitz. 1979. *Retaining the wicked: the incapacitation of the dangerous criminal.* Lexington, Mass.: Lexington Books.

Van Ness, Daniel. 1989. *Restorative justice; theory, principles, practice.* Washington, D.C.: Justice Fellowship.

Vermont Department of Corrections. 1988. Montpelier, Vt.: Relapse Prevention Program.

Viano, Emilio. 1990. *The victimology handbook: research findings, treatment and public policy.* New York: Garland Publishing.

Visher, Christy A. 1986. The Rand inmate survey: a reanalysis. In *Criminal Careers and Career Criminals,* edited by Alfred Blumstein, Jacqueline Cohen, Jeffrey A. Roth, and Christy A. Visher. Washington, D.C.: National Academy Press.

von Hirsch, Andrew. 1993. *Censure and sanction.* Oxford: Clarendon.

———. 1976. *Doing justice: the choice of punishments.* New York: Hill and Wang.

————. 1990. The politics of "just desert" *Canadian Journal of Criminology* 32: (July) 187–91.

————. 1985. *Past and future crimes: deservedness and dangerousness in the sentencing of criminals*. New Brunswick, N.J.: Rutgers University Press.

————, and Kathleen Hanrahan. 1979. *The question of parole: retention, reform, or abolition?* Cambridge, Mass.: Ballinger Publishers.

————, and Nils Jareborg. 1991. Gauging criminal harm: a living-standard analysis. *Oxford Journal of Legal Studies* (1) 1–24.

Walker, Samuel. 1989. *Sense and nonsense about crime: a policy guide*, 2nd ed. Pacific Grove, Calif.: Brooks/Cole.

Wallace, Shawn. 1991. *The fever*. London: Faber and Faber.

Wallerstein, J. F., and C. J. Wyle. 1947. Our law-abiding law-breakers. *Federal Probation* 35 (April), 107–19, 145.

Weber, Robert J. 1969. The goals of community corrections: A redefinition. In *Problems, thoughts and processes in criminal justice administration*, edited by Alvin Cohn. Paramus, N.J.: National Council on Crime and Delinquency.

Weed, Frank J. 1987. Grass-roots activism and the drunk driving issue: A survey of MADD chapters. *Law and Policy* 9, 259–79.

Weisburd, David, and Ellen Chayet. 1989. Good time: an agenda for research. *Criminal Justice and Behavior* 16, 183–195.

West, W. Gordon. 1978. The short-term careers of serious thieves. *Canadian Journal of Criminology* 20, 169–90.

Westermarck, Edward. 1932. *Ethical relativity*. London: Kegan Paul.

Wexler, Henry, and Douglas Lipton. 1985. Prison drug treatment: the critical ninety days of reentry. Paper presented to the American Society of Criminology, San Diego, Calif.

————, and R. Williams. 1986. The stay 'n' out therapeutic community: prison treatment for substance abusers. *Journal of Psychoactive Drugs* 18:22, 221–30.

Whitaker, Catherine J. 1990. *Black victims*. Washington, D.C.: Bureau of Justice Statistics.

The White House. 1991. *National drug control strategy*. February Washington, D.C.: Government Printing Office.

The White House Conference for a Drug Free America. 1988. *Final report of the White House conference for a drug free America*. Washington, D.C.: White House Printing Office.

Wilbanks, William. 1986. *The myth of a racist criminal justice system*. Monterey, Calif.: Brooks/Cole.

Wilkins, Leslie T. 1991. *Crime and market forces*. Dartmouth, N.H.: Dartmouth University Press.

———. 1969. *Evaluation of penal measures*. New York: Random House.

———. 1965. *Social deviance: social policy, actions and research*. Englewood Cliffs, N.J.: Prentice-Hall.

———, and Ken Pease. 1988. The public demand for punishment. *Issues in contemporary criminology: international journal of sociology and social policy* 7:3, 16–22.

Williams, Terry. 1989. *The cocaine kids: the inside story of a teenage drug ring*. Reading, Mass.: Addison-Wesley.

Wilson, James Q. 1983. *Crime and public policy*. San Francisco: Institute of Contemporary Studies.

———. 1975. *Thinking about crime*. New York: Random House.

———, and Richard J. Hernstein. 1985. *Crime and human nature*. New York: Simon and Schuster.

———, and George L. Kelling. 1982. Broken windows: the police and neighborhood safety. *Atlantic Monthly* 249, 29–38.

Wolfgang, Marvin E., Robert M. Figlio, and Thorsten Sellin. 1972. *Delinquency in a birth cohort*. Chicago: University of Chicago.

Wright, Erik. 1973. *The politics of punishment: a critical analysis of prisons in America*. New York: Harper and Row.

Wright, Kevin N. 1989. Race and economic marginality in explaining prison adjustment. *Journal of research in crime and delinquency* 26:1, 17–30.

Yankelovitch, Skelly and White, Inc. 1984. *Taxpayer attitudes study: final report*. Prepared for the Internal Revenue Service.

Young, Jock. 1973. *The new criminology for a social theory of deviance*. London: Routledge and Kegan Paul.

Zamble, Edward, and Frank Porporino. 1988. *Coping behavior and adaptation in prison inmates*. New York: Springer-Verlag.

Zedlewski, Edwin W. 1987. Making confinement decisions. *The economics of disincarceration.* Washington, D.C.: U.S. Department of Justice.

Zeisel, Hans. 1982. *The limits of law enforcement.* Chicago: University of Chicago.

Zimring, Franklin E. 1991. Ambivalence in state capital punishment policy: an empirical sounding. *Review of Law and Social Change* 18:3, 729–42.

————, and Gordon Hawkins. 1991. *The scale of imprisonment.* Chicago: University of Chicago Press.

————, and Gordon Hawkins. 1988. The new mathematics of imprisonment. *Crime and Delinquency* 34, 425–36.

Name Index

Subject Index